P9-DUS-018

ERAS AND MODES IN ENGLISH POETRY

ERAS & MODES IN ENGLISH POETRY

By Josephine Miles

UNIVERSITY OF CALIFORNIA PRESS

Berkeley and Los Angeles · 1964

University of California Press
Berkeley and Los Angeles, California

Cambridge University Press
London, England

Second edition, revised and enlarged
(First paper-bound edition)

Library of Congress Catalog Card Number: 57-7384

Manufactured in the United States of America

Preface

The idea of temporal change is important in literary history. We have a sense that one work leads to another, that one artist influences another, that an author matures, that we can discern stages in development from era to era. We have a sense of a whole and ever-changing pattern of artistic progression, not always to better, but always to remarkably different, sorts of work. We name the stages of change for leading literary or political figures, as if there were some natural representation. Or we name the stages for styles, as if we discerned clearly that one style in literature lasted just so long and then gave way to another.

The idea of style is important too. We have a sense that despite its complexities the manner in which thought and attitude are given artistic form is somehow describable and identifiable, by substance, tone, syntax, and the shapes of genres. The style is taken to be not only the man but also the group, as if epoch and group and even individual did not stir with conflicting, increasing, and subsiding forces of interest and manner.

It seems to me possible that by specifying certain characteristics within style and era and by tracing their changes within individual and group usage, we may learn more definitely what are the interrelationships of time and manner and what are the qualities and tempos of artistic change. Basic to both the general speech of an era and its literary constructions is the language of the era, already socially structured and selective, and made more so by artistic impress. In the characteristic selections and arrangements of this language we may find one part of style, its simplest substance and ordering, and this I propose to consider as "mode."

Languages which use a subject-and-predicate construction, as most Indo-European languages do, provide the possibility of basic variations in modal emphasis. Their sentences may be dominantly predicative, with many active verbs and clausal subordinations; or they may be dominantly qualitative, with many adjectival and phrasal modifications; or, at least in theoretical possibility, they may balance these two emphases in equilibrium. Any persistent usage or choice among these possible modes is apt to be stylistic, to be connected with traits and attitudes of the users and with purposes of use; and that which is social choice may then also become artistic choice by compliance, or anti-artistic choice by reaction. Certain linguistic emphases may be associated with certain literary forms, as, for example, classical Sanskrit employed a highly phrasal and substantival language for its mode.

What do we know about these modal traditions in English? We have some sense of whole linguistic styles: Anglo-Saxon, for example, and then the Italianate English of the Renaissance, the formalizations of neoclassicism, the force of Biblical measures in translation, the metaphysical re-creations of the romantic nineteenth and twentieth centuries. But are specific modes of language-structure characteristic of, or even pertinent to, these largely discerned social and literary styles? We may learn that from Chaucer through Surrey the mode of English language in poetry was strongly predicative, establishing what might be called a clear native pattern. But was English poetry to be limited to that pattern? Was it interested, consciously or unconsciously, in possible alternatives?

One may look quickly through our five hundred years of poetic practice, to get a general answer to these questions, and this is what I have tried to do in this book. I have looked at what seemed to me representative works of representative poets, and found that almost every poet has a predilection for one certain mode; that groups of poets in certain eras agree in such predilection; and that emphases follow each other in certain sequences. All that I note and suggest is tentative. The great mass of English poetry has yet to be observed, as has its relation to English prose usage and to usage in other languages. Concerned with basic traits of language and the changes in these traits over a long span of time, this study tells little of precise context, little of the tone, manner, and shade of meaning of words in particular contexts. But one sort of context is pertinent to such material study, though not that of the single passage or work: the context of usages which, one may find, tend to accompany the structural usage. Certain sound patterns, certain meters and linear organizations, tend to be found with clausal as distinguished from phrasal or balanced modes. Certain main words and groups of references are used in connection with these other patterns. In short, a complex of traits seems discernible, combining the most basic facts of language—sound, reference, and statement structure—so that the name for the mode may imply them all. There is relevance at more consciously artful levels of language also, at the various levels of figure, of symbolic connotation and association, or of normative intensification, the biases of manner; and again there is relevance for attitude and genre. Every word is potentially metaphoric, potentially connotative, potentially intensive or normative, potentially ambiguous in all these ways, as we have learned; and every sentence as it limits also empowers every word. My concern here is, as historian, to offer evidence of complexes of power and limitation in the linguistic medium that are of interest to poets and groups of poets, as apparent in their poetic usage, and as altering from poet to poet, from era to era, in certain definable patterns of choice. These are strands, not necessarily in themselves artful, which enter into the pattern of art.

The chapters in this book are based on the following hypotheses: first, that formal analysis of basic materials helps us to understand literature as an art; second, that formal analysis is meaningful not only for single works but for groups of works, on the basis of repeated formal organizations of components, which we call style; third, that a part of style more clearly limitable than tone or theme or genre or even manner, and thus most accessible to scrutiny, is what may be specified as mode: the selective use of the elements and structures of language.

Certain modes of poetry are discernible in the structures of language, and certain eras seem to have aptitudes for one or another of these modes. The history of English poetry gives us in part, then, a pattern of centers of emphasis changing both recurrently and cumulatively, one extreme of structural emphasis moving toward another by way of gradual modifications and renewals, and all moving in some respect in a single direction. This process I hope to describe more fully, first looking at the whole sweep of English poetry from 1500 in terms of eras of emphasis, and then focusing upon examples of single modes and their developments, particularly in the seventeenth, eighteenth, and nineteenth centuries.

An earlier work, *The Continuity of Poetic Language* (University of California Press, 1951), was a first step, as it distinguished certain complexes of extreme traits at each mid-century and suggested certain possible tendencies in the development from one to the next. The present work studies the whole of each century, finding an apparent period of moderation in the latter part of each, which seems to mediate the preceding and ensuing extremes, to provide a "classical" Latin balance between Saxon and Greek-Hebraic forces in the language.

Certain chapters have been printed in earlier forms, as follows: "The Sweet and Lovely Language," in *Gerard Manley Hopkins* (New Directions, 1945); "The Language of the Donne Tradition," in the *Kenyon Review,* Winter, 1951; "The Language of William Blake," in English Institute *Essays,* 1950; "The Romantic Mode," in the *Journal of English Literary History,* Vol. XX, No. 1, March, 1953; "The Language of the Ballads," in *Romance Philology,* Vol. VII, No. 1, August, 1953; "The

Sublime Poem," in *The Image of the Work* (University of California Press, 1955); "Eras in English Poetry," in *PMLA,* Vol. LXX, No. 4, Pt. 1, September, 1955; "Wordsworth: The Mind's Excursive Power," in *The Major English Romantic Poets: A Symposium in Reappraisal* (Southern Illinois University Press, 1957).

As at the completion of any work, one thinks of those to whom one is most indebted: to the University of California Faculty Committee on Research, for grants in aid; to Mary Jackman, Harriet Polt, W. L. Stover, for aid rendered; to Harold A. Small for editing, and to Ariel Parkinson for emblem-making; to Elizabeth Scott of the Statistical Laboratory for checking generalizations; to George P. Elliott, A. L. Kroeber, Yakov Malkiel, Elizabeth Nitchie, John Crowe Ransom, William R. Steinhoff, Clarence D. Thorpe, and Bennet Weaver, for good ideas; to my colleagues Bertrand Bronson, Bertrand Evans, John Jordan, Charles Muscatine, Thomas Parkinson, Mark Schorer, and Ernest Tuveson, for patient guidance, and beyond these, as they would wish, to Benjamin Harrison Lehman.

J. M.

Berkeley, 1956

PREFACE TO THE SECOND EDITION

I HAVE BEEN stressing time; now an additional chapter traces in more detail the coming and going of major poetic words through time; then the final chapter raises questions about place and distinguishes American poetry from British as much as the poetry will permit itself to be distinguished by its language. The Tables include the American materials and have been revised to indicate word-lengths of all texts, for the sake of more accurate comparisons.

In the interval between editions my concern has been also with prose, and the specifying of differences between poetry and prose in the use of language. The two forms have much in common, and one of their likenesses leads me to make a caution about terminology. In *Eras and Modes* I have used the terms *phrasal* and *clausal* as synonymous with *adjectival* and *predicative*. The scale of distinction has been simple: from most to least adjectives in proportion to verbs. As a whole a scale from phrasal to clausal usage is similar; but for some, especially modern, writers of prose and poetry, the phrasal-clausal choice provides a different though relevant scale. Please consider then that these terms are used generally and may be further specified in a following study.

Increasing critical attention to the structure as well as the language of literature seems to me all to the good, and I take the opportunity to cite at least the following: Francis Berry, *The Poet's Grammar,* 1958; Wayne Booth, *The Rhetoric of Fiction,* 1961; Phillip Damon, *Modes of Analogy in Ancient and Medieval Verse,* 1961; Donald Davie, *Articulate Energy,* 1955; E. H. Gombrich, *Art and Illusion,* 1960; *Poetics,* ed. Donald Davie, 1963; Samuel Levin, *Linguistic Structures in Poetry,* 1962; Josephine Miles, "Language of Lycidas," in *Lycidas,* ed. Dean Patrides, 1961, and "Song of Roland," *Romance Philology,* May, 1958; Winifred Nowottny, *The Language Poets Use,* 1962; Richard Ohmann, *Shaw: The Style and the Man,* 1962; Leo Spitzer, *Essays in English and American Literature,* 1962; and George T. Wright, *The Poet in the Poem,* 1960; as well as the many new concordances.

Additional acknowledgments are due: to the *Journal of Aesthetics and Art History* for permission to reprint "Style and Change," Fall, 1963; to the *Kenyon Review,* for "The poetry of Praise," Winter, 1961; to the University of California Press for Tables from *Renaissance Eighteenth Century, and Modern Language in Poetry,* 1960, now out of print. The fifth Table appears here in summary form.

Acknowledgment, too, to Mr. John Paul Graff, for steady mind and eye.

J. M.

Berkeley, August, 1963

Contents

CHAPTER ONE

INTRODUCTION: ERAS AND MODES IN ENGLISH POETRY

Conventionally, we have distinguished the boundary lines of centuries as significant to the history of poetry and of literature in general. We speak with a sense of unities when we speak of sixteenth, seventeenth, eighteenth, or nineteenth-century poetry. Then also we have tended to divide each century in two, speaking of pre-Elizabethan and Elizabethan, divided at 1557 with Tottel's *Miscellany;* of metaphysical and neoclassical, divided at the Restoration; of neoclassical and preromantic, divided by the death of Pope in 1744; of romantic and Victorian, divided by Scott's death in 1832 or the crowning of Queen Victoria. Often the divisions waver all across the mid-century: from 1640 to 1660, for example, or from 1744 to 1770, as if we had a sense of a middle period as well as of a beginning and end to each century. I have used such vague words as "sense" and "tend" for our divisions, because I do not think we have an actual philosophy for them, any taxonomical principle of temporal classification. We feel that a literary period begins and ends when a certain kind of writing, or spirit of writing, begins and ends; we set and reset these boundary lines as we redistinguish kinds; yet all the while the century marks seem to preserve their significance, as if writers were apt to end one kind and begin another with the changing of the numerals. Perhaps these divisions are merely "arbitrary," merely "convenient"? Then would they be convenient if they seemed to run counter to the facts as we felt them to be?

Wondering whether a closer technical look at poetic practice might not discover some descriptive principle of period sequence, I have found that neither diction nor metrics alone seems to provide a pattern regular enough to mark change; but that, on the other hand, both are closely involved with sentence structure, which does reveal a sequential pattern. Both serve by certain emphases to support the pattern of basic sentence form.

The distinction which I have found pertinent in kinds of sentence structure is between the sort which emphasizes substantival elements—the phrasal and coördinative modifications of the whole statement—and the sort which emphasizes clausal coördination and complication of the statement. The first or phrasal type employs an abundance of adjectives and nouns, in heavy modifications and compounding of subjects, in a variety of phrasal constructions, including verbs turned to participles; it is a cumulative way of speaking. The second or clausal type emphasizes compound or serial predicates, subordinate verbs in relative and adverbial clauses, action, and rational subordination; it is a discursive way of speaking. The first might say, "Rising and soaring, the golden bird flies into the stormy night of the east"; the second if given the same terms would say, "The golden bird rises and soars; it flies into the night which storms in the east." The motion and concept both differ; and, indeed, the discursive type is less apt to be speaking of "golden birds" at all than to be dealing with abstractions or complex events.

Theoretically, there might be a third type between these two: not merely a scale of degrees between extremes, but a mode of statement characterized by a balance between clausal and phrasal elements. And actually, just as we do in fact find kinds of poetry which are dominantly phrasal or dominantly clausal, so we find a kind of poetry in which sentence structure is balanced between the two. We have, then, three modes technically describable in terms of dominant sentence structure and emphasized by usage in meter and vocabulary; these I call provisionally the adjectival, predicative, and balanced modes of poetic statement.

Classifying the poetry written from 1500 to 1900 in accordance with this distinction, we discover a sequence which runs as follows: predicative, then balanced; predicative, then balanced; adjectival, then balanced; predicative, then balanced. In other words, there are four groups, one in each century, each begun by an extreme and terminated by a balance. No periods of extreme come immediately together, because each is followed by moderation in a balanced form.

These four groupings appear to coincide closely with the four centuries. The Skeltonic satiric poets of 1500 wrote an extremely clausal poetry, as did Wyatt and Surrey and their followers in mid-century; then the final thirty years were the golden Elizabethan years of a relatively balanced mode. The seventeenth century began with the clausal verse of Jonson, Donne, and Herbert, and continued with that of Cowley and Vaughan; after 1670 came again the balance of the neoclassicists. The eighteenth century began with Prior and Thomson and continued with Collins and the Wartons the opposite extreme of phrasal emphasis, countered slightly by the classicism of Pope and Johnson, until finally in 1770 the new balance began to be achieved with Goldsmith, Crabbe, Rogers, even finally Wordsworth. The nineteenth century then began with the active clausal balladry of Coleridge, Byron, Moore, Landor, proceeded with that of the Brownings and the Pre-Raphaelites, and ended again, after 1870, with the balanced modes of Swinburne, Bridges, Thompson, Phillips, Hopkins—to begin again in the twentieth century the clausal revival of the Donne tradition, in Housman, Hardy, Cummings, Frost, Auden.

That there can be felt some poetic sense of century seems undeniable. Over and over the pattern recurs, of a new mode for a new era, and then of a balanced moderation at the end. Unless the structure of sentence, sound, and reference is utterly impertinent to poetry, which does not seem possible, the slightest suggestion of developing pattern is significant for poetic history; and a pattern as regularly recurrent as this one is especially so, since it coincides with many commonly accepted patterns. We may learn technically not only how structural patterns coincide with centuries, but also why internal divisions have conventionally suggested a span of middle years: the modes at beginning and end are clear, but the middle years represent modification and transition from the one to the other.

One may ask the Why of this discoverable pattern, but I have no idea of the Why, and am indeed still much concerned with the details of the How. It may be simply that artists, like others, are intensely aware of living and working in a beginning or ending century, and so suit their tones and structures. It may be some repetition we have been caught up in, as many cyclical theorists suggest. Curt Sachs in *The Commonwealth of Art,* François Mentré in *Les Générations sociales,* and Max Förster in "The Psychological Basis of Literary Periods" (*Studies for Wm. A. Read*) are three, for example, who suggest pendular swings. Agnes Young in *Recurring Cycles of Fashion* finds three eras of dress fashion in each sequence. Dialectics, whether idealist or materialist, suggest a clash of opposites and then a resolution. But the poetic pattern seems rather a matter of mediation between opposites, a pendular swing but not a smooth one, in stages, not in a continuous arc. Perhaps the stages are a matter of generations, as Mentré suggests, with epochs of rebellion, transition, and reconciliation; at least, the consciousness of era seems part of the problem.

More needs to be known before we can fairly speculate. The pattern is present in the language of poetry: could we find it in prosaic language also, in which case it would seem to be a part of social history? Or could we find it analogically in the material structures of other arts, in which case it would seem more specifically aesthetic? Or could we find it in both, as part of a more sweeping human pattern? We do not know, because we have not looked. At least we do know that it is close enough to conventional divisions in English literary history, confirming most of them, to offer alternative suggestions for a few.

We have long accepted, for example, the fact that the last thirty years of the sixteenth century brought a new richness and smoothness to English poetry. Now we may note that technically this meant, among other things, an increased balancing of typically English clausal structures by Latin participial constructions, accompanied by, as cause or consequence, a fuller and smoother pentameter line and a more aesthetic and appreciative vocabulary. Shakespeare's sonnets are representative of the new possibilities. Since it moves toward Latin and away from Saxon structure, this poetry of balance may justly be called classical, just as its kind will be a century later, from 1670 to 1700, when Waller and Dryden even more effectively succeeded in drawing away from the roughly intellectual and clausal poetry of the metaphysicals toward Rome again. Granting these two familiar end-century stages of poise, we may then recognize that they also recur in the eighteenth and nineteenth centuries, in the group of Goldsmith and Crabbe, and then again in the "decadence" of Swinburne and Bridges, a leveling, composing, classicizing of what had gone before, an enriching by sensuous and presentative vocabulary, a filling in and loading of metrical line, a stabilizing of action for the sake of reception. In each of these four end-century periods we find a strong express interest in Latin and Greek poetical style, as a necessary model perhaps for the counterbalancing of preceding native or Biblical extremes. The interests are relative, not wholly repetitive; Crabbe does not necessarily echo Dryden; nor Bridges, Crabbe; but each acts as the same sort of modifier for his immediate predecessors. In the pattern of the whole, their relative positions become clear.

So also in relation to the early and mid-century extreme of the native English clausal structure which we have conventionally recognized in Skelton and Wyatt, in Donne and Cowley, in Byron and Browning, and their respective eras, we may more clearly recognize the opposite extreme extending through most of the eighteenth century, the phrasal structure of the poetry from Blackmore through the Wartons, too excessive to be "classical" as it is often called, too vigorously opposite to the active romantic mode meaningfully to be called "preromantic" as it often is. While classical poetic usage is characterized by regularity of meter and richness of reference along with its structural balance, and while metaphysical and romantic clausal usages are characterized by conceptual vocabulary and stanzaic verse forms, the eighteenth-century phrasal extreme—for which we may supply the label "sublime," because it combines qualities of the Gothic, the Greek Pindaric, and the Biblical—is characterized by blank verse or irregular ode forms and a vocabulary of lofty ceremony and enthusiasm.

The forward motion of usages never allows a mode exactly to recur, but progressively alters materials even while it is recalling structures. Therefore historians have tended to name the periods of poetic practice seriatim, without labels of significant renewal which would indicate the pattern of tradition as well as of development. Actually our Tudor and metaphysical, our romantic and modern, all share along with a dominantly clausal structure a language of sound and reference which keeps them in close bond. They are early- and mid-century forms, and in strongest contrast to the early and middle eighteenth-century form of the sublime, which swung to an opposite extreme of language. Late-century forms, on the other hand, are persistently balanced, in grammatical structure as well as in sound and sense, and may as well be called classical for all four centuries as for the first two.

We could read the pattern of recurrence, then, as follows, generation by generation: sixteenth-century English clausal, English clausal, classical balanced; seventeenth-century metaphysical clausal, metaphysical clausal, classical balanced; eighteenth-century sublime phrasal, sublime phrasal, classical balanced; nineteenth-century romantic clausal, romantic clausal, classical balanced. This is too heavy a terminology, but it may merely indicate the close relation between what we have felt and what we may learn technically about periods of poetic development. For while subject matter and sound pattern move progressively and selectively forward in one direction, with a few significant renewals, structure moves rather periodically back and forth, in stages from extreme through balance to extreme, conditioning and altering always, as it is altered by, the developing materials of sound and sense it works with. The simple line of motion is something as follows:

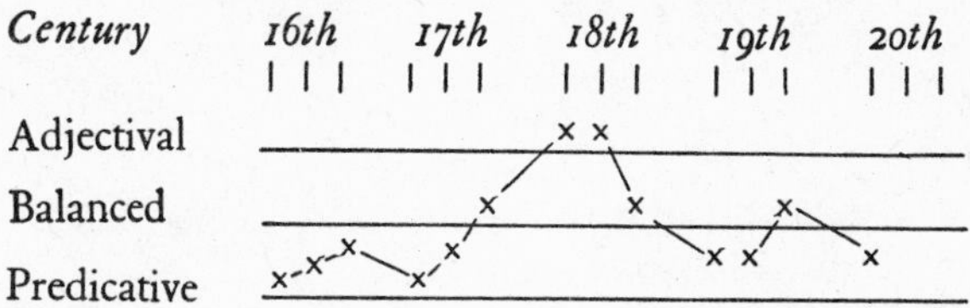

The apparent symmetry of the pattern is interesting and troubling. Does our language so regularly move, even in poetry? Are periods meaningfully marked by the sentence structures of poets? With ten poets for each X, the pattern appears as shown in the table on pages 8 and 9 (see Appendix A).

Many interesting details may be noted. Chaucer and his colloquial

TYPES OF PROPORTIONS FOR 200 POETS

England

Pre-1470	1470	1500	1530	1570	1600	1630	1670	1700	1730
Phrasal (most adjectives per verbs)									
							Thomson		
							Somerville		
								T. Warton	
							Philips	Armstrong	
							Dyer	J. Warton	
				Fletcher					Bowles
					Milton			Collins	Cowper
								Mason	Blake
						Prior		Akenside	
			Sylvester		More	Blackmore	Blair	Gray	
Balanced									
			Spenser					Shenstone	Rogers
	Hawes							Lyttelton	Crabbe
	Dunbar				Waller		Pope		Goldsmith
			Shakespeare				Young		Burns
			Fairfax			Dryden	Parnell		Churchill
						Pomfret			Wordsworth
					Crashaw		Addison		
	Douglas	Sackville		Sandys				Johnson	Chatterton
Clausal (fewest adjectives per verbs)									
Henryson			Chapman		Lovelace	Roscommon			
Gawain P.		Gascoigne		Quarles	Marvell	Vaughan			
James I	Lindsay	Breton	Sidney	Carew	Denham	Garth	Gay		
Lydgate	Skelton	Wyatt	Drayton	Herrick	Cleveland	Walsh			
Chaucer	Barclay	Googe	Marlowe	Shirley	Cowley	Oldham			
Pearl P.	Coverdale	Baldwin	Campion	Donne		Creech			
Minot	Sternhold	Turberville	Daniel	Herbert					
Gower	Ballads	Surrey		Wither					
Hoccleve	Heywood	Crowley		Jonson	Suckling				
Langland		Churchyard							

TYPES OF MEASURES FOR 200 POETS

England

Pre-1470	1470	1500	1530	1570	1600	1630	1670	1700	1730
Lines									
							Thomson		
							Blair		
							Young		Burns
Langland							Philips	J. Warton	Blake
Minot		Gascoigne	Chapman		Milton		Somerville	Akenside	Cowper
Couplets									
						Pomfret			
						Prior			
						Garth			
						Creech	Dyer		Rogers
						Blackmore	Pope	T. Warton	Crabbe
Chaucer	Lindsay			Carew	Marvell	Oldham	Gay	Johnson	Chatterton
Gower	Barclay		Marlowe	Quarles	Denham	Roscommon	Parnell	Lyttelton	Churchill
Lydgate	Skelton		Sylvester	Sandys	Waller	Dryden	Addison	Armstrong	Goldsmith
Stanzas									
		Breton							
		Turberville							
	Heywood	Googe	Fairfax	Shirley					
	Coverdale	Sackville	Campion	Herbert	Lovelace				
Henryson	Sternhold	Baldwin	Shakespeare	Herrick	Cowley				
James I	Douglas	Crowley	Drayton	Wither	More			Mason	
Hoccleve	Hawes	Churchyard	Daniel	Fletcher	Cleveland			Collins	
Gawain P.	Dunbar	Surrey	Sidney	Donne	Crashaw	Walsh		Gray	Wordsworth
Pearl P.	Ballads	Wyatt	Spenser	Jonson	Suckling	Vaughan		Shenstone	Bowles

TYPES OF PROPORTIONS FOR 200 POETS

England (continued)					America				
1770	1800	1830	1870	1900	1770	1800	1830	1870	1900
Phrasal (most adjectives per verbs)									
		Henley							
Hemans	Tennyson								
Keats	Hood								
	Horne	Wilde	Blunden			Whittier			
		Swinburne	Aldington	D. Thomas		Chivers			
			de la Mare	Spender	Barlow	Whitman		Moore	
							Guiney	Crane	Hecht
Balanced									
		Phillips			Dwight	Lowell		Pound	Shapiro
Shelley		Thompson	Sitwell		Trumbull	Poe		Williams	Rukeyser
Southey	Clough	Bridges	Graves	Barker	Bryant		Moody		Bishop
Hunt		Hopkins			Drake		Lanier	Jeffers	Wilbur
	Arnold	Yeats		MacNeice	Sigourney		Sterling		Roethke
			Masefield	Nicholson	Freneau	Timrod	Sill	Stevens	Scott
			Lawrence	Ridler	Pinkney	Longfellow	Miller	Eliot	Eberhart
			Owen	Raine	Halleck	Emerson		Cummings	
Clausal (fewest adjectives per verbs)									
Campbell			Muir	Auden	Percival	Holmes	Wilcox		
Moore	E. Browning	Hardy	E. Thomas				Robinson		
Byron	Tupper						Field	Millay	Warren
Coleridge	Meredith					Very	Dickinson	Frost	Lowell
Landor	Rossetti			Gunn					
	R. Browning								
		Housman		Jennings					

TYPES OF MEASURES FOR 200 POETS

England (continued)					America				
1770	1800	1830	1870	1900	1770	1800	1830	1870	1900
Lines									
								Crane	
								Jeffers	
								Eliot	Lowell
								Moore	Rukeyser
						Whitman		Pound	Bishop
Keats	Tupper	Phillips	Lawrence		Dwight	Timrod	Moody	Williams	Roethke
Landor	Horne	Henley	Aldington	Barker	Barlow	Lowell	Sill	Stevens	Warren
Couplets									
Campbell									
Hunt									
Stanzas									
				Gunn					
	Rossetti	Yeats	Blunden	Jennings	Pinkney		Sterling		
	Meredith	Thompson	Graves	D. Thomas	Percival	Very	Robinson		
Hemans	Arnold	Housman	Owen	Nicholson	Drake	Poe	Guiney		
Shelley	Clough	Wilde	Sitwell	Ridler	Bryant	Holmes	Wilcox		Hecht
Byron	R. Browning	Hopkins	Muir	Spender	Sigourney	Chivers	Field		Wilbur
Moore	Tennyson	Bridges	E. Thomas	Raine	Halleck	Whittier	Lanier	Cummings	Shapiro
Southey	E. Browning	Hardy	Masefield	MacNeice	Freneau	Longfellow	Miller	Millay	Scott
Coleridge	Hood	Swinburne	de la Mare	Auden	Trumbull	Emerson	Dickinson	Frost	Eberhart

tradition, for example; and the early participation of the aureate poets in the classical tradition which reaches to Yeats and Stevens. Or the ascending line from Spenser and Waller to Milton and Thomson; it is interesting that Denham, often grouped with Waller by his contemporaries, here seems far apart. Denham and Cowley are true transitional figures: most of their work was traditionally clausal, but they were interested in trying a few new forms. Marvell is listed late, for his classically formed satire; note how the more colloquial satire of Creech and Oldham, and then of Gay, with whom Swift could be grouped, is the last of the English clausal mode to fade, until it is revived again at 1800 by Coleridge's and Byron's narrative techniques. Blake's *Songs* should be linked with Coleridge; but it is rather his phrasal prophetic poetry which predominates, and which is here listed. By the mid-nineteenth century, poets as important as Morris, Bridges, Patmore have to be omitted for lack of space, but do not affect the pattern, as their works vary widely within the range of possibilities. Inclusion of Phillips in the late nineteenth-century list is based on Jerome Buckley's stress, in *The Victorian Temper,* on his importance. Other well-known modern poets would further support the full variety of possibility, with characteristic emphasis on balance. At least I think the main outlines of the pattern will remain clear through the many changes that are possible. Most readily acceptable to the reader will probably be that part of the pattern which represents the early clausal emphases of Wyatt and the metaphysicals, along with the clearly opposing mode of the eighteenth century. Least acceptable will seem the partly romantic emphasis on balance; I think we may learn a good deal more, however, about the specific nature of nineteenth-century classicism. The discrimination of modes simply fails to make many pertinent distinctions, as between Hopkins', Bridges', and Swinburne's styles, for example; on the other hand, it indicates underlying likenesses which may be worth further study.

The tendency of one sort of sentence structure to predominate in the poetry of a generation, and the tendency in the past four hundred years to move from one extreme of structure, the native clausal, through classical balance, to an extreme of elaborated phrasal structure, and then back again, is borne out by other characteristics of language such as sound structure and vocabulary. Clausal poems, we find, tend to be stanzaic and active poems, working out an argument or narrative in clearly defined stages and formal external order. Phrasal poems, and phrasal eras, on the other hand, emphasize line-by-line progression, and cumulative participial modification in description and invocation without stress on external rhyming or grouping. So the strongly stanzaic verse of the sixteenth century became moderated in the more skillful blank verse and couplet of its last generation, just as in the next century the metaphysical stanza narrowed to the neoclassical couplet, carrying its linear organization partly inward by caesural balances. Then the eighteenth century aimed for the other extreme, not only a blank verse freer from end-stop emphasis, but even the irregular lines and motions of the ode forms, settling again into such couplet moderations as Goldsmith's and Crabbe's, before turning back in the nineteenth century to the clausal ballad stanza and in the twentieth to the more metaphysical involutions of Cummings, Frost, and Auden.

In the same way, the major vocabulary, the nouns, adjectives, and verbs most used and most agreed upon in each generation, follow the periodic pattern, though their main line of development is in one direction. Certain primary words thus drop out of poetic usage not to return; others persist through all four centuries; but some come and go in periodic fashion. The persisting ones name the basic human concerns that we should expect: *God, heart, life, love,* and *man,* modified by value in *good,* by magnitude in *great,* by time in *old,* active in *coming, going, giving, taking, making, seeing.* The lost words, on the other hand, are those most closely reflecting the limitations of interest in a period: the early *cruel fortune, pain, king, lady,* and *lord,* for example; the *blood* and *fire* of the metaphysicals; or, at the extreme opposite to these socially analytic and conceptual terms of clausal poetry, the equally limited ceremonious ones of the phrasal eighteenth century: *soft, breast, maid, muse, scene, song, youth, virtue, rising* and *falling.*

Most significantly, the terms which neither persist nor vanish but recur do so along with recurring sentence and verse forms. So, for example, the early Tudor vocabulary of concept, in words like *mind* and *thought, word* and *thing, time* and *world,* recurred strongly again in the clausal poetry of the nineteenth century. So also each century in its last generation, in its classical mode, contributed a special sort of recurring term, sensory and observational, like *sweet, heaven, night, sun* for the Elizabethans, with their corresponding verbs of *lie, love, look;* then the neoclassicists' *happy, mighty, art, fate, nature, grow;* the late eighteenth century's *little, sad, tear, woe, weep;* and the late nineteenth's *young, child, dream, foot, summer, woman:* always a vocabulary of human dimension and feeling in the natural world.

As of structural continuity, we may say of this referential continuity that it begins in the sixteenth and seventeenth centuries with emphasis on social and relational terms, moves through the descriptive vocabulary of the classical generations to the sublime and ceremonious world of the eighteenth, and then back to more abstract relational terms again, though never in conceptual vocabulary so strong as at first, and with a late classicism in which direct natural and human image seems partly to have turned to symbol.

One is not surprised to learn that reference and sound work closely with sentence; that the language of poetry is integral in its characteristics. Which moves first: which new sound makes for new sense, or new structure for new sound, is a question needing more than the evidence available. At least, in generational stages, we can see that the three phases move together, though not with equal force, vocabulary the least likely, structure the most, to return to old stages. All work as one poetic unit: the relational pattern of clausal sentence with stanzaic sound and with conceptual vocabulary; or the cumulative pattern of phrasal sentence with internal and onomatopoetic sound and with sublime vocabulary; or the distinct, not merely transitional, balanced pattern of structure, line, and human nature in nature which we call classical. Here, in this nucleus of language properties, we may find some of the basis for a definition of modes; and in modes, of styles; and in styles, of eras.

Perhaps it would be useful to see each mode at work in a single poem, not as widely different as possible, but as close together in one century. Here is first, the active, Wyatt's sonnet "Against His Tongue":

> Because I still kept thee fro' lies and blame,
> And to my power always thee honoured,
> Unkind tongue! to ill hast thou me rend'red,
> For such desert to do me wreke and shame.
> In need of succour most when that I am,
> To ask reward, thou stand'st like one afraid:
> Always most cold, and if one word be said,
> As in a dream, unperfect is the same.
> And ye salt tears, against my will each night
> That are with me, when I would be alone;
> Then are ye gone when I should make my moan:
> And ye so ready sighs to make me shright,
>   Then are ye slack when that ye should outstart;
>   And only doth my look declare my heart.

The conceptual terms are typical; the metaphors, functional; the difficulty of speech, thematic. The sonnet structure is tightly woven and enclosed. The sentences are active and clausally constructed; there are seventeen verbs to ten adjectives in the fourteen lines. In general, the proportioning in the poetry of Chaucer, Wyatt, Donne, Herrick, Cowley, and later Byron, Housman, Browning, Frost, and others, is about seven adjectives to fourteen nouns to eleven verbs in an average ten lines; and this single poem by Wyatt is fairly representative of it, using just that sort of colloquial language with its *becauses, ifs, whichs,* and *whens,* which makes for an active complexity of thought and structure.

What are the simple signs of that classically balanced poetry for which some of the late Elizabethans then strove? A thoroughly symmetrical proportioning, an inner onomatopoeia and harmony of sound along with the tight outward rhyme, a sensory, normative, and emotional vocabulary. This was the less active, more responsive world of the Shakespearean sonnet, clauses balanced by modifying phrases, and some of the need for connectives smoothed away, in a proportioning of ten adjectives to twenty nouns to ten verbs in ten lines. For example, Shakespeare's sonnet I is near the pattern:

From fairest creatures we desire increase,
That thereby beauty's rose might never die,
But as the riper should by time decease,
His tender heir might bear his memory:
But thou, contracted to thine own bright eyes,
Feed'st thy light's flame with self-substantial fuel,
Making a famine where abundance lies,
Thyself thy foe, to thy sweet self too cruel.
Thou that art now the world's fresh ornament
And only herald to the gaudy spring,
Within thine own bud buriest thy content
And, tender churl, mak'st waste in niggarding.
    Pity the world, or else this glutton be,
    To eat the world's due, by the grave and thee.

Adjectives and verbs are nearly balanced here, because many clausal constructions have been made phrasal, in the classical fashion. *But thou, contracted,* and *self-substantial,* and *making a famine,* and *And, tender churl,* all, by participial, appositional, or compounding construction, turn verbs to adjectives, smooth the transitions, integrate the sound.

Each late-century generation called itself classical, and strove consciously for what it thought to be a Roman mode of language. Sidney's age and Dryden's, and later Wordsworth's and Bridges', wrote of their pleasure in what they called classical proportions. Wordsworth withdrew to the simplicities of classicism under the early influence of Goldsmith, away from the eighteenth-century "gaudy and inane"; and Bridges and Hopkins in turn tried to win back some of that gaudiness, to make a balance against the stringencies of the ballad tradition. Furthermore, the great Latin poets themselves wrote the sort of syntax in the sort of line which we, following Dryden, have been calling classical. That is, the proportioning of language by Ovid, Virgil, and Horace was just that balanced one adjective to two nouns to one verb which Dryden together with his poetic colleagues achieved and which he praised in his preface "On Translation" as the "golden" line of classical literature. It suited the rhymed pentameter as it had suited unrhymed hexameter, and it dealt explicitly with emotion and sense of the natural world for Shakespeare and Marvell and Dryden as for Virgil. *Laetus, magnus, amicus, caelum, nox, video* were among the major terms for Roman classicism as for English. The mode was one literally worked for and achieved in England, and was renewed again and again as extremes of English experiment outwore themselves.

The outstanding classical poets to offer the model of a different mode were Pindar and Lucretius. Their cosmic and ceremonious overload of sublime epithets and phrasal constructions indicated a kind of extreme which English poetry did not reach until the eighteenth century. But Biblical richness and the Platonic tradition early offered to such poets as Spenser and Sylvester, and then Milton, the idea of a poetic language as free as possible from clausal complication, as resilient as possible in richly descriptive participial suspension. The signs of such a mode are more adjectives than verbs, some free variation in line length as in the ode, much inner harmony and less rhyme, and a vocabulary of physical presence, ceremony, and pleasure. The proportioning of statement ranges from about twelve adjectives, sixteen nouns, ten verbs in ten lines for Milton and Collins and Keats to fifteen adjectives, eighteen nouns, eight verbs for Thomson and the Wartons in the height of the mode. Even so early as Spenser, to say nothing of the aureate poets, the mode of speech is visible; in Spenser's *Amoretti,* sonnet 1:

> Happy ye leaves when as those lilly hands,
>   which hold my life in their dead doing might,
>   shall handle you and hold in love's soft bands,
>   lyke captives trembling at the victors sight.
> And happy lines, on which with starry light,
>   those lamping eyes will deigne sometimes to look
>   and reade the sorrowes of my dying spright,
>   written with teares in harts close bleeding book.
> And happy rymes bath'd in the sacred brooke,
>   of *Helicon* whence she derived is,
>   when ye behold that Angels blessed looke,
>   my soules long lacked foode, my heavens blis.
> Leaves, lines, and rymes, seeke her to please alone,
>   whom if ye please, I care for other none.

The poem is an exclamation, not an argument. It rests in its adjectives, *happy, trembling, starry, lamping, bleeding, blessed,* in the physical sense of bodily images which are also symbols. *Handle, look, behold,* and *please* are the few significant actions, and they are subordinate to the substance. Connections are provided by participles, and these together with the descriptive adjectives are half again as many as the verbs.

This is the mode which would give us the heavens and earth of *Paradise Lost,* the cosmological reaches of Akenside, the rich details of Thomson, the personifications of Collins, the great aesthetic and social divine wars of Blake, the figure of Keats's Autumn, the vigor of symbol and celebration in Whitman and Henley. In our own day, such poets as Dylan Thomas may lead us back to it. The style of which this mode is an enduring part has been given no name by the literary historians, though the eighteenth-century poets themselves often called it "sublime." It is an extreme we have not met in our language strongly for almost two centuries, but an extreme that some of the Imagists, under Pound's guidance, may have been aiming at, and may aim at again.

The examples of the three modes, representing as they do the range within one century and within one genre, do not represent the full reach of variation from century to century, particularly in patterning of sound. The Elizabethan classicism did manage to free itself somewhat from the tight stanzaic forms of the clausal mode, into more straightaway couplets and blank verse, but the height of the couplet form for classicism did not come until the next century, and the height of blank verse and freer odal forms not until Milton and his eighteenth-century followers. What I have tried to illustrate in the quotation of the three sonnets is, first, the power of the three modes to work within one genre; and, second, the temporal concurrence of modes, the latent potentiality of all, while one may dominate.

Neither genre nor era seems to control mode, though of the two era seems the stronger. Perhaps individual aptitude may be the controlling force, though I suppose it might be strongly conditioned by era or by genre models. At any rate, we find sonnets, epics, pastorals, satires written in any of the modes, apparently depending largely upon period; and we find some versions of each mode, however scant, in every period. The sense of language complex, the core of fitting-together structure, sound, and reference, seems to be the basic force for choice and emphasis. Some poets experiment with one and another, as Blake for example tried the clausal mode in his *Songs of Innocence and of Experience,* and then turned back to elaborate in his prophetic poems the phrasal pattern with which he had begun. But many poets, Donne, Dryden, Thomson, Keats, for example, stay by one identifying mode for their work, sometimes even when they are translating others of a different sort. Sometimes, within an era, the idea of a certain suitability of mode to genre or topic does occur, perhaps even is debated; then we see, for example, Pope modifying his structure, to suit what he considers the satiric tradition. As a whole, we may surmise from present evidence, first, that a poet has an aptitude for a mode as basis for development of his individual style; second, that his own and his era's general concept of the importance of distinct genres may condition his adaptation of modes; and third, that much agreement of usage in any one era seems to suggest some temporal conditioning force in the language itself, or at least in the poets' attitude toward it.

At any rate we may testify to the persisting use of all the modes in English poetry, with some correlation in Latin and Greek backgrounds, and we may even surmise that the traditional high, middle, and low styles had some basis in language structure. At least in English we may see a simple correspondence. The phrasal mode of Sylvester, Milton, and the eighteenth century, with its lofty phrases and cadences, its figures larger than life, and its high passions, was a clear part of what the century itself called the high or sublime style, not so much heroic as cosmic, not so much active as receptive and "passionate," in Pindar's richly ceremonious sense. The balanced and medial mode has been traditionally recognized as classical, the golden mean in the golden line of an adjective, two nouns, and a verb, as Dryden described it, the sharing of ethos with pathos in human heroism in moderated language. The relation of clausal mode to low style is somewhat less clear in tradition, perhaps because the mode was not so strong in Latin as in English, and the English put it, like the iambic, to uses not all simple, common, and low. Nevertheless, there was some recognition. Elizabethans were troubled that the clausal English was low, as Richard Foster Jones has shown us; the long critical argument against monosyllables in poetry was also an argument against English clausal construction and connection; Donne's rough "masculine" style was recognized as low and English, not classical enough; and Wordsworth, when the style was renewed two centuries later in the balladry of Coleridge, had come round to praising the low and common, as Emerson did and as Frost did, not only for the ethos of social tradition, but for the pathos which nature had drawn down to man from the Bible and the sublime. In other words, though there was a shift in meanings by the nineteenth century, a new notion of the low as natural, and a new use of natural vocabulary and colloquialism in clausal construction, the structure itself had persisted and seemed steadily to be recognized as part of the tradition of common or lowly style. The scholarly work of Ernst Robert Curtius, of J. V. Cunningham, Klaus Dockhorn, Sister Miriam Joseph, Erich Auerbach, F. W. Bateson, and Samuel Monk has interesting bearing on the problems of spirit and intention behind the modes we have here distinguished.

The study of modes should lead to the study of the styles of which they are a part. The question of complexes of usage in language should lead to questions of the ideas and attitudes that are conveyed through these complexes, and of the power of stylistic indirections like figurative speech, like metaphor, symbol, hyperbole, and irony, to alter the quality and effect of the medium. But my present concern is the modes themselves, to try to distinguish them clearly so that they may be recognizable, to suggest their usefulness as characteristic of poets and of eras in poetic history. How strong was the Chaucerian tradition of speech in English, how close were Donne and Jonson as opposed to Spenser, how different was Jonson's classicism from Dryden's, how different was Keats's romanticism from Byron's, how vividly new was the renewal of an old mode by the ballad makers of the nineteenth century—these are the sorts of questions which discrimination of modes may help to answer.

CHAPTER TWO

THE LANGUAGE OF THE DONNE TRADITION

DONNE's is a good example of what we may call the native predicative mode in English, following Chaucer and Wyatt, and leading to the modern metaphysical, the mode of discursive speech, in which one thinks aloud and argues aloud, assuming the presence of a vocal listener. Different as Donne and Ben Jonson were in many ways, they shared a liking for this manner, which they called masculine in conscious opposition to Spenser's "sweeter" feminine; and perhaps no poet was more successful than they in giving us the art of the language in its most natural early form, which all its particles, monosyllables, clausal constructions, and thoughtfully laborious articulations.

In his book *The Donne Tradition* George Williamson's central question was, "What do we owe to the Donne tradition as an inheritance of genuinely poetic value?" I should like to ask the question again more technically and more narrowly. What do we owe to the *language* of the Donne tradition as an inheritance of genuinely poetic value? The problem is a double one, concerning both description and evaluation. What is the Donne tradition, or even one small part of it, and what do we mean by "genuinely poetic value"? I limit the question to language in order to be observant of the main materials and their main lines of construction, as these participate in theme and style. The medium serves in part to characterize the art and to define its tradition. The selections and arrangements of material characteristic of Donne's poetry represent his poetic habit and a poetic habit through history, one which may be our inheritance, but one which, despite our liking for it, is not wholly ours.

Donne's primary language is vocative, predicative, abstract. The sentences he uses most are sentences of address and argument, in which verbs are proportionately strong in both active and logical subordination. The sound patterns he most uses are stanzaic in organization, employing meter and rhyme to group the lines and emphasize their control over a large amount of internal rough variation. The words he most uses are terms of evaluation, of time, soul, anatomy, and of constructive action. So *make, know, see, tell, think* are major verbs for him; *day, death, year,* and *eye, tear, face, heart, soul,* major nouns; and *good, true, new,* major adjectives. All these terms are used so frequently throughout Donne's verse that by sheer quantity they provide a base and an insistence. Meter and rhyme accent them. Argument and logic require them.

In poem after poem, from beginning to end, Donne reasons against anatomy, argues against time and the sun's marking of it, rhymes against certainty, makes and is made. So the first Song, "The Good-morrow":

> My face in thine eye, thine in mine appeares,
> And true plaine hearts doe in the faces rest,
> Where can we finde two better hemispheares

Without sharpe North, without declining West?
What ever dyes, was not mixt equally;
If our two loves be one, or, thou and I
Love so alike, that none doe slacken, none can die.

Or again, "The Anniversary":

  All Kings, and all their favorites,
  All glory of honors, beauties, wits,
The Sun it selfe, which makes times, as they passe,
Is elder by a yeare, now, then it was
When thou and I first one another saw:
All other things to their destruction draw,
  Only our love hath no decay;
This, no to morrow hath, nor yesterday,
Running it never runs from us away,
But truly keepes his first, last, everlasting day.

Or, later, "Of the Progress of the Soul: The Second Anniversary":

Nothing could make me sooner to confesse
That this world had an everlastingnesse,
Then to consider, that a yeare is runne,
Since both this lower world's, and the Sunnes Sunne,
The Lustre, and the vigor of this All,
Did set; . . .

Or, the first of the "Holy Sonnets":

Thou hast made me, And shall thy worke decay?
Repaire me now, for now mine end doth haste,
I runne to death, and death meets me as fast,
And all my pleasures are like yesterday;
I dare not move my dimme eyes any way,
Despaire behind, and death before doth cast

Such terrour, and my feeble flesh doth waste
By sinne in it, which it t'wards hell doth weigh; . . .

And the fourteenth:

Batter my heart, three person'd God; for, you
As yet but knocke, breathe, shine, and seeke to mend;
That I may rise, and stand, o'erthrow mee, and bend
Your force to breake, blowe, burn and make me new. . . .

All these active verbs, these references to time and good, to body and soul, these addresses, these metered and firmly rhymed exhortations, make up the woof, the basic weave, of Donne's poetry. His theme of love, both earthly and divine, is given a body and a duration and a value by the explicit argument of the verse.

Such a material is not peculiar to Donne, but is characteristic of many, perhaps of a majority, of English poets up to and through his time. The evaluative, metered, and predicated mode is the mode of his era as a whole: *good, great, true,* the human *heart,* and the abundant constructive verbs common to all in their recurring pattern of rhyme and reason. In this sense we may call the Donne tradition the tradition of English Renaissance poetry, different from our and from any poetry since, because the era is so powerful in the shaping of the primary language. But also with this sense of majority we may distinguish Donne's tradition from another, lesser in his age, but increasing to full power in the eighteenth century—the line of Sylvester and Milton. The vocabulary of the Milton line is more simple, sensuous, and passionate, with a stronger literal naming of qualities and feelings; the sound qualities are more internally harmonious, more assonantal and onomatopoetic; the sentence structures are simpler, more exclamatory, more substantival. Where the Donne tradition uses only one verb for every two substantives (nouns and adjectives), the Miltonic uses one verb for every three substantives; or even for four; the difference is a deeply structural one, therefore. Miltonic substantive poetry is phrasal, qualitative, coördinate; Donnic predicative poetry is clausal, conceptual, full of logical subordination. The two modes still function for us today, though many of our poets, like T. S. Eliot, try to strike a balance between them.

In Donne's time, most of his friends and associates wrote in the mode we call his, with a direct inheritance from Wyatt and Surrey and even from Chaucer and Langland. Within the common agreement of the era was this further agreement in selection and emphasis, this intensification of the human, the temporal, the active and rational, which the predicative structure of poetry supported. Chaucer, Wyatt, Surrey, Jonson, Suckling, Carew, Cowley especially agreed with Donne in the sort of sentence structure, the primary vocabulary to be used, in opposition to the greater richness of a Spenser or a Milton. When Donne differed from his colleagues, when he stood alone in primary usages, it was by intensification of negative terms, like *bad* and *false*, within the very realm of agreement.

In fact, only the slightest of variations in material set Donne apart as individual. His likeness to Jonson, Cowley, and the rest is strong at the level of medium, his choice of words and syntax in agreement with theirs. A fine distinction between Donne and the Donne tradition therefore would have to be made at more complex levels of style and thought, and this fact itself is significant for those who would search out his singularities. But even his small singularities in material are partly defining. His treatment of stress within the norm of the line has been much discussed. His treatment of the vocative in argument appears usually personal and individual, often because it is so complex. His usual proportioning of about eight adjectives, sixteen nouns, twelve verbs in ten lines throughout most of his work except the closest imitations, like the Satires, indicates a stress on verbs usually steadfast through a variety of forms. Not only his negative evaluations like *bad* and *false* identify his major vocabulary, but also his combination of *death* and *soul,* least frequent Cavalier terms, with the common Cavalier substance of *heart, face,* and *tear,* and the relatively new specification of *sun.* The omissions which serve to define by their absence are mainly the aspects of handsome vision which increase toward the eighteenth century: *nature, art, beauty, grace, grow, move, rise.* Such pleasures are not Donne's. His is the active, negative, human, complex poetry of individual relationships both earthly and divine which was characteristic of him particularly, but also of his line from Chaucer more generally, and of a great deal of the poetry before 1650 most generally of all.

That the eighteenth century abandoned both Donne and his tradition many modern critics have pointed out. In the mid-eighteenth century I find no poet who uses much of the Donnic vocabulary or proportioning. Verbs never exceed adjectives; substantives dominate by three or four to one; argument has been given over to exclamation and generalization in parallel and harmonized structures. But in the nineteenth century the tradition is restored in a new and modified fashion.

Renewal of the ballad brought back active predication, but with a new vocabulary of color and sensation. Wordsworth in the *Lyrical Ballads* wrote a poetry active in its motion, but structurally still strong in nouns, especially in the nouns of nature: *sun, moon, sky, sea, field, forest.* But with Coleridge, Byron, and Landor, and especially in mid-century with Browning and the Pre-Raphaelites, a stronger version of the Donne tradition came into play. These were its variations:

The proportioning was like Donne's, the domination of verbs over adjectives, indicating a syntax which again used logical subordination as well as motion. The sound patterns again encouraged effects of irregularity, of difficult and personal thinking, within a regular versified frame. The sentences were less often vocative, but still in first and third person managed the technique of deliberation and of argument in effortful process. The primary vocabulary was more evaluative than it had been in a long time. This Donnic group stressed *good* rather than *bright; great* and *little* rather than *dear, deep,* or *dim,* which were fashionable among their colleagues in the nineteenth century. They stressed *day, eye, God, heart, love, man, sun, world* rather than the more atmospheric new terms of *light, air, star, spirit, flower, hour.* They used most of the traditional primary verbs and added some of their own. Like Donne in his century, the Brownings in theirs opposed with their abstract and intellectual vigor and their lively ingenuity the more receptive and sensory poetry of the Miltonic tradition, of Keats, Tennyson, Lowell, and the later Wordsworth.

At the same time, all these nineteenth-century poets as contemporaries made some agreements which Donne would not have made. In the first place, the Browning group were renovative rather than traditional for their day, and in the second place they were renewing abstraction in an era of atmospheric detail the validity of which for poetry they did not deny. So they used with pleasure much of the *sweet, fair, soft, hand, father, mother, night, nature, song, fall, lie, feel* vocabulary of sense and passivity by which the nineteenth century is characterized and which was alien in the Donne tradition.

Browning, at the beginning of "Transcendentalism," warns against too much abstraction:

> Stop playing, poet! May a brother speak?
> 'Tis you speak, that's your error. Song's our art:
> Whereas you please to speak these naked thoughts
> Instead of draping them in sights and sounds.
> —True thoughts, good thoughts, thoughts fit to treasure up!
> But why such long prolusion and display,
> Such turning and adjustment of the harp,
> And taking it upon your breast, at length,
> Only to speak dry words across its strings? . . .

In the language of speech itself, Browning demands more color and more song. Just such aesthetic substance is what he gives, in "Soliloquy of the Spanish Cloister," or "The Bishop Orders His Tomb," thereby making a characteristic combination of the substantial and the colloquial, the latter establishing the frame. Notice the speaking and Donnic language of "Andrea Del Sarto," at its beginning:

> But do not let us quarrel any more,
> No, my Lucrezia; bear with me for once:
> Sit down and all shall happen as you wish.
> You turn your face, but does it bring your heart?
> I'll work then for your friend's friend, never fear,
> Treat his own subject after his own way,
> Fix his own time, accept too his own price,
> And shut the money into this small hand
> When next it takes mine. Will it? tenderly? . . .

Here is the Cavalier vocabulary, quiet and minor but active, in nineteenth-century aesthetic.

In the poetry of the present day the Donne tradition of language is an oddly varied one. The Cavalier lyricism of Cummings and Millay is one part of it; the metaphysical meditation of Frost and Auden, another. What all these share, and what they share with Donne, is a sense of colloquial speech, the difficulties of thought in process, the need of judgment. Their high degree of predication is devoted to personal statement yet evaluative statement; their form preserves more of stanzaic order than most in the twentieth century; their vocabulary is most abstract, least innovative. Primary terms of agreement are *little* and *old, death* and *sun, great, earth, nothing,* and *come, go, know, make*—as close to abstract construction as the twentieth century gets. The group tends to ignore the primary sensory words of the Pound-Eliot line, the *white* and *dark* and *green,* the *light, bird, moon, dream, wind* of current specification, and the most passive verbs. It is difficult to think of these modern predicative poets as a school, to group Millay and Auden together in any way, and yet we see that they share a desire for external control, for irony in statement, for the effects of men thinking and evaluating, for the useful making of sentences.

Frost's narratives meditate as they go. His lyrics, "The Road Not Taken," for example, or "Desert Places," draw their singleness of mood from active situation. Cummings' experiments with parts of lines, parts of syllables, and parts of speech all work within the framework of orthodox sentence making, and the play of statement against line. Auden's accordion-pleated dicta contain verbs, however quiet the verbs may be, and deal less in objects and qualities than in a series of thoughts which add up in the end to a sort of sum, or at least have a line drawn beneath them. Both in convention and experiment some measure of the Donnic line prevails against the ripe plums and maple leaves of many.

So Cummings in *1 × 1:*

> let it go—the
> smashed word broken
> open vow or
> the oath cracked length
> wise—let it go it
> was sworn to
>   go
>
> let them go—the
> truthful liars and
> the false fair friends
> and the boths and
> neithers— . . .

the external formalities, the address, the terms of truth and goodness.

Auden gives us a much heavier version of the material. His interest is more descriptive and general, and as a consequence his nouns are more important. But abstract considerations keep his work in motion. "Always in Trouble" begins:

Can speak of trouble, pressure on men
Born all the time, brought forward into light
For warm dark moan.
Though heart fears all heart cries for, rebuffs with mortal beat
Skyfall, the legs sucked under, adder's bite.
That prize held out of reach
Guides the unwilling tread, . . .

Or, "The Diaspora":

How he survived them they could never understand:
Had they not beggared him themselves to prove
They could not live without their dogmas or their land?
No worlds they drove him from were ever big enough:
How *could* it be the earth the Unconfined
Meant when It bade them set no limits to their love? . . .

Because we are able to perceive through the poetry of five centuries the persistence of a certain choice of language, a relatively stable pattern of structure, sound, and vocabulary, we are justified in speaking of a tradition in language, and may even conveniently, since Donne participated in it, call it the Donne tradition. It is also Chaucerian, Tudor, metaphysical, romantic, and modern; it belongs to all those poets who, whatever the peculiar materials of their day, tend to emphasize the materials of controlled process in thought and speech as distinguished from the data of sense and status.

By this distinction, in our own day, T. S. Eliot would not be a part of the Donne tradition, nor would Pound, Spender, Thomas, Stevens. Theirs is a school either of strong aesthetic and substantival emphasis or of a poised balance in selection; none of them is devoted strongly to the terms and the structures of predication. Where the Donne tradition uses verbs, Eliot uses nouns and adjectives. Where the Donne tradition uses words of evaluation like *good* and *false,* Eliot uses words of sense like *white* and *dry*. Where the Donne tradition uses strong external controls in structure of line and sentence, Eliot uses powerful internal connections. The two characteristics closest to a bond are the characteristics of strong negatives and of colloquial speech; but here too the differences persist: Eliot's negatives are of sense rather than of abstract standard, and his speech is not his own, but quoted ironically: his not the drama, but the observation.

I make this explicit contrast because Eliot himself has been most articulate in calling to mind the likenesses between modern and metaphysical. Indeed all these likenesses exist, and they have made Jacobean poetry come especially alive in our time. The main qualities which Williamson and others have attributed to Donne: the "actually realized object," the early "symbolist imagery," the "felt thought and aftersense," the "direct sensuous apprehension of thought," the "unified sensibility," of "the poetry of that past age that is most like our own," are all traits which we have most admired in the poetry of our own day; and their presence in Donnic poetry has made it for us admirable too.

Nevertheless, it is important to remember that for Donne at least one major characteristic of style, the choice of medium, was based not on the sensuous apprehension of objects, the images and symbols which were, rather, Spenserian or Miltonic, but on concepts of the process of thought. This is the ratiocination, the "brainwork," which Williamson points out; but it is a special kind: not the generalizing and coördinating reason of the eighteenth century, which was in its own way equally rational, but the logically subordinating reason of the metaphysicals. It was a reason which employed metaphors more than images, similes, or symbols; abstract more than concrete reference; complex more than compound sentences; argument more than declaration. It was in many important ways quite opposite to the aesthetic rationale of our day.

Merritt Hughes, Rosamund Tuve, and others have warned against "kidnapping" Donne for our own interests; it is possible that too much identification is dangerous not only to knowledge of Donne but also to our own self-knowledge. The weight of much modern poetic material, the character of the language medium for Eliot as for a possible majority of modern poets, is closer to nineteenth-century than to seventeenth-century choice and value.

Having described only one aspect of the Donne tradition, its language, I can suggest little concerning internal relationships or intrinsic values. But I can consider the apparent value of the one part, the language itself. Extrinsically, does the language of concept, address, predication, and external sound pattern seem a good medium for poetry? Many modern critics would say it does not. They emphasize the poem as aesthetic object, and they emphasize its materials as directly aesthetic also, by a theory of denotation or correspondence. Dewey, Eastman, MacLeish often make such choice. On the other hand, many modern critics while still emphasizing the poem as aesthetic object would allow its materials to be only indirectly, in context, aesthetic, by such theory of contrast as that of Cleanth Brooks or, often inconsistently, I. A. Richards. Neither kind of critic, then, would praise Donne's primary language of conceptual reference and argument as such. The first kind praises what language of sense it finds in his work, though it is subordinate; the second kind praises the subtle interrelation by conflict between the poetry's conceptual language and its total aesthetic effect. So both sorts of critics as they value the language of the Donne tradition alter it toward the language of the present, in the very process of discussion.

But I think that even more strongly in its original and enduring character the language of the Donne tradition may be said to have value for the present: value in the sense of qualities which we like, and value in the sense of qualities which we often lack. The colloquial communicativeness and rational complexity of Donnic language we both admire and need. Much of our best verse now is rich and deep, heavy and not resilient, symbolic and not active. Yet we speak wishfully of the active argument in Donne, his sense of good, his terms of human relation. We do not prefer Frost and Auden to Eliot and Stevens, yet we hear in them a tone we are apt to ponder and praise. Though substance is the cliché of our time, the weight of objects with which we drift, the process of thought in Donne moves us to some recognition and pleasure. The very sparseness of his language in our poetry, then, may heighten our sense of its rare worth to future design.

Materialist and organicist philosophies of the eighteenth and nineteenth centuries, still making judgments for the twentieth, tend to stress by their theories of correspondence the sheer stuff of poetry, the need of a directly aesthetic medium, the beautiful material as poetic. The philosophy of the poet as maker, on the other hand, asks not the material parts but the constructed whole to be beautiful, and gives to the poet rather than to the tool or symbol the active responsibility. Such a view of construction is the one that Donne, and the Donne tradition, has taken. In the midst of the richness of Elizabethan experimentation, a group of poets early affirmed the Chaucerian mode of construction, the strong predication of human standards and relationships in colloquial verse. Poets as different as Donne and Jonson, Cowley and Herbert, maintained the affirmation, and it was renewed by some romantics. Now it is renewed again, however variously, by a New England narrator, a New York lyricist, an English and American moralist. In the sense that such a pattern of language, carrying a pattern of thought, has been useful over five centuries to a number of poets whose work we think good, the inheritance seems descriptively poetic. And in the sense that such a pattern carries values still clear to it, the inheritance seems prescriptively poetic, a language for thought to come to life in.

CHAPTER THREE

DRYDEN AND THE CLASSICAL MODE

Sometimes we may wonder whether we can recognize a classical style in English poetry. Did Ben Jonson write it, or Samuel Johnson, or between them John Dryden? Was it plain or elaborate, modest or highflying, narrative or meditative, or all of these in some special combination? We think of it as flourishing in the Augustan era, the late seventeenth and early eighteenth centuries; and we think of it as formal, balanced, reasonable. How may we learn when it began and how long it lasted, what was the endurance of its particular collocation of traits?

One way is to begin by observing a hypothetical mid-point, the work of Dryden. If we find in many poems by Dryden a repeated pattern of usage embodying a clear attitude and idea, and if we find this pattern and attitude shared by a number of his contemporaries, then I think most readers would grant the presence of a sort of nucleus of the classical, and from it we could look further to observe its extensions and attenuations.

I propose to establish here not a whole view of the style, not the special patterns given the material by figure and association, by metrical detail and conventions of genre, but merely some of the bases for discrimination of style, in the simplest material of language as it is selected and arranged: the most used referential words, metrical structures, and sentence structures. What does Dryden have to say over and over, in what topics and constructions?—That may be our first concern as we ask about neoclassicism.

In the first place, his steadfast use of the iambic pentameter couplet is familiar to us. From his first published poem, "Upon the Death of Lord Hastings," 1649, through the occasional poems of the 1660's, excepting only the "Heroic Stanzas" and "Annus Mirabilis," through the satires and philosophical poems of the 1680's and the panegyrics of "Eleonora" though not the pindarics of the odes, and finally through the translations of Juvenal, Ovid, Virgil, and Homer, and the adaptations of Chaucer, Dryden saw that the rhymed pentameter should prevail. It was his "golden line," as he called it in his essay on translation, his classical unit of poetic presentation, allowing a substantial number of nouns and adjectives per verb, demanding thought organized by measure and by rhyme. The "tag" of the rhyme which Milton permitted him in the adaptation of *Paradise Lost* was a tag as much for the one line as for the couplet: a way of pointing the thought by regular expectation, with a minimum of internal or external carry-over, so that the unit itself was to be valued. Deeper study could clarify for us the norms of his variation in this precious form, but for our general purposes here it is enough to note its thoroughgoing presence in his work.

Secondly, a certain sort of sentence structure went along with the pentameter. Like the couplet lines, it was *balanced,* not only in the usual literary sense that it set one term or statement over against another, but also in the more technical sense, that it weighed equally the force of verb and adjective in predication. In this verse, adjectives and verbs were just equal in number. The result was that phrasal and clausal structures were balanced, that the writing was neither excessively passive nor excessively active, but moderate in blend of action and quality. The most meditative pieces are given some narrative temporal structure by which the simplest narratives are slowed and stilled with epithet. Before Dryden's time England had had only a little of such moderation in the structure of statement.

Thirdly, what were these statements about? What were the topics of concern, whatever the occasion or genre? Some terms, of course, were stressed and shared by most of the poets in his era—key value terms like *good, day, eye, God, heaven, man,* and actions like *find, give, know, make, see.* It was a vocabulary of scope and range, and Dryden used it as the others did, evaluating large actions and perceptions both heavenly and human, conceived in a strongly visual landscape. Further, Dryden repeatedly emphasized terms which were characteristic of his own work, or of a small group, as distinguished from the times as a whole. If we can generalize at all about the quality of this group of much-used terms, apart from their contexts, we may surmise that their emphasis is upon four special interests: emotion, as in *pleasure, fear, friend,* and *love;* abstraction, as in *mind, care, power, life, fate, name, place, way;* descriptive physical detail, as in *blood, hand, head;* and especially heroic combat, as in his most individual *arms, force, foe, ground, king, war, fly, fall,* and *stand.* Together, Dryden's major words give us a view of his persistent subject: the state, the social order human and divine; emotional, moral, abstract in concept, yet in action imagible. This range of interest is observable not only in certain major poems but in the whole concordance of his work, as edited by the late Professor Guy Montgomery at the University of California. (See Appendix B.)

Balanced predication and pentameter serve to order and consolidate such a vocabulary. In each successive poem, Dryden reconstructs the architecture of the state, with the same basic materials, to an effect of the same basic pattern, allowing for a wealth of minute variation. In the elegies, those mourned for shine from a realm analogous to the human, but patently divine. In the *Absalom,* the disturbed political world of Charles II partakes of the disturbed political and moral world of Scripture and the disturbed heroic worlds of Adam and Samson Lost, and so absorbs these more cosmic landscapes and passions into English affairs. In the *Religio* the abstractions are given their own visual cosmic path. In the translations of Ovid, Virgil, Homer, the machinery of Zeus and Juno is set to operating for English royal analogy; and the lively new natural terms of wind and sea, even the bees in the fourth *Georgic,* set up their own human and divine society:

Then to their common standard they repair;
The nimble horsemen scour the fields of air;
In form of battle drawn, they issue forth,
And ev'ry knight is proud to prove his worth.
Press'd for their country's honor, and their king's,
On their sharp beaks they whet their pointed stings,
And exercise their arms, and tremble with their wings. . . .

Thus, in the season of unclouded spring,
To war they follow their undaunted king,
Crowd thro' their gates, and in the fields of light
The shocking squadrons meet in mortal fight.
Headlong they fall from high, and, wounded, wound,
And heaps of slaughter'd soldiers bite the ground.

These are the loyalties and oppositions of *Absalom* also, as the king speaks at the end:

"Nor doubt th' event; for factious crowds engage,
In their first onset, all their brutal rage.

Then let 'em take an unresisted course;
Retire, and traverse, and delude their force;
But, when they stand all breathless, urge the fight,
And rise upon 'em with redoubled might;
For lawful pow'r is still superior found;
When long driv'n back, at length it stands the ground."
 He said. Th' Almighty, nodding, gave consent;
And peals of thunder shook the firmament.

From the Almighty, through Zeus, David, Charles, Flecknoe, to the bee king runs the chain of generality, of nature, power, and order. And to this order, passion and atmosphere are devoted.

Others in Dryden's time were devoted to this same complex of materials for poetry. Marvell was one, in his State Poems. Addison was another, in his translation of Virgil. Parnell was another, in his poems on several occasions, and Pope another, in his *Rape of the Lock*. We are willing enough, by previous expectation, to consider this as a classical group. They wrote during some fifty years from 1670 to 1720, and they were friends of a sort and mutual admirers at times. In the basic materials with which we are concerned they had a common interest: they all stressed balanced predication and pentameter couplet, and they shared with Dryden a group of dominant terms which few others used, which bespoke their central interests: such terms as *happy, high, mighty,* and *arms, fate, king, name, nature, lie, rise,* a royal, political, and natural order, to be described or praised, or satirized, with a great deal of feeling and sense impression under tight technical control.

We may note within the group certain variations which do not alter the basic agreement. For example, Marvell's early octosyllabics and sensory stress, his *grow, green, flower, grass,* and *tree,* make his early poetry differ from his late more greatly than Dryden's. But still nature and fate are pervasive. Then again, Addison is a poet far more limited in his poetic devotions. But his translation of the fourth *Georgic* is even more closely balanced than Dryden's, and his vocabulary for translation even more classically agreeable, in its *great, high, mighty, fate,* and *state.* Parnell, sponsored by Addison as well as by Pope in the second decade of the century, wrote some famous decasyllabics in "The Hermit" and "Queen Anne's Peace," to a total effect of balanced proportion and rich atmospheric feeling in the words of *glory, joy, name, nation, peace, power, praise, war,* and *view.* And Pope, sometimes more epithetical, sometimes less, within a small range, persists, with Dryden, in the pentametric social order, in *air, fate, heaven, king, love, name, power, prayer, sky,* in the brilliant scene of human and divine, mocked or recommended. All inhabit and write about the same series of unfolding worlds joined by the generality of analogous order.

If, then, we may accept the Marvell-Dryden-Addison-Pope-Parnell group as representative of the classical style in English, with Parnell, as Goldsmith later wrote, "the last of that great school that had modelled itself on the ancients, and taught English poetry to resemble what the generality of mankind have allowed to excel," we must pursue and accept also the consequences of the assumptions which led to this grouping. These assumptions are, as I have suggested above, that a number of poets who live in one era and share many concepts, attitudes, and purposes, who share also some major poetic materials of sound and sentence structure and dominant reference, may well be at least provisionally considered as a group, their basic likenesses being so much stronger than their differences; and, more particularly, that since Dryden is traditionally at the center of what is called neoclassicism, we may test the traits of the mode through him and those who most agree with him.

The first consequence of the assumption is that we should expect classical poetry itself, the poetry of Horace, Ovid, Juvenal, Virgil, Homer, to possess the dominant traits that we have noted in Dryden and his group. That is, we should expect Dryden and his friends to take over from Latin and Greek not just any minor qualities they happened to admire, but the dominant qualities of the poetry itself, if they have understood it, and if they have the skill to master it in English.

And so, in fact, we find they have done. A predominant trait of Horatian and Juvenalian satires and epistles, of Ovidian metamorphoses, of Virgilian georgic and epic, in contrast to a more active Homer on the one hand and a more ceremonious Pindar on the other, is the use of the balanced sentence structure, with equal use of adjectives and verbs. This balance the neoclassicists had a sense for, in their "golden" proportion which they strove to make English meet. The somewhat shorter line of English pentameter necessitated a reduction to a proportion of just one verb and adjective per line instead of somewhat more, but the balance is the same. The pentameter was also weaker than the Latin hexameter in its line ends, and the couplet rhyme appeared partly in order to help make up that deficiency, out of a sense of the formal unit of the verse. As for vocabulary, the very terms we see as characteristic of the Dryden group are characteristic also of the Roman, the *magnus, bonus, malus, longus, animus, honor, urbs, nox, populus, do, facio, fero, video, volo, opto, timeo,* of Horace and Juvenal, and the additionally atmospheric and emotional *altus, summus, laetus, caelum, terra, tellus, unda, sol, ventus, arma, fatum, gens, urbs, nomen,* of Ovid and Virgil, in addition to their more poetically standard *amor, deus, pater, tempus, vir, homo,* and in addition to such abstract terms as *locus, via, populus,* which the English brought to slight stress in such terms as *place, way, crowd,* and *mankind.*

The Roman offered to the English of 1700 a form and subject adaptable to English needs. Indeed, the satisfaction probably worked two ways: the English admired the Roman for itself, its artistic authority, and had long tried for correspondence; the literary effort may have served to develop English interests in the direction of the spatial generalities of scene and kingdom. On the other hand, what were clearly English concerns, social and religious order, universal human psychology and association, and "greatness" on all levels of a society which yet wished to encourage the middle way—all these led to a natural artistic preoccupation with materials newly recognized as classical. The satirists' *magnus* and *parvus, animus* and *amicus,* and even more the Virgilian *altus* and *laetus, caelum, fatum, ventus, unda,* helped the senses, waked theoretically by Hobbes and Locke, to report in a newly emphasized vocabulary bolstered by social feeling and divine abstraction; while classical balanced sentence and full regular line helped control this new natural and general material, checking the gods firmly by kingship and the passions by the weather, tempering action and observation so that neither outran the other.

So Dryden and his group were classical not only by self-nomination, but by artistic discrimination. They literally adapted a style, conveying line and sentence structure and a special vocabulary with its concomitant frame of vision, expertly from one language to the other. Consequently, their practice defines them. It is the classical poet in English who balanced line and sentence and who stresses concepts such as *happy, high, mighty, hand, friend, king, mind, name, nature, night, sky, war,* and *world* in recurring context and combination, wherein cosmic, social, and personal levels run parallel, with *sky* or *king high* or *happy* or *fearful,* and the war one of *minds,* of *friends,* of *nature,* or of *world.*[1]

Where does such proposal for definition leave the early "classicists" like Sidney, or Daniel, or Ben Jonson? It leaves them in Old England, a century past. It demands that we look back to observe their practice, and the possible sources of the classical style in English; but it suggests that we shall find in poetry's earlier years a very different syntax and vocabulary. For example: from the poetry of Chaucer, Skelton, and

[1] Note in R. F. Jones's *Triumph of the English Language* the recurrent attitude toward Latin as natural, human, pagan, as opposite to Saxon logic and metaphysic. Note also a parallel contrast between Bunyan's prose and Johnson's in S. Krishnamurty's "Frequency-Distribution of Nouns in Johnson's Prose," *Journal of the University of Bombay,* XX, Pt. 2 (September, 1951), 1–16.

the ballads, through Wyatt, Marlowe, Sidney, through Jonson, Donne, Vaughan, Herrick, and into the mid-seventeenth century of Cowley and Denham, the English poetic sentence structure was persistently unbalanced toward the predicative, that is, highly clausal rather than phrasal, subordinate rather than coördinate, active rather than participial. This one trait was enough, I think, to keep any of the poetry which it characterized from seeming classical in any basic stylistic way. Of the great models, only Homer approached this sort of construction, and he by no means so radically as most of the English. Poetic thinking, like prosaic thinking, in the Renaissance was still more "Senecan" or "Ciceronian" than "modern," more clausal, that is, than modificatory in the later fashion. English jumped with verbs, and though some of the would-be classicists were troubled by their lack of "smoothness" in English, they blamed the articulations of the language, especially its monosyllabic Saxon inheritance, without apparently realizing the power of what epithets and participles they did possess to soothe and subdue in the classical way. Perhaps closest to grasping the norm was Sackville in the *Mirror,* in that rich new style of his which made such a contrast to Baldwin's Englishness; and Chapman, who caught Homer's proportions exactly. Such lively and confident poets as Donne and Jonson did not, of course, even aim at the balanced style. They called their own active verse sinewy and masculine in contrast to the smoother feminine extreme of the Spenserians.

Spenser represented what was in his day a minor tendency in English construction but was to become, with Milton, major in its force. This was the tendency to overbalance statement in the other direction, that of epithet, to make verbs into participles and suspend action in a frame of description. In agreement with him were such followers as the Fletchers and Joshua Sylvester, who translated into English the highly influential *Divine Weekes* of Du Bartas; and one wonders how much the combination of Platonism and Protestantism had to do with this descriptive mode, that it could so fully develop to absorb Milton and the eighteenth century. At any rate, between Donne and Milton the contrast in structural method was a strong one, and neither extreme seemed to portend a feeling for classical balance.

Shakespeare's *Sonnets* give us the first clear view of a smoothly balanced structure. The other main sonneteers, except for Spenser, were predicative in their emphasis, in the general tradition of their poetry; Shakespeare achieved a basic alteration of tradition in his sentence pattern, of the sort that Waller later was to get so much credit for from Dryden and his friends. This was the "marble" in the architecture of the language, the substantializing of action by quality and clause by phrase, to the effect of a surface smooth and solid.

Did genre have anything to do with this problem of structure? Of course yes, but possibly less than one might imagine. At least it does not happen, as one might imagine, that sixteenth- and seventeenth-century narratives are all strongly predicative while the pastorals and lyrics are descriptive and adjectival. As we have noted, the predicative emphasis persisted in all genres through both centuries. On the other hand, some further discriminations can be made. Consider the works which first seem to have employed the balanced mode. One was Shakespeare's *Sonnets,* lyrical with narrative elements; another was Sackville's *Induction;* a third was Joseph Hall's *Satires.* Here are the main genres, then, all participating in the new tendency. Hall's *Satires* are particularly interesting because they provide such contrast to the satires of John Hall, his contemporary, and of Donne, as of Oldham and Roscommon later; and it was his work which gained the outspoken approval of the master satirists when classicism had been more generally achieved. Joseph Hall anticipated, then; he caught the new possibility, as Shakespeare did. And when Dryden, Marvell, Pope, and the others later developed the possibility, they did so in various forms, in elegy and epistle as well as in satire and narrative. So that we find no clear establishment in genre *per se.* Nevertheless, the clue we get from Sackville, Hall, and Shakespeare, as distinguishd from the extremes of a Jonson or a Milton, is a deliberating quality, neither dramatic argument on the one hand nor celebration on the other, which may bring them close to the compromise of the classical temper, and which may suggest a combination of meditative genres distinguished at least from the dramatic action of Homer, as from the rhapsodies of Pindar and Lucretius: a genre of middle way, and in that sense, in Aristotle's terms, closer to epic than to drama or dithyramb. "All poetry has three styles; the descriptive, the dramatic, and the mixed," J. E. Congleton in his *Pastoral Poetry* (p. 14) quotes from Kynaston's translation of the Codex Ambrosianus. The middle is the mixed for the new classicism, as heroes and kings have left the gods for the state.

Vocabulary follows sentence structure in giving only scattered evidence of classical adaptation before Dryden's time. The rhymed pentameter was not consolidated till then, except in uses of it such as Joseph Hall's, though Sackville's and Shakespeare's pentameters had done much to prepare the way; and the new sort of reference was a part of this whole complex. Terms peculiar to Virgil, Horace, and the Dryden group we find in isolated use by certain earlier poets: *happy* by Shakespeare and Cowley, *common* by Gascoigne, *high* by Spenser, Sandys, Waller, *friend* by Breton, *name* by Googe, Cowley, and others, *nature* by Surrey and Shakespeare and Cowley, *power* by Sternhold and Sandys and Waller, *state* by Sackville, *air* by Milton, *sea* and *fate* by Waller. One notes here an accumulating atmosphere: a few main references by single poets, which gradually get caught up into a tissue of agreements among those immediately preceding the classical period, Cowley, Sandys, Waller, Milton—poets of the Spenserian rather than the Jonsonian tradition.

Indeed, we may see that the Jonson-Donne tradition, as it summarizes the Chaucerian and most of the modes before 1650 and includes the most of dialogue, commentary, argument, and satire, is the native intellectual tradition, has along with its clear predicative structure and colloquial tone a special and persisting vocabulary, lasting through Roscommon and some of the satires of Pope into the nineteenth century. This is a vocabulary of human commentary, beginning with Chaucer, and drawing partly from Latin satire: active, with *give, make, tell* stronger than *see, hear, know;* temporal, with *new, old, time, age, young, year;* socially evaluative, with *good, bad, poor, rich, just, kind, false, true, wise;* verbal, with *speak, word, tale;* urban, with *town* and *city* and some royal command; in all, discursive and abstract, except in terms of human relationships. This was not to be the vocabulary of the classicists. It would set Joseph Hall apart from Dryden, who grew more spacious and various and added the *fate, heaven, nature, power* terms of the richer descriptive traditions of Spenser, Sandys, Waller, and even Milton.

It is in terms of Milton that we are led by poetic practice further to understand Dryden's classicism, because neither the native satiric modes nor the Roman poets fully provide the materials which we see flourishing at 1700. Dryden's classicism was not only an expert imitation but also an expert compromise, and the compromise was between the Jonsonian and Miltonic extremes. In the major vocabularies of such poets as Spenser, Sylvester, Waller, heightened in Milton, we find at once the more sensuous and more spiritual terms which were characteristic of much Augustan emphasis, a kind of Whiggery; and, in the structures of these same poets, that overbalance of descriptive and participial modification which was most vividly to spread and characterize the style of the mid-eighteenth century. *High, mighty, heaven, nature, power, sea, world* were such words, often equivalent to the classical terms, and adopted by Dryden's group. *Bright, dark, eternal, air, light, spirit* were the further Sylvestrian and Miltonic kinds which would later help establish the tone of the sublime "pre-romantic" period. Of the fifty nouns, adjectives, verbs he used most, Dryden shared twenty-seven with Milton, only twenty-one with Pope; with

Milton the atmospheric *high, place, night* and significant verbs of *falling* and *lying;* with Pope, *care* and *friend.*

The cumulative force of the sort of verse atmospheric in its terminology, cosmic in its reach, Platonic and Biblical and Protestant, overbalanced in structure and least regular in linear metrics in ode and blank-verse forms, steadily grew through Sylvester and the Spenserians to Milton and from Milton to the whole group encouraged by Addison: Pomfret, Blackmore, Akenside, Prior, Philips, Thomson, Collins, the Wartons, Blake, and many others in the eighteenth century, providing that century's major mode. Only a few, notably Young and Johnson, resisted this pressure of cosmic atmosphere strongly enough to preserve a classical balance; only these, with a wavering Pope, maintained the middle way which Dryden had unwaveringly established.

This middle way, this classical golden mean, we see poised at 1700, medial and balanced then in more ways than one. The native English style, active, colloquial, and humanistic, which had persisted from Chaucer through Donne and Jonson and even much of Cowley and Denham and was not to be seen again until almost 1800, met in Dryden, under the direct mediation of Virgil and Horace, with that other style, rapidly increasing its sweep of epithet and cosmic atmosphere, which Milton, the Bible, and Longinus fostered and the eighteenth century enthusiastically embraced. The result of the meeting was a great strengthening of earlier efforts at classicism, a more thorough recognition and capacity for reproducing technically the moderations of the Latin style. Joseph Hall on the one hand brought a moderate colloquialism close to Dryden in the humanistic world; Marvell, Waller, and the later Milton tempered, on the other, their cosmic wealth and scope to the affairs of state. Two sets of vocabularies, sound patterns, sentence structures, as different from each other as we have ever had in English poetry, partly blended and combined for one or two generations of poets at that time which we called neoclassical, with the result of poise: a poise of metrical and sentence forms in the pentameter couplet and the balance of adjective and verb per pentameter line; a poise of diverse materials, native, Biblical, classical in a harmony at once social and cosmic.

Marvell, Waller, the later Milton, Dryden, Addison, Parnell, Pope, Young, Shenstone, Goldsmith, Johnson, wrote this verse. The group of classicists is not large, as determined technically by its blend of form and material. It excludes Jonson as radically English; it excludes most of the eighteenth century as radically Gothic; but it includes both Johnson and his opponent Young as both are tempered to balance and moderation. This sort of classicism is not the rule of reason in any logical way that we have heard of. Rather it is emotional; *happy* is its Virgilian term, and *care, fear, joy* its contribution. *Truth* and *wisdom* are much less important to it than *nature* and *power,* the sense of extended universal forces and controls. Time and space are poised in it, the first a subsiding, the second a growing concern. Abstraction takes the form of generality, not personal but pervasive, in terms of physical or social law. Actions still create, but accept much also; the senses are alert to receive and observe. The *Georgics* are the model of mediation, because they draw the levels of thought together: the natural, the social, the divine. All are externalized and synthesized as the English world; the world of Charles II in *Absalom,* for example, is caught up into both Rome and Judea and thence to both Olympus and Eden, even to Heaven and Hell.

Of the three great traditional styles, low, middle, and high, this of Dryden's seems to be the middle. It is not the high; that was the highest Milton's or Blake's. It is not the low; that was Jonson's, with all his zest for the native tradition and his absorbing of the classics into it. Dryden's very point in the *Absalom* is that it not be the traditional low English satire, but high in mockery, and thus a compromise in effect. The *Georgics* works the same way, elevating its men and bees to make the simple tasks divine and the divine simple. Pope's *Rape* works this way, and Parnell's social poems, and Gray's *Elegy,* and Johnson's surveys; even, indeed, the domestications of much of *Paradise Lost* and *Paradise Regained.* As God, king, and man are seen to feel much alike and to work much alike, in the same rich realms, as even the fields and skies are humanized, as Homer is seen in Virgil, and the Old Testament in the New, classicism establishes its time of balance, between the England of Jonson and the England of Blake, in Dryden's golden line and golden mean.

CHAPTER FOUR

THE SUBLIME POEM

WE CAN, I think, construct a clear image of a sublime poem if we are willing to consider the basic simplicities of the modes in which most eighteenth-century poets wrote. If we were to look at all the leading poets of the century, thirty or forty of them perhaps, we should find a few, especially at the beginning, writing in that balanced, coupleted, cultivated mode which has been called classical; we should find a few, especially at the end, writing in that narrative lyrical ballad mode which has been called romantic; and we should find the rest, in the years from 1700 to 1770 and beyond, writing enthusiastically in a clearly definable harmonic and panoramic mode which has so far been called by no name of its own. One might call it picturesque or Pindaric, to suggest its artistic allegiances; Georgian, to suggest the reigns during which it prospered; Gothic, to suggest its sweep above and beyond classicism. All these terms, however, have limiting connotations awkward for the poetry. Closest to stylistic terms are Warton's "sublime" and "pathetic," representing a realm of emotional and dimensional discriminations adopted with interest by the critics in the century.

I propose to use sublime as a descriptive term for the whole realm of interest including the pathetic, for the whole ethos-pathos range of discernment; it too has its disadvantages of connotation, as in some of the specifications of Burke; but at least it is the era's own term, and suggestive even now of the sweeping, lofty, harmonious, emotional concerns which characterized poetic choices in the eighteenth-century mode. I shall try progressively to substantiate and clarify my use of it for that poetry which had its specific complex of traits: an epithetical, phrasal, participial, and compounding sentence structure, an unrhymed or irregular ode line, a vocabulary of passion and magnitude.

We may remember the classical distinction between ethos as human action and pathos as human suffering—suffering at the hands of fate, of the gods. Pathos was the wider, the more mysterious, the encompassing and tragic term; ethos was the term of social choice and custom, even of comedy. In ethics, man initiated; in pathetics, the gods proposed and disposed, and man endured. The great figure of ethos carried beyond its sphere, to become the extreme of pathos, is Prometheus. It was in such great pathetic figures and scenes that the eighteenth century was interested. Ethos for them had lessened, in "manners" as a matter of fashion, and as a term almost completely subordinated; pathos remained as high and moving, and to it was added the high and moving sublime of Longinus, newly sponsored by Boileau. Klaus Dockhorn, in his two monographs on Wordsworth and the sublime (Göttingen, 1944 and 1949), has shown us how exactly the formula seemed to get reversed, the classical high pathos becoming the neoclassical low and particular pathetic; and he has been troubled, as many historians have been, about the moment and the manner of this reversal. At least it may be suggested that English sublime-pathetic poetry itself carries a clue, perhaps a clearer one than its critics articulated, in its "simple, sensuous, and passionate" subject matter.

For Sylvester, Fletcher, More, Milton, the sensuous and passionate in poetry were high and lofty and coincident with sublimity. Heroic narrative was narrative of sublime pathos, of great figures in a great scene. But with and after them,[1] as narrative declined and description gained in literary force, as nature in its way took over the heights from man, and the gods became more and more a part of natural force, more mountainous, stormy, cosmic, yet retaining Longinus' Biblical sublimity, the human seemed to be diminished, its suffering set against the great storms of natural forces, made more local and perceivable, and so "pathetic" in its newly diminished sense. The mass of eighteenth-century poetry, the Dodsley collection for example, shows this new quality vividly: the new subject matter of natural force towering over and sublimating human passion, as in image it is a counterpart and analogy. We must turn to look at the poetry more closely to watch the development of the mode.

Intimations of sublimity grew slowly through the seventeenth century. The rich note of Spenser and his followers came to seem antiquated. The newer and more cosmic tone was Sylvester's in the *Divine Weekes,* and this is the sound that grew, for Milton especially, and for the later Cowley, Denham, Waller, and the Pindarists: the high style as it resounded in the spheres. We remember how at mid-century Hobbes and Davenant reargued the levels of style, and set again the highest as courtly and heroic. But courtly and heroic materials were not to be the active ones; rather, Protestantism was to turn them even further toward satire. For Protestantism it was the heavenly court, the heavenly city, the heavenly hero that mattered. So

[1] Josephine Waters Bennett points out (English Institute *Essays,* 1951) that Spenser and Milton are the first great poets of Protestant revolt. See also Norman Maclean's "From Action to Image," in *Critics and Criticism,* ed. R. Crane (Chicago, 1925), and the Ramist models for Fraunce in Sister Miriam Joseph's *Shakespeare's Use of the Arts of Language* (Columbia Univ. Press, 1947).

the style gradually rose up from the secular to the cosmic, with the combined aids of heroic theory, Sylvestrian practice, and Longinian *Peri Upsous*.

Davenant wrote to Hobbes in his Preface to *Gondibert* (London, 1651), "And surely Poets (whose business should represent the World's true image often to our view) are not less prudent than Painters, who when they draw Landschaps, entertain not the Eye wholly with even Prospect; and a continued Flat; but (for variety) terminate the sight with lofty Hills, whose obscure heads are sometimes in the clouds." He wrote also that "wise Poets think it more worthy to seek out truth in the Passions, than to record the truth of Actions; . . . it being nobler to contemplate the general History of Nature, than a selected Diary of Fortune." Davenant wrote with conscience, he said, and he chose to deal with Christian characters, with distant scenes, with wit, "the dexteritie of thought, rounding the world, like the Sun, with unimaginable motion; and bringing swiftly home to the memorie, universal surveys."

Hobbes replied with assent, equating heroic with celestial: "For there is in Princes, and men of conspicuous power (anciently call'd *Heroes*) a lustre and influence upon the rest of men, resembling that of the Heavens, and an insincereness, inconstancie, and troublesom humour of those that dwell in populous Cities, like the mobilitie, blustering, and impuritie of the Air; and a plainness, and (though dul) yet a nutritive facultie in rural people, that endures a comparison with the Earth they labour."

The universal analogies were so clear that the poet could easily proceed, in theory, but Davenant himself had not the sense of the new heroic meter and vocabulary. Too conceptual, too homely, too popular, his quatrains rattled:

Of all the Lombards, by their Trophies known,
  Who sought Fame soon, and had her favour long,

King Aribert best seem'd to fill the Throne;
And bred most bus'ness for Heroick Song.

What Cowley and Waller praised him for in their introductory verses was his generality, his breaking away from the antique fictive spell of pagan gods and magic toward a more social and religious truth, in lines

Which no bold tales of Gods or Monsters swell,
But humane Passions, such as with us dwell.

What Davenant needed to fulfill his motives was a fuller power of elaboration, and it was this that Cowley began to capture in the *Davideis,* as Denham and Waller did in their surveys, so that the great power which Milton achieved had been anticipated by a growing purpose and familiarity. For all the relative failure of Cowley's heroics, his fellow Denham could praise them,

When Heroes, Gods, or God-like Kings
They praise, on their exalted wings
To the Celestial orbs they climb,
And with th' Harmonious Spheres keep time; . . .
("On Mr. Abraham Cowley," *Poems,* London, 1668)

And for all Denham's own immersion in the metaphysical style, he could begin to try the sort of line and phrasing which Dryden in turn would praise: the descriptive and lofty analogy, as in the middle of "Coopers Hill":

But his proud head the aery Mountain hides
Among the Clouds; his shoulders and his sides
A shady mantle cloaths; his curled brows
Frown on the gentle stream, which calmly flows,
While winds and storms his lofty forehead beat:
The common fate of all that's high or great.

Part of this increasing sense of nature's divinity and humanity came from Protestantism, from Platonic and Biblical sources, as in the work of Spenser, Sylvester, the Cambridge Platonists and Thomas Burnet, as, indeed, from the King James version of the Bible itself and the sublimity of preaching based upon it. Cowley's support of Davenant in his poem of praise was explicitly anti-Catholic, pro-Hebraic; and we can watch in paraphrases like those of Sandys the growth of a sensuous Biblical vocabulary into English.

Part of the sublime style, too, was to be found in classical poets, even the most mundane like Horace. In pastoral scenery, Christian and pagan could join to find significance. While Ovid had been the classical poet for the sixteenth century, and Virgil would be for much of the eighteenth, in between Horace provided a good guide, and everybody from Jonson to Roscommon tried him in translation. The English which translated him grew more and more suitably furnished and proportioned, though his true rich classical balance was difficult for native English to achieve. The famous beginning to his Ode IX, of Book I, much liked in the seventeenth century, even in its simple translation by Thomas Creech, suggests the new vocabulary of scene and sense:

> See how the Hills are white with Snow,
> The Seas are rough, the Woods are tost,
> The Trees beneath their Burden bow,
> And purling Streams are bound in Frost.

Or, even more lofty, the end of Ode III:

> With Wings, which Nature's Laws deny,
> First Daedalus did boldly dare
> To beat the Empty Air,
> And wander thro' the liquid Sky.

Thro' Hell the fierce Alcides ran,
He scorn'd the stubborn chains of Fate,
And rudely broke the Brazen Gate;
    Nought is too hard for Man.

Grown Giants in Impiety,
Our Impious Folly dares the Sky,
We dare assault Jove's glorious Throne;
Nor still averse to his Command,
Will we permit his lifted Hand
    To lay his Thunder down.
        (*Odes, Satyrs, Epistles, of Horace,*
        6th ed., London, 1737)

This is soaring as "unclassical" as Blake's, and in Blake's vocabulary.

Horace's very consciousness of the varieties of style brought new possibilities to seventeenth-century attention, as he discussed suitability of method and subject in his "Art of Poetry":

Some scatter here and there few gawdy Lines,
Which glister finely, when a Grove's their Theme,
A pleasant Wood, or else a purling Stream:
How with the Flood, their Fancies smoothly flow!
How variously they paint the Heav'nly Bow!
But now perhaps none of these Themes agree.
Perhaps thou hast some Skill to paint a Tree,
But what of that? What will this Art perform?
Wert thou to draw a Shipwrack, or a Storm?

These had not been the subjects or the problems of English poets. They were the problems of painters, as Horace said; and of this likening the English now took strong note. How to paint a tree? How to paint a storm? It would remain for James Thomson to try the problem most wholeheartedly.

In Creech it was already the new "classical" Horace that was speaking and advising toward the new poetry. Hear how different the old colloquial Horace sounded, in the more English English of Oldham's translation: the same passage has for Oldham the miscellaneous jumble of earlier satire.

> Some, who would have us think they meant to treat
> At first on arguments of greatest weight,
> Are proud, when here and there a glitt'ring line
> Does through the mass of their coarse rubbish shine.
> In gay digressions they delight to rove,
> Describing here a temple, there a grove,
> A vale enamell'd o'er with pleasant streams,
> A painted rainbow, or the gliding Thames.
> But how does this relate to their design?
> Though good elsewhere, 'tis here but foisted in.
> A common dauber may perhaps have skill
> To paint a tavern sign, or landscape well;
> But what is this to drawing of a fight,
> A wreck, a storm, or the last judgment right?
> (*Poetical Works* of John Oldham, London, 1854)

This is the Oldham of the "Satires against the Jesuits" of 1683, the great admirer of Ben Jonson, one of the poets of the dregs, whips, and scourges of the satirical tradition; and both his technique and his vocabulary are strongly traditional, making little allowance for the mood of the classics which was dawning on the landscaped world of Dryden. In the satirists we see the conventionalists, the holders to English tradition, against the sweep of Miltonism; even in Marvell we see the force of the old terms in his State Poems, crowding out the green shade of his earlier rich pastoralism. Therefore the change was slow; the rational and bitter persisted; but translation by translation Horace was sweetening and his countryside winning out.

Swift in most of his poetry [2] and Gay in his *Fables* prolonged the vernacular satiric line a short way into the eighteenth century, but after them there was little of colloquialism in poetry until Burns and Coleridge and Byron brought it back again under different auspices, the active narrative simplicity of lyrical balladry.

Meanwhile, the Roman classical mode of the late seventeenth century had also somewhat subsided in the eighteenth. The balanced terms and structures of Joseph Hall, Marvell, Dryden, Addison, and Parnell continued temperately in some of Pope's work, and in Johnson's and Goldsmith's. But otherwise its force was minor, not to be renewed until late in the century, in the new classicism of Crabbe and Wordsworth.

The prevailing eighteenth-century poem was the sublime poem, risen from sources in English efforts at heroic poetry, strengthened by new versions of classical practice, and fully established by the combined forces of the Bible, Milton, Fénelon, and Longinus. The sublime poem was written throughout the century, from Pomfret, Prior, Blackmore, Brooke, and Thomson, through Gray, Akenside, and Collins, through Blair and Dyer and Armstrong, through Mason, Lyttelton, and Somerville, to the Wartons and Blake and Bowles, even to Keats. Thereafter, with exceptions in Whitman,[3] Wilde, Henley, and some of the Imagists, we have had less of its nature. But for one whole century it dominated the world of English poetry.[4]

How may the sublime poem be distinguished? First of all, by its cumulative phrasal sentence structure, its piling up of nouns and epithets, participles and compounds, with a very minimum of clausal

[2] Swift's *Battle of the Books,* like *The Rehearsal* earlier and Pope's *Peri Bathous* later, mocked the new sublimity.

[3] Gay Wilson Allen in his *Whitman Handbook* (Packard, 1946) clearly describes for Whitman the mode I have called "sublime": the panoramic images, linear units, cumulative structures, and phonic iterations.

[4] John Arthos' *Language of Natural Description in Eighteenth-Century Poetry* (Univ. of Michigan Press, 1949), pp. 2, 14, 42, makes this point particularly clear in his own terms, relating to the styles of Lucretius and Du Bartas.

subordinations and active verbs. Second, by its vocabulary of cosmic passion and sense impression. Third, by its internal rather than external patterning of sound, the interior tonal shadings and onomatopoeias of its unrhymed verse. In combination, these three major traits make for an exceptionally panoramic and panegyric verse, emotional, pictorial, noble, universal, and tonal, rising to the height of heaven and of feeling in the style traditionally known as grand or sublime.

We may look at John Philips' "Blenheim" or "Cyder" as examples, to see how the consciously Miltonic style functions in blank-verse pomp, at the century's beginning. "Blenheim" begins:

> From low and abject Themes the Grov'ling Muse
> Now mounts Aerial, to sing of Arms
> Triumphant, and emblaze the Martial Acts
> Of Britain's Heroe; may the Verse not sink
> Beneath his Merits, but detain a while
> Thy Ear, O Harley, . . .

The lines proceed to show Albion in action:

> Now from each Van
> The brazen Instruments of Death discharge
> Horrible Flames, and turbid streaming Clouds
> Of Smoak sulphureous; intermix't with these
> Large globous Irons fly, of dreadful Hiss,
> Singeing the Air, and from long Distance bring
> Surprizing Slaughter; on each side they fly
> By Chains connex't, and with destructive Sweep
> Behead whole Troops at once; the hairy Scalps
> Are whirl'd aloof, while numerous Trunks bestrow
> Th' ensanguin'd Field; . . .
>
> (Lines 143–153; *Poems,* ed. M. G. Lloyd Thomas, Blackwell, 1927)

This is the sort of sublime excess we have found even more in Blake's Prophetic Books than in Milton; it has the drive and richness of much compacted detail in massive range. The more famous "Cyder" is more pastorally peaceful, but still in its destruction scene reaches magniloquent heights.

> Horrible Chasm, profound! with swift Descent
> Old Ariconium sinks, and all her Tribes,
> Heroes, and Senators, down to the Realms
> Of endless Night.
>
> (Bk. I, lines 227–231)

Fall and *rise* were, indeed, the characteristically most used verbs in eighteenth-century poetry; along with the nouns *air, sky,* and *scene,* they indicated the sort of cosmic atmosphere and activity that prevailed, while *dear, soft, tender, virtue, song, joy* for the first time in English poetry made feeling explicit, and the nouns *breast, head, maid, muse, youth* bodied forth the feeling figures. They were, as we may see from Philips and others, partly classical figures, the presences of gods and muses, more than life-size; they were partly and increasingly northern titanic figures, with a Jehovan presence; the first were often related to the "beautiful," the second to the "sublime," but even beauty in the eighteenth century grew more and more sublime as it grew from the classical terms of *happy* to late-century *sad,* from *new* to *wild,* from *nature* to *cloud,* from *art, fate,* and *friend* to *woe* and *weeping,* even from *mighty* to *little,* as the sublimity of passion came down to smallest essences, and the whole realm became one with the pathetic. This was the road which sublimity traveled: it grew out of classical beauty and it grew into classical pathos, moving always by way of the heights and the depths.

So Pomfret begins in 1699 with the classical picture in "The Choice":

> Horace and Virgil, in whose mighty Lines
> Immortal Wit, and solid Learning, shines;

Sharp Juvenal, and am'rous Ovid too,
Who all the Turns of Love's soft Passion knew:
He that with Judgment reads his charming Lines,
In which strong Art with stronger Nature joins,
Must grant his Fancy does the best excel:
His Thoughts so tender, and express'd so well;
With all those Moderns, Men of steady Sense,
Esteem'd for Learning, and for Eloquence.
(*Poems,* London, 11th ed., lines 19–25)

Then he proceeds to intensify, as in the last sections of "Love Triumphant over Reason":

The glorious Fabrick charm'd my wondring Sight;
Of vast Extent, and of prodigious Height:
The Case was Marble, but the polish'd Stone,
With such an admirable Lustre shone,
As if some Architect Divine had strove
T' outdo the Palace of imperial Jove, . . .

And then, in the "Divine Attributes," more wildness (sec. VI):

Did not th' Almighty, with immediate Care,
Direct and govern this capacious All,
How soon would Things into Confusion fall!
Earthquakes the trembling Ground would tear,
And blazing Comets rule the troubled air;
Wide Inundations, with resistless Force,
The lower Provinces o'erflow,
In Spite of all that human Strength could do
To stop the raging Sea's impetuous Course.
Murder and Rapine ev'ry Place would fill,
And sinking Virtue stoop to prosp'rous Ill; . . .

Such variety and degree of power in 1699 presaged the range and variety of the whole century to come, all in a style "higher" than even Homer or Virgil had managed to achieve. Their lines and structures were classically balanced; these reached out to an evangelist heaven and hell.

The early practicers did not at first manage to break away from rhyme, as Pomfret here did not, and Blackmore even earlier (see *A Collection of Poems* by Sir Richard Blackmore, London, 1718 ed.). The mode was not yet clearly established, and Blackmore received the scorn of the wits for his high appeals to imagination and passion. But even in couplets the sublimity was evident. For example see "Advice to the Poets," fifth section:

> The Solar Orb did from the South retreat,
> And thro' the Air diffuse reviving Heat,
> Solace the Soil, exhilerate the Swain,
> And Nature loose from Winter's Chrystal Chain,
> When the Great Chief, at Anna's high Command,
> Return'd to chear Batavia's joyful Land:
> Dreadful in Arms he march'd to Brabant's Coast,
> And Terror struck thro' Gallia's shuddring Host,
> Whose Cohorts o'er the Ground, like Locusts, spread,
> Each Herb devour'd, and crop'd each verdant Head.

The rhymes and antitheses are of the 1690's; the emotions and images, of the next generation; Blackmore, like Pope, was pulled two ways, and Pope, as in *Peri Bathous,* recognized the conflict, but would have been the last to give Blackmore any credit for the pioneering. Consciously and earnestly Blackmore followed Davenant's and Cowley's recommendations for Christian subjects; faithfully he advised the use of noble Spenserian diction; too humorlessly for the school of Dryden, he set about stretching the "radiant Wings" of poetry's messenger to "Heavn's eternal Gate." And he treated his detractors, the wits, like invading insects which "crop each budding Vertue's tender Head," in the same locust simile he had used before, now made central to the "Satyre upon Wit."

Even the prose of the preface to his most famous "Nature of Man" works in the terms of the new poetry. "The Design of this Poem, is to express how far the Disparity of the intellectual Faculties, Dispositions and Passions of Men is owing to the different Situation of their Native Countries in Respect of the Sun; . . ." And the poetry:

> Bright Humane Nature does no less demand
> An Air adapted, and peculiar Land.
> In vain you hope Illustrious Youth will shine
> Beneath th' Æquator, or th' Ecliptick Line;
> Where Sun-burnt Nations, of a Swarthy Skin,
> Are sully'd o'er with blacker Clouds within.
> Their Spirits suffer by too hot a Ray,
> And their dry Brain grows dark with too much Day.

But for the purposes of clarification of the mode, rather than praise the maligned Blackmore for being ahead of his day we had better scrutinize a poet more thoroughly characteristic, James Thomson for example. He was one whom his contemporaries and successors praised for just those qualities which he thoroughly contributed to the sublime: the fidelity of descriptive image, the vocabulary of nature and emotion, the smooth cumulative sound and structure of the verse. His "Winter" begins:

> See, Winter comes, to rule the varied year,
> Sullen and sad, with all his rising train—
> Vapours, and clouds, and storms. Be these my theme;
> These, that exalt the soul to solemn thought,
> And heavenly musing. Welcome, kindred glooms!
> Cogenial horrors, hail! . . .

In his preface, it was Job and Virgil that Thomson praised, and "the choosing of great and serious subjects, such as at once amuse the fancy, enlighten the head, and warm the heart," as an influence "towards the revival of poetry." His ostensible subject, the seasons, served to parallel both the history of civilization in survey, and the anatomy of man's passion in detail. See, for example, such description of a parallel emotion some hundred of lines into "Spring":

Senseless and deformed,
Convulsive Anger storms at large; or, pale
And silent, settles into full revenge.
Base Envy withers at another's joy,
And hates that excellence it cannot reach.
Desponding Fear, of feeble fancies full,
Weak and unmanly, loosens every power.
Even Love itself is bitterness of soul,
A pensive anguish pining at the heart; . . .

Then see again how closely parallel runs the phrasing of his politics, as in "Liberty," IV:

"Awhile my spirit slept; the land awhile,
Affrighted, drooped beneath despotic rage.
Instead of Edward's equal, gentle laws,
The furious victor's partial will prevailed.
All prostrate lay; and, in the secret shade,
Deep-stung but fearful, Indignation gnashed
His teeth. . . ."

The whole long poem is a compendium of the language of eighteenth-century Whiggish verse which would reach its height of power in Blake. Or again, as in the "Castle of Indolence," we may see that somewhat softer version of the sublime, which was to find its final elegance in Keats. Canto I, stanza XXXIX:

Each sound too here to languishment inclined,
Lulled the weak bosom, and inducèd ease.
Aerial music in the warbling wind,
At distance rising oft, by small degrees
Nearer and nearer came, till o'er the trees
It hung, and breathed such soul-dissolving airs
As did, alas! with soft perdition please:
Entangled deep in its enchanting snares,
The listening heart forgot all dutie and all cares.

In all these ways, in the poetry of sensuous sensibility, the poetry of politics and universal survey, the poetry of massive personification, the poetry of patient detailed description, Thomson built up the book of eighteenth-century verse. He drew from the psychology of sense impression, from the painterly tradition, from the new philosophical feeling of cosmos and of anatomy more than life-size, and from the literary developments we have been observing, making even Spenser serve the new landscape. His work was the center of a century's mode.

Even so early as Parnell's writing of his "Essay on the Different Styles of Poetry," in 1714, the relation of new mode to old was so clear that it could be assumed and generalized upon. Parnell treated four difficulties for poetry: metaphysical verbalism, dry sententiousness, artificial pastoralism, and bombast. Then he treated the parallel virtues: the beautiful images of description, the forms that rise from reflection, the narrative liveliness of court or countryside, the true height of poetry of the passions.[5] The virtues are virtues of what he feels to be reality: observable images of natural scenes, thoughts, actions, and passions. The vices are the tricks of unreality in correspondent realms: image distorted into far-fetched metaphor, thought abstracted rather than personified,

[5] Note how these have been elaborated toward nature and passion from more technical medieval distinctions (J. W. H. Atkins, *English Literary Criticism: The Medieval Phase,* Cambridge Univ. Press, 1943; and Ernest R. Curtius, *Europäische Literatur und lateinisches Mittelalter,* Bern, 1948).

the countryside made unnatural, the natural sublime made fantastic or monstrous. He recommends as devices, modest metaphors, beauteous similes, repetitions, questions, emotions, personifications, exclamations, rising sentences, and smooth transitions, the very characteristics of eighteenth-century poetry as distinguished in itself:

> Whence images, in charming numbers set,
> A sort of likeness in the soul beget,
> And what fair visions oft we fancy nigh
> By fond delusions of the swimming eye,
> Or further pierce through Nature's maze to find
> How passions drawn give passions to the mind.

For this early conservative critic, as for Trapp and many other conservative theorists in the century, as indeed for Bysshe[6] in his standard compendium, the criteria of the naturalists from Hobbes and Locke and the deistic admirers of the observable universe had been acceptable and assumable; poetry lay in the sky, the mountain, the field, the human breast. It grew from sensation into thought and passion. It was essentially literal, essentially reportorial, reflecting a literally and reportorially sublime universe.

Not only Samuel Monk's *The Sublime,* but also such recent studies as Cecil Moore's *Backgrounds of English Literature, 1700–1760,* Ernest Tuveson's *Millennium and Utopia,* J. E. Congleton's *Theories of Pastoral Poetry in England, 1684–1798,* Donald Davie's *Purity of Diction in English Verse,* John Arthos' *Language of Natural Description in Eighteenth-Century Poetry,* Samuel Kliger's *The Goths in England,* John Butt's *The Augustan Age,* R. L. Brett's *The Third Earl of Shaftesbury,* and Jean Hagstrum's *Samuel Johnson's Literary Criticism* have made us increasingly aware of the brief tenure of neoclassicism in the eighteenth century, and the looming power of a cosmic art beyond the

[6] For contemporary recognition of Bysshe's "sublimity" see Preface to *The British Muse,* ed. Thomas Hayward, London, 1738.

classic. In pulling away from the metaphysical fictive extreme, the century moved to another, natural, extreme, that of the sublime, where trope gave way to simile, and concept to body, and microcosm to the natural world. Thus the "Whiggish" poetry of the Shaftesburians, in the wake of Milton and Addison and Locke, the central century's poetry of Shenstone, Akenside, Thomson, Collins, the Wartons, even at times by Pope. Thus the poetic debate in Joseph Spence's *Essay on Pope's Odyssey,* 1626, between the classicist who loved plain nature, as Wordsworth later would, and the *modernist* (not a metaphysical reactionary) who loved "pictures! passions! charming imagery!" (Austin Wright's *Joseph Spence,* p. 17), all the "glittering and elevation" against which Wordsworth would eventually rebel.

The orderly harmonies of classicism had seemed and would seem again a relief after the extremes of metaphysical speculation, of sublime embodiment and extension. But meantime the reaches of sublimity were invigorating to eighteenth-century poets, and all tried to see how much particularity, how much error and flaw, the rising harmony might be able to sustain, beyond the confines of mere beauty and ethos. As early as the 1690's, while forty were reading Rochester to every one reading Milton (John H. Wilson, *The Court Wits of the Restoration,* p. 106), Robert Wolseley was nevertheless writing in his "Preface to Valentinian" (*Critical Essays of the Seventeenth Century,* ed. Spingarn, III, 12), "every ass that's romantick believes he's inspir'd." By 1761 Shenstone was writing to a friend: "The taste of the age, as far as it regards plan and style, seems to have been carried to the utmost height, as may appear in the works of Akenside, Gray's Odes and Church-yard verses, and Mason's Monody and Elfrida. The public has seen all that art can do, and they want the more striking efforts of wild, original, enthusiastic genius. It seems to exclaim aloud with the chorus in Julius Caesar,

" 'O rather than be slaves to these deep learned men,
Give us our wildness and our woods, our huts and caves again!' "

(Quoted by John Butt, *The Augustan Age,* p. 138)

Akenside himself, along with Goldsmith, in his "Pleasures of Imagination (Enlarged)," stressed the inclusive powers of the sublime:

> . . . what human breast
> E'er doubts, before the transient and minute,
> To prize the vast, the stable, the sublime?

And though conservative critics like Johnson liked the vast to be magniloquent rather than mysterious, explicit rather than implicit, others like the Wartons were working constantly for more particularity, implication, speaking simplicity. As Edward Young phrased what Longinus and Boileau had said (*Night Thoughts,* IX, 1634 ff.):

> There dwells a noble pathos in the skies,
> Which warms our passions, proselytes our hearts, . . .
> Demonstrating great truths in style sublime,
> Though silent, loud! . . .

As these few lines represent the richer treasures of Collins and his contemporaries, we may let one quotation from Richard Hurd (*Works,* Vol. II, pp. 8–9) represent the vast store of mid- and late-century critical praise of sublime subject and style as distinguished from classical:

"For there is something in the mind of man, sublime and elevated, which prompts it to overlook all obvious and familiar appearances, and to feign to itself other and more extraordinary; such as correspond to the extent of its own powers, and fill out all the faculties and capacities of our souls. . . .

"Hence it comes to pass, that it deals in apostrophes and invocations; that it impersonates the virtues and vices; peoples all creation with new and living forms; calls up infernal spectres to terrify, or brings down celestial natures to astonish, the imagination; assembles, combines, or connects its ideas, at pleasure; in short, prefers not only the agreeable, and the graceful, but, as occasion calls upon her, the vast, the incredible,

I had almost said, the impossible, to the obvious truth and nature of things."

The rationale for the phrasal and cumulative mode, with its language of sensory embodiment, is implicit in these terms; and they are not merely "Gothic" but also Biblical and classical terms, in the Grecian classicism of Plato, Longinus, Lucretius, and Pindar, as well as in what T. S. Eliot was to call, in "The Function of Criticism" (*Criterion,* II, 31 ff.), the Whiggery of the Inner Voice.

The "specific sort of feeling in the face of the awful and great" which Shaftesbury's *Characteristics* called sublime here blends with feeling itself, with greatness, with personification and implication, so that we may be sure of its all-encompassing power. By the late century, when there was a reaction toward classical balance, many poets, like Rogers, Blake, Bowles, and Keats, found still such satisfying wealth of both soaring statement and implicative height in the sublime style that they enthusiastically prolonged the use of it.

To Rogers' *Pleasures of Memory* the Introduction (1793) reads:

Oh could my Mind, unfolded in my page,
Enlighten climes and mould a future age;
There as it glow'd, with noblest frenzy fraught,
Dispense the treasures of exalted thought;
To Virtue wake the pulses of the heart,
And bid the tear of emulation start!
Oh could it still, thro' each succeeding year,
My life, my manners, and my name endear;
And, when the poet sleeps in silent dust,
Still hold communion with the wise and just!—
Yet should this Verse, my leisure's best resource,
When thro' the world it steals its secret course,
Revive but once a generous wish suppress,
Chase but a sigh, or charm a care to rest;

In one good deed a fleeting hour employ,
Or flush one faded cheek with honest joy;
Blest were my lines, tho' limited their sphere,
Tho' short their date, as his who trac'd them here.

These lines provide a standard context for the decade's key terms. Eighteenth-century *mind, clime, age, thought,* glow in increasing light. *Heart* and *tear* wake to *virtue, cheek* flushes with *joy*. *Life* and *name* endure through *world* and *time,* a *fleeting hour*. The wish or prayer in its cumulative couplets here gives us accustomed generality atremble with sensibility. The concluding lines of the "Ode to Superstition" are even more elaborate, in their physical sense of truth as light.

Lord of each pang the nerves can feel,
Hence, with the rack and reeking wheel.
Faith lifts the soul above this little ball!
While gleams of glory open round,
And circling choirs of angels call,
Canst thou, with all thy terrors crown'd,
Hope to obscure that latent spark,
Destin'd to shine when suns are dark?
Thy triumphs cease! thro' every land,
Hark! Truth proclaims, thy triumphs cease:
Her heav'nly form, with glowing hand,
Benignly points to piety and peace.
Flush'd with youth, her looks impart
Each fine feeling as it flows;
Her voice the echo of her heart,
Pure as the mountain-snows:
Celestial transports round her play,
And softly, sweetly die away.
She smiles! and where is now the cloud
That blacken'd o'er thy baleful reign?

Grim Darkness furls his leaden shroud,
Shrinking from her glance in vain.
Her touch unlocks the day-spring from above,
And lo! it visits man with beams of light and love.

Truth with glowing hand points to peace, feeling flows, voice echoes heart, the cloud shrinks, the dayspring visits man with beams of light and love—here again we have the central scene anatomized as in the earlier eighteenth century, but, in *nerve, feeling, echo, smile, voice,* and *touch,* that anatomy made now more inwardly expressive.

Southey is another to present this norm, in his "Bion" poems of 1795. His proportioning is average, his verse forms vary from old couplet to new sonnet, and of his subjects, as he says with Lovell in the Preface, "Much novelty cannot be expected." So he too writes of Memory in "The Retrospect," its closing lines of invocation,

Why wilt thou, Memory, still recall to view
Each long-past joy, each long-lost friend anew?
Paint not the scenes that pleas'd my soul of yore,
Those friends are gone, those long-past joys no more;
Cease to torment me, busy torturer, cease,
Let cold oblivion's touch benumb my soul to peace!

Older friends and scenes are blended with new joy and peace. And in "Romance":

Fain would the grateful Muse, to thee, Rousseau,
Pour forth the energic thanks of gratitude;
Fain would the raptur'd lyre ecstatic glow,
To whom Romance and Nature form'd all good:
Guide of my life, too weak these lays,
To pour the unutterable praise;
Thine aid divine for ever lend,
Still as my guardian sprite attend;

Unmov'd by Fashion's flaunting throng,
Let my calm stream of life smooth its meek course along;
Let no weak vanity dispense
Her vapors o'er my better sense;
But let my bosom glow with fire,
Let me strike the soothing lyre,
Altho' by all unheard the melodies expire.

In standard phrases and linear variations, Southey calling on Rousseau brings new and old together, *glowing, pouring, soothing* the era's sort of verb, and *calm stream of life* its metaphor, and *all unheard* the melodies. In the Sonnets are ruins, knells, nightingales, and other such appurtenances, yet such remarked simplicities as "My friendly fire, thou blazest clear and bright."

In satire, however crudely used, the same interplay is stressed, as by Gifford in the *Baviad,* which achieves the norm by making fun of it:

If comedy be yours, the searching strain
Gives a sweet pleasure, so chastis'd by pain,
That e'en the guilty at their sufferings smile,
And bless the lancet, tho' they bleed the while.
If tragedy, th' impassioned numbers flow
In all the sad variety of woe,
With such a liquid lapse, that they betray
The breast unwares, and steal the soul away.

His vocabulary is more of past than of future, more sweet fate, power, and bodily terms than the language of nature, soul, and truth in its more evanescent forms; but such it must be to keep poetry's feet on the ground, as he feels, and he feels in a very suitable and orthodox way. Amused by the vogue he makes fun of, his readers may also directly enjoy it, so strong are eighteenth-century forces still.

Some of the poets of the 1790's were even more than the average devoted to middle eighteenth-century measures: Blake, who pushed many measures to their limits, and Campbell, who preserved them faithfully over a long span, and William Bowles, who meant inspiration to the young Wordsworth. These were poets of full flowing lines, who shared especially the terms of power and sublimity, *eternal, dark, divine, beautiful, sacred, stormy, fate* and *rapture, cliff* and *vale* and *view*. Yet they are deeply personal, as Bowles says in introducing his sonnets. The very first provides an example:

As slow I climb the cliff's ascending side,
  Much musing on the track of terror past,
  When o'er the dark wave rode the howling blast,
Pleas'd I look back, and view the tranquil tide
That laves the pebbl'd shore: and now the beam
  Of evening smiles on the grey battlement,
  And yon forsaken tow'r that time has rent:—
The lifted oar far off with silver gleam
Is touch'd, and hush'd is all the billowy deep!
  Sooth'd by the scene, thus on tir'd Nature's breast
  A stillness slowly steals, and kindred rest;
While sea-sounds lull her, as she sinks to sleep,
Like melodies which mourn upon the lyre,
Wak'd by the breeze, and, as they mourn, expire.

Bowles's are not what we think of as lyrical sonnets; they are heavily descriptive in the same way that blank verse and heroic couplet might be: so devoted were these late-century poets to the emotional and substantial *mass* of verse, that even Blake's long lines (in *America*) do not seem alien:

. . . the vale was dark
With clouds of smoke from the Atlantic, that in volumes roll'd
Between the mountains; dismal visions mope around the house . . .

and Campbell could give the sense of vast and mournful scope whether he used the newest experimental stanza forms or the conventional couplets with which he opened and closed his career. His youthful and famous "Pleasures of Hope" in 1798, despite its forward-sounding specific vocabulary of romantic usage in *dim, dream, father, child, home, star, wind,* the infiltration of new content into old form, was on the whole a model of a sublime poem, outdoing itself in the old glooms and splendors of expression and unable to suffer any real sea-change.

Auspicious Hope! in thy sweet garden grow
Wreaths for each toil, a charm for every woe;
Won by their sweets, in Nature's languid hour,
The way-worn pilgrim seeks thy summer bower;
There, as the wild bee murmurs on the wing,
What peaceful dreams thy handmaid spirits bring!
What viewless forms th' Aeolian organ play,
And sweep the furrowed lines of anxious thought away!

Angel of life! thy glittering wings explore
Earth's loneliest bounds, and Ocean's wildest shore.
Lo! to the wintry winds the pilot yields
His bark careering o'er unfathom'd fields;
Now on th' Atlantic waves he rides afar,
Where Andes, giant of the western star,
With meteor-standard to the winds unfurl'd,
Looks from his throne of clouds o'er half the world!

Now far he sweeps, where scarce a summer smiles,
On Behring's rocks, or Greenland's naked isles:
Cold on his midnight watch the breezes blow,
From wastes that slumber in eternal snow;
And waft, across the waves' tumultuous roar,
The wolf's long howl from Oonalaska's shore.

Poor child of danger, nursling of the storm,
Sad are the woes that wreck thy manly form!
Rocks, waves, and winds, the shatter'd bark delay!
Thy heart is sad, thy home is far away.

It is difficult to stop quoting from Campbell; he blends with such enthusiastic unoriginality the homely pathos of Goldsmith and Cowper with the sublime natural forces of Bowles and Blake into the finest sort of "preromantic" mélange.

Now how did this century-old pattern of cosmic, emotional, exclamatory pentameter change gradually into the romantic poetry of stanzaic implication? I think it did not. The preromantic sublime does not become romantic poetry, but goes on in its own way for Wordsworth, Keats, Campbell, Kirke White, and others high and low, to Tennyson, Whitman, Wilde, and to Dylan Thomas. Romantic starts new and individual, a fresh spring beside the old tumultuous river. The sources of this spring were in the Ballads wherever they might be found and read; but for a long time, as in Chatterton and some of Percy's *Reliques* themselves, these sources were swamped and overgrown with Spenserianism in the eighteenth-century antiquarian form which served to conceal the pure new motion of ballad lyric and ballad narrative.

In the 1790's there were manifold unconcealable new signs: Blake's *Songs,* Scott's narratives, Burns's hesitant new beginnings. The short implicative line of song demanded a different vocabulary and a different sentence structure, with less of exposition and more of echo.

"Does spring hide its joy
When buds and blossoms grow?
Does the sower
Sow by night,
Or the plowman in darkness plow?"
(Blake, "Earth's Answer")

or,

Such is the fate of artless Maid,
Sweet flow'ret of the rural shade!
By Love's simplicity betray'd,
And guileless trust,
Till she, like thee, all soil'd, is laid
Low i' the dust.
(Burns, "To a Mountain-daisy," 1786)

For Scott and Coleridge, as for Burns, the deepest source of invention appeared in a minor form, not in prime vocabulary or mode but in lines of lyrical understatement—"Does the spring hide its joy . . ." and "Low i' the dust."

But not alone the bitter tear
Had filial grief supplied;
For hopeless love and anxious fear
Had lent their mingled tide:
Nor in her mother's alter'd eye
Dar'd she to look for sympathy.
(Scott, *Last Minstrel,* I, x)

So acceptance of the ballad tradition subtilizes old materials for the *Last Minstrel,* and adds the new particularity of detail.

From the sound of Teviot's tide,
Chafing with the mountain's side,
From the groan of the wind-swung oak,
From the sullen echo of the rock,
From the voice of the coming storm,
The Ladye knew it well!
It was the Spirit of the Flood that spoke,
And he call'd on the Spirit of the Fell.

"Sleep'st thou, brother?" . . .

(I, xiv, xv)

From such writing it is a step, though a magical one, to the lines of *The Ancient Mariner:*

And the coming wind did roar more loud,
And the sails did sigh like sedge;
And the rain poured down from the black cloud;
The Moon was at its edge.

The thick black cloud was cleft, and still
The Moon was at its side:
Like waters shot from some high crag,
The lightning fell with never a jag,
A river steep and wide.

The loud wind never reached the ship,
Yet now the ship moved on!
Beneath the lightning and the Moon
The dead men gave a groan.

They groaned, their stirred, they all uprose,
Nor spake, nor moved their eyes;
It had been strange, even in a dream,
To have seen those dead men rise.

This poetry of implication, of half-heard sound and meaning, of active predicative structure, is as far as we can get from the sublime poem, and was its immediate successor as the metaphysical had been its immediate predecessor, with a brief era of classical balance to temper each change. Wordsworthian classicism worked between his most soaring predecessors, sublime masters such as Blake, and the new extremes of suggested depth in Landor, Byron, Coleridge. The one great follower of the sublime tradition in the romantic era was Keats. No real ballad man, he chose rather the old eighteenth-century inheritance of Spenser and the richest classical poets, the vocabulary of sense and passion, the phrasal and harmonic abundance unchecked by balanced structure. What he did draw from his own contemporaries was the sense of suggested depth as well as height, the nameless as well as the namable in the anatomy of sensation, so that he was able to blend the effectiveness of two whole traditions in his intensification of them. His is one more, and an intenser one, of the sublime odes to Melancholy.

No, no, go not to Lethe, neither twist
  Wolf's-bane, tight-rooted, for its poisonous wine;
Nor suffer thy pale forehead to be kiss'd
  By nightshade, ruby grape of Proserpine;
Make not your rosary of yew-berries,
  Nor let the beetle, nor the death-moth be
    Your mournful Psyche, nor the downy owl
A partner to your sorrow's mysteries;
  For shade to shade will come too drowsily,
    And drown the wakeful anguish of the soul.

2.

But when the melancholy fit shall fall
  Sudden from heaven like a weeping cloud,
That fosters the droop-headed flowers all,
  And hides the green hill in an April shroud;
Then glut thy sorrow on a morning rose,
  Or on the rainbow of the salt sand-wave,
    Or on the wealth of globed peonies;
Or if thy mistress some rich anger shows,
  Emprison her soft hand, and let her rave,
    And feed deep, deep upon her peerless eyes.

3.

She dwells with Beauty—Beauty that must die;
And Joy, whose hand is ever at his lips
Bidding adieu; and aching Pleasure nigh,
Turning to poison while the bee-mouth sips:
Ay, in the very temple of Delight
Veil'd Melancholy has her sovran shrine,
Though seen of none save him whose strenuous tongue
Can burst Joy's grape against his palate fine;
His soul shall taste the sadness of her might,
And be among her cloudy trophies hung.

Here in the combination of extremely sensuous particularity with emotional forms and personifications, the varied and interior odal structure, the full vowel harmony, the language of anatomy and ceremony, we read an essence of the poetry which Hobbes early blessed, which Milton and Thomson and Collins forwarded, which was the eighteenth century's own; in the sublime poetic scene of the universe, the enduring passionate figures, larger than life.

CHAPTER FIVE

THE SUBLIMITY OF WILLIAM BLAKE

WHAT is the community of the poet Blake, not the painter, not the engraver, not the dreamer or good fellow, but the poet? With whom did he share the materials of his art? Some say with the metaphysical poets like Donne and Vaughan; some say with the romantic poets like Wordsworth and Shelley; some say with none—that Blake had no community.

It is true that his late eighteenth-century era liked to stress originality, real novelty, which might preclude the copying of other authors and the sharing of vocabulary and sentence structure. And indeed, though Blake was not so averse as Reynolds to copying, making patient and profitable exercises in the *Poetical Sketches* as Miss Lowery has shown us, he tended to agree explicitly with Edward Young and the rest that classical unifications were less to be trusted than the unities of individual spirit. One might well expect him then to take the lead in breaking away from the use of generally shared materials, in an era which was devoted to such breaking away.

But the medium of poetry, language, is a social material, and one finds within it at any certain time coherences and qualities characteristic of that time and a part of contemporary invention. The basic changes in it from era to era are gradually made, by poets as by people as a whole, and the changes are fairly regular, so that there is always transition and also always persistence. Blake in his choice of materials provides no particular exception. He seems to have participated congenially in usages which were changing as gradually as in other centuries and carried as much weight of tradition. This participation in basic practice encourages us to study him not only as different but as similar, not only as odd but as representative of poetic community, first in his choice of major poetic language, and then in the contexts of his use of it.

Blake does differ from most poets by his strong use of repetition, so that in a thousand lines of his verse not merely the normal thirty or forty, but more like seventy or eighty nouns, adjectives, and verbs are repeated more than ten times apiece. I have studied the thousand lines from the beginnings of almost all his major works, a hundred lines from each, so that the resulting list of terms represents emphases not temporary but continued through Blake's life. Much as he changed, in theme and form, Blake persisted in the use of well-worn and apparently valued materials of language, all the way from the *Poetical Sketches* in the 1770's to *Jerusalem* in the 1810's.

The major language in force in Blake's day was still the language of mid-century, of Pope, Young, Gray, Collins, Mason, Thomson, and the Wartons. The pervasive terms were those of atmosphere and emotion, of *fair, soft, sweet, gay, happy, proud, tender, air, day, night, life, nature, flower, land, scene, sky, song, world;* of *eye, hand, heart, joy, love, youth, friend, soul,* with a few abstractions like *divine, power, beauty, fate, time* and *virtue;* and rather scant verbs, mostly of observation and reception, like *hear, see, bear, behold, find, fall, rise, stand, take*. This was a major vocabulary, in other words, of natural and cosmic scene, observed, felt emotionally, and generalized by amenable human beings. This poetic continuum differed from that of the mid-seventeenth century, a hundred years earlier, by its decrease in active constructive verbs and in abstract terms of value both positive and negative, and by its increase in words of physical and emotional description. It differed, in turn, from the continuum of the coming mid-ninteenth century by its greater generality, its verbs not as passive as they were to become, the shades, colors, and sizes in its atmosphere not so precisely delineated, the night side of nature and the child side of man not so selectively emphasized. The nineteenth century was to recall goodness, time, and death to poetry and to refine details like feeling, spirit, prayer, childhood, and dream. Meantime the eighteenth century consolidated as fully as possible its gains of aesthetic substance, the physical actuality of cosmic scene and human form, the occasions for emotional and rational generalization.

Into this world Blake entered with a good deal of sympathy. The simple listing of his main vocabulary helps indicate how much. These were terms which persisted through the *Sketches,* the *Songs, America,* the *Zoas, Milton,* and *Jerusalem:* the adjectives *black, bright, dark, divine, eternal, golden, human, little, red, silent, soft, starry, sweet, terrible,* the nouns *air, bosom, child, cloud, daughter, day, death, earth, emanation, eye, fire, flower, foot, furnace, hand, head, heaven, God, joy, life, love, lamb, man, morning, mountain, night, son, song, soul, sun, time, valley, voice, wheel, worm;* the verbs *awake, bring, come, fall, find, give, go, hear, know, look, rise, see, sit, sing, sleep, smile, stand, take, turn, walk, weep.* This is a fine and special vocabulary, I think you will agree; possible in its entirety only to Blake, but possible in its main texture just to that period between the eighteenth and nineteenth centuries when the vast scope of visible nature was being observed and felt by men increasingly aware of their own small size, the mystery of their childlike joy and terror.

Consider the poetic status of these terms in Blake's day. As we should expect from the usage of other poets, about half of Blake's major terms are strongly established and traditional in the major language of the era, about half are either newly used in a growing tradition or used individualistically, without further agreement. In Blake's list, the traditional half are the words of scene and feeling: the *dark, soft, sweet, air, day, night, love, joy, soul, song, eye, hand, head,* and the standard verbs of perceiving. Noteworthy terms of the eighteenth century which Blake does not stress are *fair, gay, proud,* and *tender,* the lighter and more affectionate of adjectives, and the major traditional noun *heart,* and the classical abstractions of *nature, power, youth, fate, virtue, mind,* and *thought.* These omissions indicate the direction of the nineteenth century: away from light affection and from generality. Positively too, a fourth of Blake's terms anticipate the nineteenth century: the *little, child, daughter, death, earth,* the *bring, sing,* and *weep,* of more active and particular expression.

Finally, there are the words which are most especially Blake's own, his *eternal, red, starry,* and *terrible,* his *sit* and *sleep,* his *cloud, lamb, morning, valley, worm, furnace,* and *wheel.* Most of these are terms which particularize in a special way others of the major ideas: as *lamb* and *worm* particularize the natural and lowly, for example; as *starry, cloud,* and *sleep,* the night, and *morning* the day. The words *furnace* and *wheel,* on the other hand, represent a realm of reference less common to poetic tradition.

Though these most individualistic terms and others are not major in the usage of many other poets, Blake shares most of them with at least one or two poets of the past, and the consistency of these parallels is again illuminating of his interests. His special colors *red, black,* and *golden* are distinctively Ballad terms; his *eternal,* like *divine* and others, is shared with Young and Collins; *cloud, lamb,* and *sleep* are in the seventeenth-century tradition of Vaughan, Crashaw, Quarles, Wither, and Milton which pervades Blake's materials. If one looks for the presence of Blake's major terms in the work of earlier English poets, one finds it, therefore, either in a majority of them, in the central tradition of common usage, or in one particular minority, the line of Sylvester and Milton through Gray, Collins, Thomson, and the Wartons, with Ballad variations. This is the line of scenic and spiritual concern, not humanistic in the Tudor or metaphysical or Johnsonian neoclassical sense, but directly physical rather, as the physical suggests cosmic symbol. Spenser's *sweet* and *little, hear* and *look,* Crashaw's *bright, black, dark, heaven, fire,* and *night,* Vaughan's *cloud, death, sun, fall, weep,* and *sleep,* Milton's *air* and *sit* and *sing,* Young's *human* and *eternal, time, earth,* and *song,* and Collins' and the Wartons' development of these, all represent, in Blake's terms, the special sort of poetic selection and emphasis, vastly increased and focussed in the eighteenth century, which establishes the physical landscape as a value and portent of the divine, and sits, looks, hears, and sings in a ceremony of aesthetic celebration.

This tradition of song, this bardic line, leads to some thought about the sound of Blake's language as well as its sense. What are the major uses of sound that accompany the major vocabulary? Again we find them, for all their individuality, to be part of eighteenth-century experiment and of the Miltonic line. When Blake wrote, at the beginning of his last great poem *Jerusalem,* that he was abandoning the "Monotonous Cadence, like that used by Milton and Shakespeare and all writers of English Blank Verse, derived from the modern bondage of Rhyming," in favor of "a variety in every line, both of cadences and number of syllables," he was trying to extend even further the principle on which so many blank-verse and ode writers of the eighteenth century had worked—the principle of onomatopoeia, of inner harmony and suitability. Said Blake: "Every word and every letter is studied and put into its fit place; the terrific numbers are reserved for the terrific parts, the mild and gentle for the mild and gentle parts, and the prosaic for inferior parts; all are necessary to each other. Poetry Fetter'd Fetters the Human Race." In other words, the external bonds of linear arrangement, by variations in measure and in rhyme at line ends, are least valuable to Blake; the internal variations of accent and sound echo in the line are most valuable. The frame of line and stanza is not to be stressed, but rather the interior correlation of sound with sense.

Therefore, in most of the other prophetic books as well as in *Jerusalem,* and to a lesser degree in the early *Sketches* and *Songs,* the devices of sound were varied, echoing, and internal, as they were considered to be in the eighteenth-century Pindaric tradition. Even Pope, within what Blake called his "metaphysical Jargon of Rhyming" (Descriptive Catalogue; in Keynes, p. 625), had fostered this idea of poetic harmony, this line-by-line suitability of tone; and such poetic prose as Macpherson's had easily intensified it. So in the early first lines of *Tiriel,* as in *America, Milton,* and the others, whatever regularities there are of iambic foot and seven-accent line and caesural pause and alliterative and repetitive balance are tempered by much variation:

And Aged Tiriel stood before the Gates of his beautiful palace
With Myratana, once the Queen of all the western plains;
But now his eyes were dark'ned and his wife fading in death.
They stood before their once delightful palace, and thus the Voice
Of aged Tiriel arose, that his sons might hear in their gates:

The line endings vary in masculine and feminine syllables without pattern. The balance of phrases, liked *Aged Tiriel . . . beautiful palace,* and *his eyes were dark'ned and his wife fading,* and *Tiriel stood . . . Tiriel arose, . . . gates,* gives us the sense of massive deliberate motion, with repeated order and echo.

Or again, the lines ending *Milton* add rich qualities of imitative sound:

Immediately the Lark mounted with a loud trill from Felpham's Vale,

And the Wild Thyme from Wimbleton's green and impurpled Hills,
And Los and Enitharmon rose over the Hills of Surrey:
Their clouds roll over London with a south wind; soft Oothoon
Pants in the Vales of Lambeth, weeping o'er her Human Harvest.
Los listens to the Cry of the Poor Man, his Cloud
Over London in volume terrific low bended in anger.

The hurry of syllables in *immediately,* the spondaic or sprung force of *loud trill,* the softening from *Wild* to *Wimbleton,* the stress on *rose over,* the liquids and sibilants of Oothoon's weeping, the phrasal unity of alliteration in *Human Harvest,* the lowered tones of Los's anger, these are characteristic qualities for Blake and his time, putting the stress of pattern on phrase and atmosphere in long rising and falling cadence. Song, like painting, worked for correspondence, for tone color. The suiting of stresses and vowels and consonants was accented by slight but not constraining patterns of alliteration, assonance, and basic measure. This was a mode of sound which, though extended and freed by Blake, did not develop strongly into the nineteenth century, except in individuals like Tupper and Whitman. Rather it was the ballad or couplet rhyming of the *Songs of Innocence and of Experience,* the melodic rather than the harmonic version of song, that moved into nineteenth-century experiment. Nevertheless, even these most stanzaic forms have been altered by Blake from their seventeenth-century and ballad tones of speech toward the harmonic consonances of the more prophetic style:

Calling the lapsed Soul,
And weeping in the evening dew;

That might controll
The starry pole,
And fallen, fallen light renew!

The structure of this stanza, from the first of *Songs of Experience,* the calling, weeping, fallen, fallen, suspension by participles, is important to Blake for structural sense as well as sound. The participial sort of meaning is a major meaning for him, the motion observed in process and seen as qualitative rather than as active. As his vocabulary is strong in its stress on descriptive adjectives, as his poetic sound is also descriptive, and suspensive in its lack of frame, its use of carry-over and echo, so his structure too is descriptive, his sentences heavy with adjectives and substantives, his verbs turned to participial constructions. This was in its whole, in its natural complex, the language Blake got from the eighteenth century, definable as physical, descriptive, onomatopoetic, invocative, and declarative, fond of participles.

Notice the recurrent structure of Blake's sentences and their progress in his poems. The season poems in the early *Sketches* are characteristic: they begin, "O Thou . . . ," then move to a relative clause, then to invocations, "turn thine eyes . . . ," "come and let us . . . ," and so forth. If the vocative does not begin, then simple declaration may, as in the *Songs,* "Earth rais'd up her head," or "I wander thro' each charter'd street," or "My mother groan'd"; usually such beginnings lead to dialogue or invocation. For Blake, the simplest of declarative statements seem to be bound up both with further sweeping description and with ceremonious address either in question-and-answer or in prayer form. "Enslav'd, the Daughters of Albion weep; . . . O Urizen! Creator of men! mistaken Demon of heaven! . . . Thus every morning wails Oothoon; but Theotormon sits / Upon the margin'd ocean conversing with shadows dire. / The Daughters of Albion hear her woes, and eccho back her sighs."

Such sentence structure cumulatively sets forth a vast panorama, active in time and space, yet so encompassed by eternity, so structurally repetitive, poised, and echoing, even as the sounds themselves are, that one accepts the whole at once, not as narrative or picture merely, but as simultaneous vision; the rising and falling, the dividing and fusing are endless. Almost every individual sentence echoes another. One way I think these sentence forms may be more technically identified is in terms of their proportioning. The main tradition of English poetry, from Chaucer, through the Tudors and the metaphysical poets, used substantives (that is, nouns and adjectives) in proportion to predicates (that is, verbs) in a ratio of two to one; and this proportioning still holds today for many poets. But the line of poets beginning with Spenser, Quarles, Crashaw, Milton, and strengthening in the eighteenth century, used rather a proportion of three to one, and even, for Thomson and the Wartons, an extreme of four to one; this was the line, this the extreme, which Blake approved.

The proportioning of four to one, four adjectives and nouns to one verb in a line of verse, indicates a special structure. Modification must be strong, and verbs made into adjectives by participial construction. Nouns must be many, and listable, and cumulative. Verbs must be used mostly to keep the work going; there cannot be much play of subordination, or of reasoning. Phrases, rather than clauses, must be the units of expression. This was Blake's mode of choice in most of his work, from *The French Revolution* through *Jerusalem.*

Considering these characteristics of sentence structure together with those of sound and vocabulary, one sees that certain qualities of language are apt to function together as a basic material for certain poets and for certain times, and that Blake as wholeheartedly as any accepted the material of his kind and time. In the mid-eighteenth century the language of poetry, developed from tentative minority beginnings in Sylvester, Milton, and their line, provided a complex of sound and reference unlike that of any other era. Sentences were more phrasally compounded, less clausally complex than ever before or since. Nouns and adjectives, in natural consequence, strongly dominated verbs and took over verb meanings. Sounds, like sentences, stressed not limits, periods, bounds, and conclusions as regular feet, line forms, rhymes, and stanzas would do, but rather interior units and correspondences, in echo and onomatopoeia. Reference stressed the objects and qualities of such sensory concern, the scenes, atmospheres, and feelings which could be onomatopoetized, the natural and human items of emotional description with their minor and parallel actions of observation and acceptance.

We may think of Blake as too active, rebellious, and eccentric to use such material; yet we find it basically his. What additions he made to it were, as we have seen, not so much changes as extensions of the basic material. He increased the characteristic reference to color, scope, and feeling; he increased human anatomizing, scenic atmosphere, and passive and expressive verbs. He used a fuller load of substantives and descriptive declaration, and a freer play of interior sound. He liked what he had, and carried it further in its own realm. The one great addition which carried him toward the nineteenth century was the diminutive, his lambs and worms, the children, sons and daughters in family relation. Otherwise, his reference, sound, and statement were all far closer to eighteenth-century than to nineteenth-century modes. This is the language of Blake and of Blake's day. Now perhaps we should look at this language in some passages of poetry, to remind ourselves how it works and sounds. The repetitions of structure and vocabulary make for a basic substance. Note the first of *Jerusalem:*

"Awake! awake O sleeper of the land of shadows, wake! expand!
I am in you and you in me, mutual in love divine:
Fibres of love from man to man thro' Albion's pleasant land.
In all the dark Atlantic vale down from the hills of Surrey
A black water accumulates; return Albion! return!
Thy brethren call thee, and thy fathers and thy sons,
Thy nurses and thy mothers, thy sisters and thy daughters

Weep at thy soul's disease and the Divine Vision is darken'd,
Thy Emanation that was wont to play before thy face,
Beaming forth with her daughters into the Divine bosom:
Where hast thou hidden thy Emanation, lovely Jerusalem,
From the vision and fruition of the Holy-one?
I am not a God afar off, I am a brother and friend:
Within your bosoms I reside, and you reside in me:
Lo! we are One, forgiving all Evil, Not seeking recompense.
Ye are my members, O ye sleepers of Beulah, land of shades!"

In these lines the exclamations, the vast declarations, the descriptive phrases like *dark Atlantic vale,* the anatomy of *face* and *bosom,* the *sleep* and *shade,* the joining of human and divine, the family terms and weeping, the phrasal alliteration and balance, the tonal echo, are characteristic. They appear also earlier, in the *Songs,* in "Earth's Answer," for example:

Earth rais'd up her head
From the darkness dread and drear.
Her light fled,
Stony dread!
And her locks cover'd with grey despair.

"Prison'd on wat'ry shore,
Starry Jealousy does keep my den:
Cold and hoar,
Weeping o'er,
I hear the father of the ancient men.

"Selfish father of men!
Cruel, jealous, selfish fear!
Can delight,
Chain'd in night,
The virgins of youth and morning bear?

"Does spring hide its joy
When buds and blossoms grow?
Does the sower
Sow by night,
Or the plowman in darkness plow?

"Break this heavy chain
That does freeze my bones around.
Selfish! vain!
Eternal bane!
That free Love with bondage bound."

Except for its greater regularity of line-end echoes, this passage is much like the later one in its language. The basic unit of statement carries six or seven stresses, sentences exclaim and implore, phrases are dominant, terms are terms of scene changed to anatomy and involved in family conflict and bondage. This is the major sort of context for most of Blake's writing. In the early work, in *Tiriel, Thel,* and the *Songs,* there are more mild and pleasant scenes and more active verbs, but even here runs strongly the strain which becomes dominant in *The French Revolution,* the sublimity of darkness, conflict, and oppression, in language heavily substantival. Of Blake's social and personal contraries, this was the one which pervaded his text.

We should remind ourselves that this sublime strain was pervasive in the eighteenth century also. The peaceful externalities of classical pastoral had come to blend with Biblical pastoral, and the wide wings of Lydian survey had encompassed the more frightening Biblical cosmos. Song was more and more often hymn. The low language of satire accorded with the threatening language of prophecy. Everywhere the lambs and smiling fields of Quarles and the pastoralists were being subjected to dark clouds and emotions filled with awe, as the combining powers of Biblical and epical influence, northern and Gothic atmosphere, the critical recommendations of Longinus, and the growing awareness of social tyranny all made for a dark and terrible world. Only the most middle-of-the-road classicists like Samuel Johnson maintained a real poise of generality. Most of the rest, from Pope to Gray to Rogers and Campbell, were apt, as Blake was, to combine their primarily scenic, anatomical, and emotional terms with a sense of vast force and portent. Consider the substance of a few passages: first, one of simple scenery from Thomson's "Winter," much like Blake's "Winter," which, as Mark Schorer has suggested, is a forecast of *Jerusalem*. Blake's begins,

> O Winter! bar thine adamantine doors:
> The north is thine; there hast thou built thy dark
> Deep-founded habitation. Shake not thy roofs,
> Nor bend thy pillars with thine iron car. . . .

Winter's storms are unchained, sheathed in ribbed steel over the yawning deep, the direful monster strides o'er the groaning rocks, withers all in silence and freezes up frail life till heaven smiles and he is driven back. Thomson's proceeds in similar though milder fashion:

> . . . Those sullen seas,
> That wash'd the ungenial pole, will rest no more
> Beneath the shackles of the mighty north,
> But, rousing all their waves, resistless heave.
> And, hark! the lengthening roar continuous runs
> Athwart the rifted deep: at once it bursts,
> And piles a thousand mountains to the clouds.
> Ill fares the bark, with trembling wretches charg'd,
> That, tossed amid the floating fragments, moors
> Beneath the shelter of an icy isle,
> While night o'erwhelms the sea, and horror looks
> More horrible. . . .

Here are not only the pervasive terms, but the pervasive contexts: the tyrant north and night, the mountainous heights and depths, the participial suspensions, the human wretches and their horror. Or, again, in "Liberty" we get the more smiling conclusion:

> The tempest foamed, immense; the driving storm
> Saddened the skies, and, from the doubling gloom,
> On the scathed oak the ragged lightning fell;
> In closing shades, and where the current strays,
> With Peace, and Love, and Innocence around,
> Piped the lone shepherd to his feeding flock;
> Round happy parents smiled their younger selves;
> And friends conversed, by death divided long.

In such passages we may see just how it is that the century's primary language works. The lines are descriptive, parallel, and cumulative in their survey. The natural forces are given human power and form, and emotional correspondence. The focus on bodily shape and feeling was one which Wordsworth was to criticize, but which Blake accepted strongly. And it had strong precedent in the figures and personifications recommended by the critics. Even so early as 1700, Samuel Wesley, whom Professor Hooker calls representative of his day, wrote to encourage, as Dryden had, the blend of Christian forms with classical scenes. (See Augustan Reprints, Series II.) Defending the use of angels and even of God, "cloth'd in divinity," and attacking the abstraction of classical "Fates," Wesley used the argument that Blake was to use, that " 'tis singulars and particulars which give an Air of Probability, and the main Life and Beauty to a Poem, . . ." He used also Blake's argument for internal sound, "Now soft, now loud, as best the matter fits." He proposed Blake's sort of scenes and machines for epic survey, "the Waste of Chaos," "the Porch of Death's Grim Court," "the chains of Britain," and "Sweet Angel-Forms, Peace, Virtue, Health and Love," and wrote the sort of descriptions as models in which "thick sulphureous vapours load the sky," and "Iron Whips and Clanks of Chains are heard" ("Concerning Poetry," lines 1009–1011)—a very handbook for eighteenth-century development. Poets as various as Young, Pope, Cowper, Chatterton, Beattie, the Wartons, Samuel Rogers, men all with some religious, social, or "Gothic" concerns, set up the tempestuous or sunny scene, the enormous allegorical figure, the emotional and social comment.

So Joseph Warton's "Ode to Superstition" in mid-century beings:

> Hence to some convent's gloomy isles,
> Where cheerful daylight never smiles:
> Tyrant! from Albion haste, to slavish Rome,
> There by dim taper's livid light,
> At the still solemn hours of night,
> In pensive musings walk o'er many a sounding tomb.
>
> Thy clanking chains, thy crimson steel,
> Thy venom'd darts and barb'rous wheel,
> Malignant fiend, bear from this isle away,
> Nor dare in errour's fetters bind
> One active, freeborn, British mind;
> That strongly strives to spring indignant from thy sway.

The poem goes on to screaming infants and wolves and lions, and ends at the thrones of Locke, Newton, and Plato, enshrined above. A half century later, in another "Ode to Superstition," Samuel Rogers repeats the phrasing of Warton as of Blake:

> Hence, to the realms of Night, dire Demon, hence!
> Thy chain of adamant can bind
> That little world, the human mind,
> And sink its noblest powers to impotence.
> Wake the lion's loudest roar,

Clot his shaggy main with gore,
With flashing fury bid his eye-balls shine;
Meek is his savage sullen soul to thine!

The phrasing as it proceeds includes the main terms of such writing in the century, the *reign* and *chain* of *winter,* the *tiger,* the *sheeted spectre,* the *cloud, web, iron hand, giant errour, labyrinth, imperial eagle, druid-rites, angels, tempest's howl,* and *rack* and *reeking wheel.* So certain main lines of connection developed: the landscape, a human body; the country of England, Albion personified; winter, a tyrant, along with kings and priests; wisdom and reason old and lordly; innocence as a naked boy, the path of childhood flowery, the daughters and sons of the father trembling and fearful, the seasonal cycles of peace and war and hope and fear, the caves of memory, the tools of oppression.

Lest it be thought, despite Samuel Wesley's early prescriptions for such materials, that they were mainly built up by the revolutionists of the late century, we should look to them also in the work of Pope, who seems in many ways as far away as possible from Blake his colleague. Pope had not Blake's message, nor his temper, nor his view. Yet the two poets as they worked within the century shared a good deal of its established substance. Both were social psychologists and satirists, both inherited and mocked the literary mode of epic conflict, while they recognized its truth to human limitation.

Pope in satire describes the mode of panegyric:

Oh, could I mount on the Mæonian wing,
Your arms, your actions, your repose to sing!
What seas you travers'd, and what fields you fought!
Your country's peace, how oft, how dearly bought!
How barb'rous rage subsided at your word,
And nations wonder'd while they dropp'd the sword!
How, when you nodded, o'er the land and deep,

Peace stole her wing, and wrapt the world in sleep;
Till earth's extremes your mediation own,
And Asia's tyrants tremble at your throne— . . .
(Trans. Horace, *Epistles,* II, 1)

The Maeonian Homeric muse had already come in Pope's day to personified abstraction moving over a scene of cosmic scope and making observers tremble.

Indeed, the kind of frame within which eighteenth-century rational speculation worked made for the consolidating of that kind of language which Blake was still to use even in rebellion. Blake did not want actually to follow the argument of Pope's *Essay on Man;* particularly he did not want to deal with the abstract Man of Epistle I, nor the Reason of Epistle II; yet with many aspects of the Passions—for example, the system of society, the origin of patriarchal government and of tyranny, the principles of love, fear, and happiness, all especially in Epistle III—we know the extent of Blake's concern. So even Pope's language can sound like his as in the sixth section it draws parallels between the early patriarch rulers and God himself and connections between tyranny and self-love.

Force first made conquest, and that conquest, law:
'Til Superstition taught the tyrant awe, . . .
She, from the rending earth and bursting skies,
Saw Gods descend, and fiends infernal rise: . . .
Zeal then, not charity, became the guide;
And hell was built on spite, and heav'n on pride,
Then sacred seem'd th' ethereal vault no more;
Altars grew marble then, and reek'd with gore:
Then first the Flamen tasted living food;
Next his grim idol smear'd with human blood;
With heav'n's own thunders shook the world below,
And play'd the God an engine on his foe.

So drives Self-love, through just and through unjust,
To one Man's pow'r, ambition, lucre, lust:
The same Self-love, in all, becomes the cause
Of what restrains him, Government and Laws.

Building a heaven in hell's despite, in Blake's variation of Pope's phrase here, Blake would borrow many of these materials: the stages of history, cosmic setting, personified feelings, altars and engines. Pope was in fact a particularly good source of the many engines and wheels which his successor characteristically used. Notice, for example, how the begininning of the *Dunciad* unfolds the origins of the great empire of Dulness: "The Mighty Mother, and her Son who brings / The Smithfield Muses to the ear of Kings, . . . / Say how the Goddess bade Britannia sleep, / And poured her Spirit o'er the land and deep. . . ." In the next few lines most of the terms are like Blake's:

Close to those walls where Folly holds her throne,
And laughs to think Monroe would take her down,
Where o'er the gates, by his fam'd father's hand,
Great Cibber's brazen, brainless brothers stand;
One Cell there is, conceal'd from vulgar eye,
The Cave of Poverty and Poetry.
Keen, hollow winds howl thro' the bleak recess,
Emblem of Music caus'd by Emptiness. . . .

and again in Book II:

Himself among the story'd chiefs he spies,
As from the blanket high in air he flies,
"And oh! (he cry'd) what street, what lane but knows
Our purgings, pumpings, blanketings, and blows?
In ev'ry loom our labours shall be seen,
And the fresh vomit run forever green!"

Blake's language is not only the common language of eighteenth-century religious song, pastoral, and panegyric, but also the rough and "particular" language of social satire. What he faithfully ignored in the eighteenth century was its most neoclassically smooth generalization and moral abstraction; what he faithfully used was its vigor and scope of scene and anatomy, its sublimely vast, yet satirically particular, emotional survey.

In almost every poem by Blake the mass of minor reference, as well as the major reference with which we have been dealing, sets before us first a physical scene, colored and detailed; second, a participating human form; third, an explicit emotional state; fourth, the construction of the human being, his tools and buildings. For the first three of these categories, Blake's terms were very solidly the terms of his century, the *fields, streets,* and *hills,* the *friends* and *fathers,* the *hand* and *eye,* the *joy* and *worship,* the *standing* and *hearing, rising* and *falling,* of eighteenth-century explication. For the nineteenth century, these materials tended to fuse into implication, into hints of light, shade, and spirit too fleeting for such anatomy. Furthermore, even the fourth category of artifacts, of *loom, wheel, furnace, chain, pillar, tomb, cell, bow, wedge, labyrinth, anvil, mill,* is more an extension of a traditional vocabulary, a Biblical and eighteenth-century satirical vocabulary, than the beginning of a new. The social poets of the next century did not take the apparatus of "scenes and machines" so seriously as Blake did.

Why then does Blake seem to us today a major innovator and experimenter, though we find his basic materials and his extension of them to be rather a part of the era before him? The reason may lie in his style, the individual pattern he gives to these materials, but I think part of it rests also in one main characteristic of the materials themselves: the reference and structure are conditioned by the attitude of childhood. Such substance is especially vivid in the early *Songs,* and is indeed always stressed there by Blake's interpreters. But the prophetic books seem no less determined. It is true that the sentences and rhymes of the early poems seem more naïve, the lyrical quality stronger, the words younger, in *happy, merry, little, sweet,* in *child* and *smile* and *lamb, laugh* and *sing,* while the later terms grow heavier, in *great, mighty, terrible,* in *mountains* and *furnaces, daughters* and *sons,* and *rising, standing, building, dividing.* It is true that some emphases change in this way in the mid-1790's, with *The French Revolution* and *America,* and continue to stand fast through *Jerusalem.* But I think that all, both early and late, are the terms of the child, the troubled observer. We have noted that important words for nineteenth-century stress are just these words of troubled observation: *little, child, daughter, death, sun, fall;* in these and his own special *silent, starry, cloud,* Blake accentuates the point of view, making his scenes and actions increasingly enormous and mysterious.

The nineteenth century was no great appreciator of Blake; first, I think, because he was so much involved with the explicit vision it was trying to grow away from; second, because his likeness, his stress on the partial view of childhood, was so deeply new that it was scarcely conscious. Here for the first time in English poetry there rose to the surface of major statement the vocabulary of child and parent, which Biblical epic had fostered. It is we who recognize and respond to it, we who feel its full significance in Blake, as it helps condition his whole mode of speech. The child in Blake, as briefly in his predecessors, as in the Ballads and the *Lyrical Ballads,* in Browning, Longfellow, Keble, and our modern poets, is an oppressed Biblical child, in contrast to the freer neoclassical *youth.* He observes, and his observations are either magnified, as by the eighteenth-century sublime, or only partly suggested and understood, as by nineteenth-century symbol. His sentence structures are simple and phrasal, his terms concrete and sensory. He, as still today, in present poetry, does not argue his case in the world, but tries to set forth, to present merely, the towering tyranny of his material. He is innocent, uses few of the terms of *good* and *bad;* but is afraid, in the terms of *light* and *dark, little* and *great, new* and *old*. He sees now more of seas and oceans, trees and leaves, than he did in the eighteenth century, and less pictorially. As would be natural, a small child substituted for a youthful swain or a man of feeling in that eighteenth-century field and storm would see less of the whole, more of the part and the profound particularity of mystery. So Blake has taught us.

In the *Songs,* the little chimneysweeps explicitly cry. In the *Zoas* and *Jerusalem* they are more often voiceless. But they do the watching. They see huge forms of the fathers rising and falling in the heavenly cycle of conflict. They are observers, even prophets, of creation, but not themselves creators. Their language, characteristically, does not grow more active, complex, and constructive, but rather increases its emphasis on cumulative size and mass. *Death, divinity, eternity, mountain, chariots, giants, terrors* conclude *Jerusalem,* in the perspective of a man diminished among his vast images. "Tell me the What; I do not want you to tell me the Why and the How," wrote Blake in his Descriptive Catalogue. He wished to be not a participator in process like the metaphysical poets, but a recorder, an engraver of the human image in its two great statuses of power and weakness, sublimity and pathos. And the very scope of sublimity turned everyday man to a child. This was the full history of his spiritual sufferings, as Blake wrote. "I am either too low or too highly priz'd; / When Elate I am Envy'd, when Meek, I'm despis'd." (Keynes, p. 873.) Himself, like his society, he saw at extremes, with no golden mean, but the cycles of wars between them.

The reader may say I have by this time got beyond Blake's language, and beyond his community of choice. Without touching the heart of Blake's mystery, not the tiger's not the lamb's nor Albion's, I have yet burdened them with a whole eighteenth-century landscape and even with some modern myth. But I believe that the study of major language does lead in the directions of theme and attitude. It is in the solid substance of sound and reference and statement that themes are embodied and must work. The great philosophical patterns set forth in books by Damon, Percival, Frye, Schorer, Erdman are not alien to the pervading patterns of participial construction and onomatopoeia, as the vocabulary of *hand, foot,* and *head* and *eye* is not alien to Los and Urizen.

The study of language in poetry must use, of course, the methods of Urizen. As Blake has said (Keynes, p. 806): "Demonstration, Similitude & Harmony are Objects of Reasoning. Invention, Identity & Melody are Objects of Intuition." This study has sought to demonstrate similitudes more than identities; to show Blake's concern with eighteenth-century materials, scenes, and machines; to indicate the steadfastness of Blake's choices, the extremes in his extension of tradition, his delicate suggestion of new attitude and theme. The breaking of balance by conflict of unequal forces, the loss of beauty in terror, the giant anatomy of human experience, the adjectives of emotion and verbs of ceremony, are not separately or together the whole of Blake's identity, but they are a part of it, and a part sometimes more safely arrived at by analysis than by intuition. What the poet's whole style makes of his language is a greater question, which analysis, as Blake would remind us, is not adequate to answer. Blake does not deny Urizen, but would have him keep his place.

What Urizen from his limited place can indicate about Blake is something of his weakness and something of his power. Unlike the great romantics, he did not develop the poetry of the newest materials available to him. He did not primarily start anew and re-create. In his own terms, he was too much the son and child, not enough the father, and that was a sort of weakness, never to let his eighteenth-century giants and children become actual nineteenth-century men. But on the other hand, the magnificent extremes to which he carried many of the essentials of eighteenth-century tradition preserve it now for us in its most vivid form of human figure against a landscape civic and cosmic; and, civic and cosmic, that is the sublime of Blake.

CHAPTER SIX

IN THE TERMS OF BALLADS

THE BALLAD MODE is a formally active mode of poetry. That is, the ballad is strongly predicative and structurally repetitive, using time in both substance and organization to carry its effect.

> The king sits in Dumferling toune,
>   Drinking the blude-reid wine:
> O quhar will I get guid sailor,
>   To sail this schip of mine?
>
> Up and spak an eldern knicht,
>   Sat at the kings richt kne:
> Sir Patrick Spence is the best sailor,
>   That sails upon the se.

The king has written a braid letter,
And signd it wi' his hand,
And sent it to Sir Patrick Spence,
Was walking on the sand. . . .

Here in "Sir Patrick Spence" as in other ballads we have a concentrated structure devoted to the progression of episode, the dovetailing of action. We hear the king asking his question and getting his answer, and then we move back: the letter has been written and received, and then in the present again Sir Patrick cries, "Mak haste." The lords fear, and the disaster has struck. Then we look to the future: "O lang, lang may the ladies stand / Wi' thair gold kems in their hair." And finally, in the present again to match "The king sits in Dumferling town," "It's fiftie fadom deip / And there lies guid Sir Patrick Spence, / Wi' the Scots lords at his feit." The parallelism and variation in parallelism has been constant and subtle, moving always to make the narrative point. The king sits at Dumferling, an elder advisor at his knee. Spence lies at Aberdour with the Scots lords at his feet. And he is "guid" in a far more profound fashion than the king asked for to begin with.

All the common words of the ballads work also toward this temporal progression, conventional though they may seem. *Dear* and *fair* as well as *good* may work so, by their constant repetition, and the colors such as *red,* and the qualities of *old* and *young, bold* and *proud. Lord, lady,* and *king* are the constant subjects of the narrative, along with family relations, and *day* in *hall* and *land* their setting, *hand, heart,* and *love* expressive for them, *come* their major action, along with *give* and *take, make* and *see, die* and *lie,* and *kill,* and the narrative verbs of *speak, tell, sing,* and *play.*

The verbs dominate two to one over adjectives, which are relatively scarce in the short and moving lines of the ballad. Even nouns are at a minimum, the proportions being five adjectives, twelve nouns, nine verbs per ten lines. Clauses are stronger than participial constructions, so that action is immediate rather than descriptive, and even the line structure contributes to the quality of motion as it gives us almost an action per line, coödinate and subordinate in alternation. Verbs bear the alliterative stresses: *To sail this schip, get guid, has written and signd and sent.* The familiar lordly figures in their lordly places and their noble moods and their colored array come and go, to meet, to give and take, slay or be slain, see merely, and tell; but always they accost each other and speak to each other, with resultant responsibility and resultant action.

Lord Percy to the quarry went,
  To view the slaughter'd deere;
Quoth he, Erle Douglas promised
  This day to meet me heere: . . .

And when they came to kyng Adlands hall
  Before the goodlye gate,
There they found good kyng Adland
  Rearing himself theratt. . . .

The woodweele sang, and wold not cease,
  Sitting upon the spraye,
Soe lowde, he wakened Robin Hood,
  In the greenwood where he lay. . . .

To the Newe Castell when they cam,
  The Skottes they cryde on hyght,
Syr Harye Percy, and thow byste within,
  Com to the fylde, and fyght. . . .

Or love or gramarye might make the meeting, and often in disguise. But the situations were not so many, nor the actors and their epithets so various, that they could not make the most of a rich repetition and convention.

What happened to this ballad form and style in the mid-eighteenth century when it was fondly revived after the encouragement of literary leaders like Addison? Did the core of the ballad, its main terms and forms, stay fast, to be embroidered around the edges by the new "romanticism"? Or were certain essential parts abandoned? Or was there a sea-change? Part of the answer lies in Percy's *Reliques* itself. In this collection of "ancient" poetry published in 1763 as one of the first new landmarks of antiquarian interest, the old ballads from the old manuscript were already altered toward a Georgian tone. The Percy ballads use less color and more emotion explicitly, more *bold, doughty, gentle, proud* sort of adjective, fewer nouns of family relation and more of setting like *land* and *hall* and *harp,* and less of the early active predication of *play, sing, speak, tell,* more of characteristically static eighteenth-century verbs like *stand.* The verb *kill* becomes the verb *slay* for Percy, and begins to decline as a term to be used at all. Active verbs have decreased in the Percy ballads, just as they did in the eighteenth century.

Some of these differences result from Percy's selective choices of ballads; others result from gradual modification or specific rewriting. Percy himself deplores what has happened to "Child Maurice" with its new "good green wood" for the old "silver wood" and its added descriptive scenery, and its emotions of "jealous rage," "heavy sighs," "care" and "despair." Or again, what happens specifically to "Barbara Allen" is that the simple phrase "oh, it's I'm sick" is developed to "with deadly sorrow sighing" and "heart was struck with sorrow" and so on, and we get "repentance." Also we get expurgation: of such terms as "for Christ's sake" and "by dear God." And we get cleaning up of the rhymes, so that not "gold" but "gold so good" will rhyme with "Robin Hood." But interestingly enough, not all the developments seem to be toward such conscious eighteenth-century standards, but rather are gradual, as when in "King Estmere" the familial terms of *brother* and *son* have been gradually lessened by omission or replacement with proper names.

The modifications in the Percy ballads are a guide to what more thoroughgoing poets will consciously make of the form. Even at heart they will alter it toward the heart of their own poetic practice. Strongest to survive in Scott was the ballad measure, but in Chatterton's work the pull of the blank-verse line tended to lengthen the ballad line and to fatten it with epithets in the rich Spenserian manner. Strongest to survive for Chatterton, on the other hand, are the basic terms which Percy has already preserved, evaluative *good* and *brave, day, heart, life,* and *man,* and the *come* and *go, give* and *take, sing* and *tell* verbs, and these survive for Scott also. What both poets agree in adding, different as their meters and temperaments make them, is a much richer and fuller world of furnishings: *blood* and *bloody, sun, arrow, spear,* with commentary *high, noble, woe* for Chatterton, and a varied personnel of *warrior, baron, dwarf,* and others, for Scott. Scott is a bit more the faithful of the two, both in his proportionings and sentence structure and in his emphasis on observed colors and objects rather than on emotional and moral judgments, but in a sense his devoted trappings are as alien as Chatterton's sentiments. Hear how even the faithfulest imitation sounds in Chatterton's "Bristowe Tragedie":

I

The feathered songster Chanticleer
  Has wound his bugle horn,
And told the early villager
  The coming of the morn:

II

King Edward saw the ruddy streaks
  Of light eclipse the gray;

And heard the raven's craking throat
  Proclaim the fated day. . . .

V

Sir Canterlone then bended low
  With heart brimful of woe;
He jorneyed to the castle-gate,
  And to Sir Charles did go.

VI

But when he came, his children twain,
  And eke his loving wife,
With briny tears did wet the floor
  For good Sir Charles's life.

And so on. But this sentiment is pure balladry compared to Chatterton's more usual vein, as in the rewriting of the "Battle of Hastings":

Oh Truth! immortal daughter of the skies,
Too little known to writers of these days,
Teach me, fair Saint! thy passing worth to prize,
To blame a friend and give a foeman praise.
The fickle moon, bedeck'd with silver rays,
Leading a train of stars of feeble light,
With look adigne the world below surveys,
The world, that wotted not it could be night;
With armour donn'd, with human gore y-dyed,
She sees King Harold stand, fair England's curse and pride.

Here, even more fully than in "Bristowe," it is Spenser that prevails, and, in major terms, the Spenser of the eighteenth century.

We may surmise, then, that in the basic ways of phrasing and proportioning the eighteenth-century adapters of the ballad carried over no more of it, or not much more, than the eighteenth century in general carried from earlier poetry like Spenser's. It took Scott and Coleridge to clarify the measures; it took a number of later poets to recover the vocabulary. We may say that the key terms of the ballad were the *good, dear, fair, brave, lord* and *lady, father* and *family, coming* and *going, giving* and *taking* and *playing,* with bright colors and active verbs; of these only the *lord* and *lady* and other terms of rank were retained in full strength and amplified in the eighteenth century. For the rest, verbs declined and grew more static, family relations lessened and simplified, traditional adjectives weakened, and *gold* and *silver* turned to *gray*. In return, the ballad got express emotion and nobility and a vastly enriched physical atmosphere.

The *Lyrical Ballads* were another matter. They show neither a direct development from the eighteenth century nor a return to the old ballad itself. They employ, both Wordsworth's and Coleridge's, almost a whole new set of terms, in a subtilization of the ballad measure. No noble personnel at all, but *moon, sun, stars, wind,* and *water.* Colors, but new ones, *black* and *white.* Comments, but new ones, of *holy, strange, poor, wild, cold, warm.* Verbs of loving and praying. For Wordsworth, a proportioning in sentence structure far from the ballad's predicative dominance.

The newness is so great that it has lasted all this while, into such modern ballads as Robert Penn Warren's on Billie Potts, in which the style may be seen in all its natural and nonnoble splendor.

Oh, the stars are shining and the meadow is bright
But under the trees is dark and night
In the land between the rivers. . . .
And the leaves hang down in the dark of the trees
And there is the spring in the dark of the trees
And there is the spring as black as ink
And one star in it caught through a chink

Of the leaves that hang down in the dark of the trees,
And the star is there but it does not wink.
And Little Billie gets down on his knees
And props his hands in the same old place
To sup the water at his ease;
And the star is gone but there is his face.
"Just help yoreself," Big Billie said;
Then set the hatchet in his head.
They went through his pockets and they buried him in the dark of
 the trees. . .

This whole poem of Warren's and his others like it share still the *Lyrical Ballad* vocabulary of *little, old, white, black, night, tree, water, wind,* and *stand,* though without the feelings, the *joy, loving,* and *praying* of the century past. Indeed, this has become a major vocabulary throughout modern poetry, by way of Pound especially, and it is a vocabulary as alien as possible to the ballads with which we began, for it has taken nature for its vehicle and has no praise for character or action. There was a strong break, then, between Scott and Coleridge: the ending of one development and beginning of a quite new one, both under the name of ballad. In the main, but one great trait of the earlier tradition has come over by other ways into modern poetry: the family relations of father, mother, son, though less now of brother or daughter, in such poets as Auden and Lowell. In these terms has grown up during the nineteenth century a renewed significance, but quite apart from ballad usage. Perhaps another trait is the sort of active verb which has survived from the ballad, the simplest *coming* and *going* of much of modern poetry, and *dying,* though the ballad *killed.*

Though we may discern three clear temporal stages for the ballad, then, in fifteenth-sixteenth, eighteenth, and twentieth centuries, with conscious interest in the mode acting as revivifying force, yet we cannot discern one continuous development through these stages, but rather an ending and a beginning. With Scott the simplest emphases of ballad measure and ballad trappings ended in rich atmosphere of detail; with Coleridge the measure took on a subtler variation, and the detail a new nature; the ballad structure became vehicle for new ideas and materials, away from kings on their thrones and knights on their steeds and harpers in their halls, toward the wind in the trees.

How is it that the ballad served both these shifts? In the eighteenth century, in a world of odes and epigrams, of cosmic scenery and speculation strictly reined and pointed, how did the ballad seem to serve? We may remember how concerned the Augustans were about narrative technique, the writing of the heroic poem; in the ballad, the work was done for them almost miraculously, and they dared to try it again, since the characters, if not all the words spoken, were of the highest. But blurred with the ballad was Spenser, because knights rode in both; and blurred with the eighteenth-century epic was Spenser, because of the *Faerie Queene;* and blurred with the scenic cosmos was Spenser, because of his high, noble, and sad scenery: so there was one way the ballad grew and got lost in the eighteenth century: in its Chatterton, its Collins, its Spenser.

Then again in the nineteenth and twentieth centuries there was a strong urge away from epic and epic scope and upholstery, toward depth, delicacy, and implication. And here again, other forces in the ballad seemed to serve: not its lords and ladies of high degree this time, but rather its quick and implicative narrative style, which got rid of adjectives in favor of verbs, let objects do the work of persons, and saw persons in basic family relation and in basic simple confrontation.

Viewed so, the ballad seems pretty complex, to have provided so much to so many different motives. That it was. And we have not thought of nearly all the possible recombinations of qualities.

The question arises, Have these transformations been primarily spatial, English; or rather temporal, through the ballad in other languages also? When we look at the great Spanish collection, Wolf and Hofmann's *Primavera y flor de romances,* we see even on the first page (Vol. II) the familiar beginnings:

> —Reina Elena, reina Elena,
> ¡Dios prospere tu estado!
> si mandáis alguna cosa
> veisme aquí a vuestro mandado.
> —Bien vengades vos, París,
> París el enamorado,
> París, ¿dónde vais camino,
> dónde tenéis vuestro trato?

The vocabulary develops in these poems to a stress on *king, queen, lady, lord, steed, horse,* and such noble terms, and also, as in the English poems, *day, hand, love, life,* and the familial nouns. In addition, *blood, flower,* and *land,* which are powerful in the Spanish, will appear two centuries later as important in the English. The epithets too are familiar: *grande, bueno, lindo.* The main verbs are again the same, *come, go,* and *tell* (*ir, decir, venir, ver*), and so on.

Here then in the key terms of two languages is the homogeneity of which scholars have told us. The strong linear and assonantal patterns and the sentence progressions are close to the English in Spanish also.

But what surprises me, perhaps unduly, from insular perspective of English studies, is the appearance in what seems to me a very different Spanish "romantic revival" of the same changes that we have seen in the English, and again somewhat earlier than the English. For the Duque de Rivas, surely neither a Scott nor a Coleridge, epithets have increased and verbs have declined as they did for these. The new terms in Spanish as in English are the "Spenserian" *alto,* and the *blanco* and *negro* of Coleridge and Wordsworth. And here in Rivas are all the nature terms: *cielo, mar, nube, sol,* as well as the spirit of *alma* and *pecho* and *parecer.*

Turbó la apacible luna
un vapor blanco y espeso,
que de las altas techumbres
se iba elevando y creciendo.

A poco rato tornóse
En humo confuso y denso,
que en nubarrones obscuros
ofuscaba el claro cielo.
("Un castellano leal," IV)

We cannot then be more surprised, holding in mind Pound's and Warren's developments from Coleridge's ballads of night and strangeness, to read as the first lines of Lorca's *Romancero gitano:*

La luna vino a la fragua
con su polisón de nardos.
El niño la mira, mira.
El niño la está mirando.
En el aire conmovido
mueve la luna sus brazos
y enseña, lúbrica y pura,
sus senos de duro estaño.

Or again, at the beginning of "Romance sonámbulo":

Verde que te quiero verde.
Verde viento. Verdes ramas.
El barco sobre la mar
y el caballo en la montaña.
Con la sombra en la cintura
ella sueña en su baranda,
verde carne, pelo verde,
con ojos de fría plata. . . .

And then:

—Trescientas rosas morenas
lleva tu pechera blanca.
Tu sangre rezuma y huele
alrededor de tu faja.
Pero yo ya no soy yo,
ni mi casa es ya mi casa.
—Dejadme subir al menos
hasta las altas barandas,
¡dejadme subir!, dejadme,
hasta las verdes barandas.
Barandales de la luna
per donde retumba el agua.

Others of Lorca's poems which stress such episodic confrontation in the persistent terms of color, especially *green, black,* and *white,* and the nature of *night, water,* and *blood,* and the *child* (*niño*) and *son,* which link the oldest terms with the new, are "Balada de la placeta," "Baladilla de la tres ríos," "Romance de los toros," from *Mariana Pineda* I, "Muerte de Antonito el Bamcorio," and, with more transformation, "Thamár y Amnón." The flexibility of his narrative structure is freer, and the stages more oblique, than Coleridge's, and of course far more than the older ballads; yet we are able to see exactly how Coleridge's inventions within the mode are basic to Lorca as well as to Warren and the English, not necessarily by direct influence but by a common temporal development. The *blanco, grande, lleno, negro, viejo, agua, caballo, cielo, aire, estrella, flor, luz, mar, monte, niño, noche, luna, ojo, sangre, viento, voz,* and again the stress on *venir, ver, tener, cantar, llorar* share fully in the world of the terms in English also.

We seem to find parallel continuities in the ballad materials of two languages, then, which would suggest much about the homogeneity of the ballad temporally as well as spatially. Its active narrative and lyrical force seems to maintain for it a cadence, a sentence structure, and a vocabulary, changing with, yet distinctive in, the successive eras of poetic practice. Child, Morley, Entwistle, and Ruth H. Webber have all stressed in their studies of the ballad its power of convention, the stability of its terms and procedures, from language to language, through the Middle Ages.[1] As Professor Entwistle has said: "The words of ballads are, in fact, complexes of motifs just as their tunes are complexes of notes. The chances against fortuitous coincidence are scarcely less heavy than against fortuitous coincidence in melody. These two aspects of the full performance have each their history of rise, expansion, and decline." [2] Even in the modern era, a period of decline for the traditional ballad in most senses, but a period of some triumph for its literary metamorphoses, the complexes of motifs persist.

Further, we find them to be part of the motifs for poetry as a whole, in our era, as in the romantic period, as in the period of the ballad itself. So that we may still perhaps be right to say, "in this way the ballads come to be the completest definition of the community which enjoys them." [3] And in this way the community which enjoys them may be greater than any one nation or language.

[1] F. J. Child, *The English and Scottish Popular Ballads,* used, with Walter Morris Hart's *Ballads,* as text; S. Griswold Morley, *Spanish Ballad Problems* (Univ. Calif. Publ. Mod. Philol., Vol. 13, No. 2, 1925); Ruth House Webber, *Formulistic Diction in the Spanish Ballad* (Univ. Calif. Publ. Mod. Philol., Vol. 34, No. 2, 1951); W. J. Entwistle, *European Balladry* (Oxford: Clarendon Press, 1939).

[2] Entwistle, *op. cit.,* p. 74.

[3] *Ibid.,* p. 13.

CHAPTER SEVEN

THE ROMANTIC MODE

WHOM shall we call the romantics? Was there actually a sufficient number of poets in agreement at the turn of the century to make what one would call a style or mode? Certain traits of attitude, or of material, or of structure, could take us back as far as Addison with his sense of a new world, or Thomson, to whom Wordsworth went for images, or the stanzaic experiments of Collins, or any poet any time for a certain cut of jib. I think we should not answer theoretically, but look to see if there was indeed in England any whole group of poets who agreed together, if only tacitly, in abandoning the full complex of the earlier mode, its epic and panoramic pentameters, for a new complex of attitude, terminology, and construction. Did any new meter take over the poetry of 1800, any new vocabulary, any whole new sort of statement?

We know that throughout the eighteenth century there had been a strong consolidation of poetic techniques which endured even through the work of Wordsworth and Keats and included much free play of virtuosity without strain on the bonds of agreement. We know that this solid agreement had made for a thematic sense of moral universality, a full and regular pentameter line, a descriptive adjectival richness, in the sublime terms of Longinus. We recognize the primary vocabulary—that is, the nouns, adjectives, and verbs used most often, over and over, by a majority of the poets—to have been especially general and emotional, in terms of *art, beauty, fate, friend, joy, life, love, land, head, heart, mind, muse, nature, power, thought, virtue,* modified by such approving epithets as *divine, fair, gay, happy, proud, soft, sweet,* a vocabulary in all well suited to generalization about natural human forces, brought home to the heart by direct image and simile.

Poems in this mode were as various as Thomson's *Seasons,* Dyer's *Ruins,* and Cowper's *Task*. In the later years of the century the tone and vocabulary grew more gloomy, more *woe* and *weeping, cold* and *sad* came into the pattern, and more details of analysis, but the pattern was easily adaptable to such modifications, and held its own as if to last forever.

The beginning of Cowper's *Task* is a good sample of the type; the epically descriptive flights have taken in humbler and humbler objects more and more seriously:

> I sing the Sofa. I, who lately sang
> Truth, Hope, and Charity, and touch'd with awe
> The solemn chords, and, with a trembling hand,
> Escap'd with pain from that advent'rous flight,
> Now seek repose upon an humbler theme;
> The theme, though humble, yet august, and proud
> Th' occasion—for the fair commands the song.

And, in the details of description:

Nor rural sights alone, but rural sounds,
Exhilarate the spirit, and restore
The tone of languid Nature. Mighty winds,
That sweep the skirt of some far-spreading wood
Of ancient growth, make music not unlike
The dash of Ocean on his winding shore,
And lull the spirit while they fill the mind;
Unnumber'd branches waving in the blast,
And all their leaves fast flutt'ring, all at once.
Nor less composure waits upon the roar
Of distant floods, or on the softer voice
Of neighb'ring fountain, or of rills that slip
Through the cleft rock, and, chiming as they fall
Upon loose pebbles, lose themselves at length
In matted grass, that with a livelier green
Betrays the secret of their silent course.
Nature inanimate employs sweet sounds,
But animated nature sweeter still,
To soothe and satisfy the human ear.

This is all deft progressive analysis, and it can go on and on, through many long volumes of the nineteenth century, in a structure which needs three nouns and adjectives to every verb, so discriminated are the details of quality within the universal whole, so substantially and thoroughly received are the sensations and concepts.

We have said we should look for a new mode where a new complex of idea, material, and structure clearly began. But the pentameter epical description was too strong in itself to admit any new complexes. And by 1800, when we should be growing restless, most of the poetry written was still of this sort, still even-coupleted and satirical in its popular reaches, still wistfully voluminous and substantival at its most lofty. Were, then, could a new mode get a hold?

Well, on various fine mornings close to 1800, various poets had begun writing verses like these:

"And wear thou this"—she solemn said,
And bound the holly rou̇nd my head;
The polish'd leaves, and berries red,
Did rustling play;
And, like a passing thought, she fled
In light away.
(Burns's "The Vision")

My mother groan'd! my father wept.
Into the dangerous world I leapt:
Helpless, naked, piping loud;
Like a fiend hid in a cloud.
(Blake's "Infant Sorrow")

No more to chiefs and ladies bright
The harp of Tara swells;
The chord alone, that breaks at night,
Its tale of ruin tells.
Thus Freedom now so seldom wakes,
The only throb she gives
Is when some heart indignant breaks,
To show that still she lives.
(Moore's "Harp")

Now in all ways, as the quickest ear or eye will tell you, this is a new and a different mode of poetry all of a sudden. It comes of course from "Sir Patrick Spence" and "Lord Randall" and "Chevy Chase," but it comes not gradually, but freely, with full intent to transform its sources. Remember how "Chevy Chase" began?—the very first of Bishop Percy's *Reliques*—

The Persé owt of Northombarlande,
  And a vowe to God mayd he,
That he wolde hunte in the mountayns
  Off Chyviat within dayes thre,
In the mauger of doughtè Dogles,
  And all that ever with him be.

The fattiste hartes in all Cheviat
  He sayd he wold kill, and cary them away:
Be my feth, sayd the doughtei Doglas agayn,
  I wyll let that hontyng yf that I may.

This is the measure and structure of Blake in some of the *Songs,* Coleridge and Wordsworth in the *Lyrical Ballads,* Thomas Moore, and Byron. Vary it as they will to their own purposes, this is the basic pattern of what will be a major nineteenth-century mode: the lyrical narrative of dramatic confrontation.

One may ask whether, since Addison praised "Chevy Chase" so early in the century, there was not an early beginning of ballad poetry in the mid-eighteenth century, as one of the strands of pre-romanticism. We should look for such an early version of the mode in Chatterton, for example, or Smart. But poets like these, we find, were too deeply involved in their own conventions to put new forms to use. Except in his "Battle of Bristowe," Chatterton was writing the poetry of a Spenserian antiquarianism, full of rich raiments, sceneries, sorrows, and *bedights,* not the book of the ballad. Even Percy's *Reliques,* so strong was the time, presented a sort of Shenstonian structure in 1765, an array of Spenserian Elizabethans, and some pure ballads, but some so rewritten, like "Barbara Allen" and "Child Maurice," that they contain the whole vocabulary of eighteenth-century emotionalism and descriptive weight: enameled fields and deadly sorrows, rages, despairs, sighs, and repentances.

It remained for the poets of the century's end to find in Percy the actual power of a new mode, and to use it for their own new purposes. Technically, the results may be described as follows: a sentence structure of dramatic confrontation, which employs more verbs than adjectives, more subordinate than serial constructions, more actions and arguments than descriptions and invocations. That is, the structure presents people in situations, with much suggestion and implication of surroundings, rather than surroundings with a suggestion of situation as the eighteenth century did. The focus has shifted to foreground figures. At the same time, the meter breaks, to allow for the effects of silence as well as sound in the verse line. In dramatic colloquy, lack of answer may be as vivid as answer itself, and the various modifications of ballad measure allow for this, as Coleridge pointed out indirectly in his discussion of "Christabel." Coleridge sought, as his contemporaries sought, a varied and broken line pattern, the constant remission of four stresses to three, with the consequent effects of easy repetition or implication, the lightness of assonance as the shade of rhyme, feminine as the shade of masculine endings, shadings of echo and progression from stanza to stanza, and indeed in every new form of modification in sound, the quality of shadow, echo, or answer, rather than the massed and cumulative quality of the old pentameters.

It was Coleridge too who brought the full effect of a new vocabulary to play in this complex of sound and structure. The vocabulary of the ballads themselves bore four main emphases: first, the great human terms of most English poetry, *man, love, heart,* and the verbs of action; second, the terms of a concrete reality, specific colors and objects, the *red blood* and the *burnished sword;* third, the terms of family relationship, *father, mother, daughter, son, brother;* fourth, the terms of station, *king, knight, lady, lord,* and so on. What Scott and the straight ballad imitators did was to preserve and reëmphasize these special terms, adding more of the same, more colors, more brothers, barons, harps, halls, steeds, and general trappings. For them an old mode was renovated, but did not become really new. Coleridge, on the other hand, with the aid of his contemporaries Byron, Moore, and Landor, following Rogers, Campbell, Burns, and Southey, made the mode realize its new language.

This new language was hard-won from the eighteenth century; it had to break away from the antiquarian trappings of the knights and ladies on the one hand and from the whole sublime gross of descriptions and emotions on the other. What it could save from the old ballads was the family relation and the qualities of immediacy; what it could save from the eighteenth century was that century's own new sort of immediacy, the sensory world of sun, sky, sea, star, and tree. Like stars coming out one by one in the sky, these terms had appeared as primary for a few poets: *sun, wind,* and *cloud* in Thomson, *deep, little, wild* and *sad,* in Dyer, Gray, and Collins, and colors in the Wartons, in the very poets for whom Wordsworth has given us the clue of liking; and now, at century's end, the terms moved into constellation. Over and over in the narrative verses of the romantics and their colleagues, the major terms of nature take part in the action. The king has gone from Dumferling town, and in his meter and story the sea has taken over. Or even the first person "I" may have become the actor, with moon and cloud as other dramatis personae. And the child has become a protagonist, descended from the son of the ballads, now younger in age, and taking the stage from the father.

In the main, then, we may say that with the generation of 1800 to 1840 there grew up a mode which by sheer contemporality and by its integration of special characteristics we may call new and whole and romantic. The vocabulary of this poetry is in part the basic human terms which prevail through all English poetry, and in part the terms of the surrounding century, and in at least one-half the terms which serve to characterize and identify it, the sensory epithets of *bright, deep, sad, wild,* the active natural forces of *flower, light, moon, mountain, sea, star, sun,* the human concepts of *hope, spirit, father, tear,* and *woe,* and the sensitive receptive verbs of *feeling, falling, lying, looking, praying, seeming*. These materials, with their total characterizing quality of a mysterious, fearful, yet hopeful nighttime in which men meet and pray, are given shape in the implicative and dramatic structures of ballad form with results familiar to us over and over in Hebrew Melodies, West Winds, Mariners.

> I pass, like night, from land to land;
> I have strange power of speech;
> The moment that his face I see,
> I know the man that must hear me:
> To him my tale I teach.
>
> What loud uproar bursts from that door!
> The wedding-guests are there:
> But in the garden-bower the bride
> And bride-maids singing are:
> And hark the little vesper bell,
> Which biddeth me to prayer!

Of Coleridge's inheritance from the ballads, Professor Lowes has said that it was mechanically literary, not so vigorous as his use of travel books. But Lowes referred mainly to the archaic diction. Actually, I think we may see, it was the oblique narrative progression of ballad sound and structure, as he uses it here to his own moral ends, that allowed Coleridge to find moral pertinence in the books of nature and travel which would otherwise have been too strange and oblique for his purpose.

Or Byron, without the harp of the ballad, would not have broken the pentameter line into such famous melodies as

> And there lay the steed with his nostril all wide,
> But through it there roll'd not the breath of his pride;

And the foam of his gasping lay white on the turf,
And cold as the spray of the rock-beating surf.

And there lay the rider distorted and pale,
With the dew on his brow, and the rust on his mail;
And the tents were all silent—the banners alone—
The lances unlifted—the trumpet unblown.

Such lilt of measure and pure romantic vocabulary Byron continues even into his most so-called classical satires. While Shelley in steadier and more sober measure manages to blur the edges of all his images in the romantic fashion of implication and in layers of metaphor:

Methought that of these visionary flowers
  I made a nosegay, bound in such a way
That the same hues, which in their natural bowers
  Were mingled or opposed, the like array
Kept these imprisoned children of the Hours
  Within my hand,—and then, elate and gay,
I hastened to the spot whence I had come,
That I might there present it!—oh! to whom?

When we come to the very center of the romantic mode in these poems of Byron and Shelley, Coleridge and Wordsworth and Keats, we may see that there is technical justification for thinking of the five together, sheer descriptive criteria, apart from greatness and goodness. What can be said about the mode in general can be said most particularly about them. Their agreements were interwoven, with no great splits between them. Their structural sense was vividly stanzaic, their sense of narrative not epic but lyric and episodic, their ear for sound tuned to undertone, their eye for concrete detail bright but seeing always blurred edges of emotional significance, as Professor Fogle has shown us; their metaphors glancing and complex, their verbs stronger and more structurally determining than their adjectives; their own especially abundant vocabulary shared in the characteristic terms of *bright, deep, cloud, light, spirit, star, sun,* and *wind,* in lightness and darkness, sound and silence.

This is not to say that the new mode, once it had come for these five poets, came immediately to stay. The five themselves kept to the mode with varying fidelity. Wordsworth, as we know, turned back from the flexible improvisations of ballads and the poems of 1806 to the more explicit earlier modes in which *The Excursion* and *The River Duddon* are written. Keats, always half faithful to the richness of Miltonic preromanticism, wrote in the *Odes* and *Hyperion* the finest sort of culmination of eighteenth-century poetry, though he worried about the very mode as he wrote. At the same time, minor figures like Hunt, Kirk White, Campbell, and Bryant in America, carried on for a while what the earlier century had so firmly established. But there is no reason to expect that the presence of a new style should immediately silence an old one. And, on the other hand, the new style spread and grew, not only in the later work of Byron, but in the minor poetry, as of Moore and Beddoes.

What makes the extent and strength of the new mode most explicit is the pattern of simple facts like these: by about 1820 most of the leading poets' work was stanzaic in structure, while a half century before it had been mostly linear; the measures were freely trisyllabic where they had been disyllabic; by about 1820 half the major terms, the nouns, adjectives, and verbs most used by the majority, were new terms, characteristically sensory, concrete, and thus often symbolic, while oblique metaphors had taken the place of explicit similes; by about 1820 the sentence structures were more narrative than descriptive, more complex than coördinate, using more verbs and sometimes only half as many adjectives as in the century before. By about 1820, in other words, the substance and structure of poetry had physically altered in determinable degree, to carry a new attitude by a new mode of statement.

The idea which gave life to this romantic mode was the idea of the spirit's narrative, the individual's lyrical story, half articulated and half heard, but powerful in its force of implication. It is one triumphant solution to the long Augustan search for a great heroic poem or a cosmical epic, which should reconcile the inheritances of classical culture and of contemporary science, in a descriptive panorama of heroic proportions, stressing scenes and sublimities and subordinating Sir Patrick Spence to Virgil, Spenser, and Milton. When the heroic story finally came to be told, it was of the individual self, of the Mariner, the adventurer Childe, even the infant of the *Songs* and *The Prelude,* the self who was the son of Sir Patrick Spence, who said little, and felt much, and implied more, and died deeply. For such a narration, the form could be better lyrical than epical, the structure better repetitive than cumulative, the terms better active than descriptive, as the individual poet is both hero and minstrel, both tree-harp and the wind in it, both the story and the storyteller, in the romantic mode.

CHAPTER EIGHT

WORDSWORTH: THE MIND'S EXCURSIVE POWER

William Wordsworth gave poetry the power to generalize about human nature subtly and consistently. A century of poets before him had tried with all sorts of crudity of device. Desiring to speak of a general humanity, they had struggled with the appurtenances of its nobility, a lofty language, a cosmic simile, a heroic couplet, a basic psychological antithesis and balance, a sublimity of invocation and epithet. Everything got out of hand. It was either too laborious, as for Crabbe, or too elaborate, as for Blake; it rose out of sight or lay heavy and inert. Wordsworth and Coleridge undertook to remedy these extremes; Coleridge, by a deeper implication in metaphor and meter of the soaring soul, Wordsworth, by a serious refining of the literal and earthly. Wordsworth's was the force of consolidation; he gave not only hints toward a new realm as Coleridge did, but the fullness of a matured power to an old realm needing comprehension. All the stumblings of Addison and Akenside toward the achievement of psychological statement, all the gross niceties of Pope in his perception of complexity, all the shadings of Gray's exploration and the smoothness of Goldsmith's certainty came to win an eventual triumph in Wordsworth's articulation of their concern, the quality of human thought and feeling in the natural world.

Today poetry is working as it was in the eighteenth century, with a great deal of stiff effort and unease, toward the articulation of consequences and the articulation of human concerns in an impressively large universe. It shares the difficulties of Pope and Thomson, the stifling amount of device to deal with a stifling amount of objects and sensations, and it needs a Wordsworth of its own, to be the generalizer and steadfast interpreter of its own terms.

This is the integral Wordsworth of *Prelude, Excursion,* sonnets, odes, from one end of his life to the other, the Wordsworth of faith as well as glee, the classicist in an effort toward a difficult synthesis of human perceptions. This is the Wordsworth whose particularity of ego and observation is turned to a poetry as general in abstraction as any we have, with its even proportions, its sustained contours of meditation, its vocabulary of emotional abstraction, its repeated patterns of association. Such poetry attempts to tell men about themselves, how they feel, how they arrive at moral judgments, as these feelings and judgments are common and shared. It appears early for Wordsworth, as in *The Borderers* (Act III):

> Action is transitory—a step, a blow,
> The motion of a muscle—this way or that—
> 'Tis done, and in the after-vacancy
> We wonder at ourselves like men betrayed:
> Suffering is permanent, obscure and dark,
> And shares the nature of infinity.

It continues in the very beginning of *The Prelude:*

For I, methought, while the sweet breath of heaven
Was blowing on my body, felt within
A correspondent breeze, that gently moved
With quickening virtue, but is now become
A tempest, a redundant energy,
Vexing its own creation. . . .

And throughout *The Excursion:*

. . . As the ample moon,
In the deep stillness of a summer even
Rising behind a thick and lofty grove,
Burns, like an unconsuming fire of light,
In the green trees; and, kindling on all sides
Their leafy umbrage, turns the dusky veil
Into a substance glorious as her own,
Yea, with her own incorporated, by power
Capacious and serene. Like power abides
In man's celestial spirit; virtue thus
Sets forth and magnifies herself; thus feeds
A calm, a beautiful, and silent fire,
From the encumbrances of mortal life,
From error, disappointment—nay, from guilt;
And sometimes, so relenting justice wills,
From palpable oppressions of despair.

And again in the mid 1830's, "The Foregoing Subject Resumed":

To a like salutary sense of awe
Or sacred wonder, growing with the power
Of meditation that attempts to weigh,
In faithful scales, things and their opposites,
Can thy enduring quiet gently raise
A household small and sensitive . . .

This central style endures through all Wordsworth's experiments: through the ballad narratives, which *Tintern Abbey* encompasses; through the high originality of the ode on immortality, which later odes conventionalize; through the restrictive couplet and sonnet forms and orthodox feelings of the later years, in which the mind still ponders its security in delicately meditative iambic pentameters.

> bees that soar for bloom,
> High as the highest Peak of Furness-fells,
> Will murmur by the hour in foxglove bells:
> In truth the prison, into which we doom
> Ourselves, no prison is . . .

The confines of the steady and flexible pentameter, rhymed or unrhymed, and the steady literal analogy between nature and man, pressed Wordsworth to bring all his musings home to his own plot of ground. And the range of these musings was vast, through the processes of human thought and feeling, through the sympathetic powers of nature, through revolutionary force and social institution, through liberty, evil, justice, individuality, fear, death, and the horizons of mystery where he grew to see heaven. He cannot now tell us what we want to know about these matters, for they are subjects that have changed in context for us; but he can remind us how much we do want to know about them, from our own perspective, but in his patiently meditative terms; with our own answers, but with his skillful and graceful modes of excursion. The poetry of a thinking process need not be limited to any one half century, now that we have got it clear and can see the power of its workings.

The high seriousness which a century ago gave Wordsworth a rank with Chaucer, Shakespeare, and Milton, most of the critics of our own century have tended merely to excuse him for, or not even to excuse him for. We remember how hateful his style seemed to George Moore and J. B. Yeats—a harping on generalization when pure objects would do,—and how to the Imagists he seemed a very model of mistaken cosmic abstraction. Their stress on the image as an emotional complex in an instant of time directly opposed Wordsworth's encouragement of the tendency of perceptions to generalize themselves. Less specialized critics today still try to ignore the mass of Wordsworth's work and to give him credit for the fresh and natural particularity which he helped to foster and which has become the major poetic substance of our era. Herbert Read selects the "Solitary Reaper," and George Rylands a line like "Those bright blue eggs together laid" as characteristic of the best Wordsworthian style. F. R. Leavis and Helen Darbishire agree on the supremacy of the brief lyric "A slumber did my spirit seal," and in the recent collection of centennial lectures on Wordsworth at Princeton and Cornell this is the poem quoted by three of the lecturers.

No motion has she now, no force;
  She neither hears nor sees;
Rolled round in earth's diurnal course
  With rocks, and stones, and trees.

These are of course the terms, this the poetry, of our own era, and therefore the selection of it may reflect us primarily, Wordsworth only secondarily. Rocks and stones and trees—they draw their primacy from our own great concreteness, which had only some of its tentative beginnings in Wordsworth's work. Even Mark Van Doren, listening for a "Noble Voice," finds nothing in poetry better than Wordsworth's reality and fact of scenes; but fears that "the voice of the prophet is a different matter."

One should hesitate, then, to suggest that it is not only the special modern part but also the traditional whole of Wordsworth that can be important to us. One should not wish to deny the long dull stretches of verse which the author of more than fifty thousand lines is apt to write, nor try to disregard the stiffening of forms and creeds which beset the aging poet.

On the other hand, our own forms and creeds of objectivity and particularity have aged and stiffened also, and tradition may recall to us other modes of value. The small celandines to which Wordsworth gave happy infancy we have outworn and outdone, but the structures of deliberation to which he gave maturity we have yet to make our own.

I shall try to describe the Wordsworthian mode as specifically as possible in brief space, in order to justify my sense of it in its power for our day. The need is, first, to recognize its basic materials, the terms and structures of language in which it works; second, to note the temporal matrix of these materials; third, to see how style shapes them, how Wordsworth's habit of work in selection and arrangement gives pattern and tone to them and conveys ideas through them. These three questions imply an observation of all the poetry. They imply a kind of neutrality, which may turn to partisanship if one favors the answers they find.

The basic importance to Wordsworth of the iambic pentameter line is clear from its persistence in his work. Early, when he was still reciting Gray and Goldsmith to himself, he tried not the freer meters of Gray, but the more conventionally coupleted pentameter, for his own "Walk" and "Sketches." His first long narrative used the line in stanza form; his first dramatic poem, in blank verse. Even before the *Lyrical Ballads* grew famous, the early *Prelude* fragments and *Tintern Abbey* itself showed the quick mastery of the sustained blank-verse motion. Marmaduke alone in the wood on the edge of the moor in Act III of *The Borderers* says:

> Deep, deep and vast, vast beyond human thought,
> Yet calm.—I could believe that there was here
> The only quiet heart on earth. In terror,
> Remembered terror, there is peace and rest.

And the beginning of *Tintern Abbey:*

Once again
Do I behold these steep and lofty cliffs,
That on a wild secluded scene impress
Thoughts of more deep seclusion; and connect
The landscape with the quiet of the sky.

These share the traits of sound structure which Wordsworth was to continue: an iambic beat strongly sustained under the surface variation, as the alliteration of *Yet calm.—I could* strengthens what was not yet established in *Deep, deep and vast;* a five-accented norm, breaking at any point in the line, and easily run on, yet constantly bringing in such a line as "The landscape with the quiet of the sky," which, while not complete in itself grammatically, adds a phrasal poise to the pentameter; and finally, a use of tonal rhyming which may be final as in couplet or stanza but is usually subordinate and often inward, as in the sounds of *remembered* and *rest,* or in the hard *c* linkage of *connect* with *landscape, quiet,* and *sky.*

Prelude, Recluse, Excursion, and later descriptions of tours led Wordsworth to develop blank verse as discursively as possible, to pause and rest and then go on again with impressions or arguments. Often in middle years he used couplet or sonnet rhyme for shaping, but not I think to any very different effect line by line. He wrote in 1832, for example:

Calm is the fragrant air, and loth to lose
Day's grateful warmth, tho' moist with falling dews.
Look for the stars, you'll say that there are none;
Look up a second time, and, one by one,
You mark them twinkling out with silvery light,
And wonder how they could elude the sight!

And in 1842 as prelude to his *Poems Chiefly of Early and Late Years:*

In desultory walk through orchard grounds,
Or some deep chestnut grove, oft have I paused

The while a Thrush, urged rather than restrained
By gusts of vernal storm, attuned his song
To his own genial instincts . . .

In both of these beginnings is the sort of phrasal stiffening which Darbishire and De Selincourt have vividly pointed out in the *Prelude* revisions, yet both keep too the direct and personal forward motion of the earliest pentameters.

Except for a few unsustained experiments with longer lines, or longer feet, Wordsworth's two serious experiments outside pentameter were the tetrameters of the ballads, with their abrupt obvious rhyming, and the free improvisations of the ode on immortality. Both of these have a sort of magic which he could not later manage: in the first, a literalness of downright measure; in the second, a tenuosity and flexibility both of which were extremes perhaps inspired by Coleridge, or extremes of youth and rebellion and unsettled skill. At any rate, by 1802 Wordsworth tried and was resigned to the confines of the sonnet, which he had once disdained, and from then on even in his least excursive pieces his prevailing pentameter took this shapely form.

His prevailing sentence structure may best be noted in such a form, where progress from beginning to end is visible upon one page. One may remember how the early poems begin with the statement that a traveler sets forth, and then list items which he sees. The *Lyrical Ballads* are similarly declarative: I met a girl . . . I have a boy . . . There is a Thorn . . . Her eyes are wild . . . It is the first mild day of March . . . In distant countries have I been . . . 'Tis eight o'clock . . . Five years have passed . . . These are the declarative beginnings, and the conclusions, drawn out of carefully observed and listed instances, are exclamations of moral significance. "The Old Cumberland Beggar" is a good example, beginning, "I saw an aged Beggar in my walk; / And he was seated, by the highway side, / On a low structure of rude masonry," proceeding through his observations as a traveler to people's view of him and a general analysis of his social and moral status, to the concluding exclamation, "As in the eye of Nature he has lived, / So in the eye of Nature let him die!" In a sonnet the whole process is concentrated, sometimes to be sure in reverse, from judgment to descriptive statement, but more often in order like *The River Duddon,* v:

> Sole listener, Duddon! to the breeze that played
> With thy clear voice, I caught the fitful sound
> Wafted o'er sullen moss and craggy mound—
> Unfruitful solitudes, that seemed to upbraid
> The sun in heaven!—but now, to form a shade
> For Thee, green alders have together wound
> Their foliage; ashes flung their arms around;
> And birch-trees risen in silver colonnade.
> And thou hast also tempted here to rise,
> 'Mid sheltering pines, this Cottage rude and grey;
> Whose ruddy children, by the mother's eyes
> Carelessly watched, sport through the summer day,
> Thy pleased associates:—light as endless May
> On infant bosoms lonely Nature lies.

This is the normal structure of statement for Wordsworth early and late—the interconnection of particular declarative statement and of phrasal and clausal series with a framing general declaration or exclamation, and, especially in later years, an accompanying invocation.

Such a pattern makes for a classical proportioning of terms, a balance between adjectives and verbs, qualities and actions, and a moderate subordination of verbs to substantives. Wordsworth, in other words, thought not complexly as metaphysical poets would, nor yet fully descriptively as Milton or Keats would, but rather discursively, drawing a constant statement from quality and quality from statement. Even in the *Lyrical Ballads,* for which the sources and models showed a great stress on action, which Coleridge adopted, Wordsworth mildly persisted in his own standard classical proportioning of ten adjectives to sixteen nouns to ten verbs in ten lines, a proportion which he maintained closely in such various work as the 1806 and 1807 poems, the *Prelude,* and the poems of his last decade, increasing substantatives a little, and sometimes especially adjectives as in the Duddon sonnets where description was central. So we see the arrangement in the poem above: the nouns of *river, breeze, sounds, solitudes, sun, shade,* and kinds of trees, moving to *cottage, children, associates,* and *Nature,* while the verbs stress interconnection in *played, caught, seemed, flung, risen, sport, lies,* and the adjectives, *sole, clear, fitful, sullen, green, silver, sheltering, pleased, light, lonely,* and others, do the work of interpretation by the setting of emotional atmosphere and responsiveness.

Wordsworth's major terms, like his sound and sentence patterns, work steadily throughout his poetry. The Duddon terms suggest their quality: adjectives of emotional atmosphere, nouns of scene and concept, verbs of spatial motion and connection. *See* is the primary action, with *look* and *hear* and *come* and *feel* and *die* and *love* also, verbs of responsiveness in many ways. And the common nouns make human generalization—*man, life, love, heart, thought, eye, mind, hope, hand, soul, spirit, joy,* along with outer *day, nature, earth, heaven, light, power, time,* and the most clearly objective *mountain.* While they describe, in *bright, deep, high, old, little, long,* the adjectives also evaluate in *good, dear, poor,* and *sweet.* In the combination of these terms, used more than any others except of course the common particles and auxiliaries, all through Wordsworth's poetic lifetime, we can sense again, even in abstraction from context, the special quality of his thought—his concern with the process of the reception and interpretation of sensation by feeling, in verbs of perception, in adjectives of size, scope, age, and affection, and in nouns of bodily and emotional sense half combined with concept and atmosphere.

The differences as well as likenesses between early and late years are reflected in vocabulary stresses. The *Ballads* used *cold* and *warm, trees* and *woods, praying* and *weeping* more than they were to be later used; were, that is, a little more specifically objective, though they also introduced most of the major later sorts of terms, like *little* and *old* and *love* and *joy* and *mountain, sun, thought, spirit.* The materials of the 1806 poems, the sonnets of 1820, and the poems of the last decade differed mainly in small details: the increase of interpretative terms like *calm, divine, happy, silent,* the increase and return of *prayer* and *spirit,* the addition of *child* and *mother, fear* and *faith, sea* and *star,* as particularizations of earlier observations and relationships in a more stabilized state of mind.

In all these ways, in all these materials of language, its reference, sound, and statement structure, Wordsworth worked along with other poets of his time. He shared a common substance, a common selectivity and sense of style. We may see, for example, that the poets of the 1790's were like him in trying ballad measures but remaining faithful in the main to pentameters; that they tried very urgently for an objective sort of tracing of objects and dispositions, in declarative statement; that they used abundantly a vocabulary of attitude, and tentatively one of observation. Burns, Bowles, Campbell, Rogers, Southey, and others were stronger for epithets like *sad* and *weary* than Wordsworth was, more for eighteenth-century *friend, scene, tears, sorrow, virtue, crying,* and *mourning,* but quicker, on the other hand, to take up emphases he would later adopt, like those on *mother* and *child, mountain, sea,* and *spirit.* Their proportionings were often balanced like his, their modes seriously devoted to explication and understanding of man in his situation.

Changed as matters were by his last decade of poetry, with Tennyson, Browning, Arnold, and Clough beginning, the mode he wrote in was still maintained. As he had differed from his early associates in concreteness and affirmation, *green trees* and *joy,* he differed from the late in the abstractness of the affirmation, in *faith* and *truth, calm, silent,* and *divine,* yet the basic pattern of abstract and concrete terms did not, in the fifty years, greatly alter. It was rather the mode of sound and statement which altered for Tennyson, Poe, Clough, and the younger poets, away from Wordsworthian declaration toward implication and symbolizing, and away from Wordsworthian flexibility within the pentameter and the iambic, to much more experimentation like Coleridge's, with implicative timing in metrical feet. In other words, by 1850 poetry had moved farther from its Laureate in its measures than in its references; it was still deeply concerned with the statement of human sensitivity to atmosphere, though by odd syllables and phrases it was trying to temper the downrightness of such statement. Later, the general human terms themselves grew suspect, and an increasingly concrete vocabulary enforced the other forms of implication in poetry.

No wonder, then, that today critics praise the most modern Wordsworth of the "bright blue eggs" and the "single stone" and the "reflex of a star." Indeed he was one of the first to foster such detail and suffered at the hands of his own contemporary critics for such fostering, and it seems just that what he was most blamed for he be now admired for. The course of poetic history has moved steadily toward more and more implicative references, measures, and sentence structures, and Wordsworth's has been part of that progress. He prepared, as Cowper and Campbell did, for the flexible pentameters of a Shelley and a Browning, and, as Blake and Burns did, for the significant concreteness of a Keats and a Tennyson. But we lose him if we bring him down all this way in terms of what he has given us that we have used and approved. Central to his own style is what he used and approved from his own eighteenth century, what he perfected as well as what he invented. And what he perfected we have a chance to learn again; not the diverse particularity of images which, as in Ossian, he abhorred as "isolated," but the continuities and connections of perception, the wise passiveness, the smooth and steady assertion.

The complex of Wordsworth's materials was not a radical but a traditional one: terms of human feeling and thought allied to sense, meters outwardly regular, inwardly toned and shaded in the manner of his day, structures exclamatory yet deliberative. All were familiar, to the degree that he could assume and thus simplify them, let them work directly and literally, as his beliefs allowed. Most were opposed to the particular, irregular, presentative, figurative materials of present-day poetry: they were general, regular, discursive, literal; their effect of literalness was Wordsworth's especial contribution. Whereas the modern poet feels the need to invent and struggle with connections in tension and irony, Wordsworth had only, against the equal struggles of his predecessors, to observe and declare them in the syntheses of imagination.

Wordsworth himself has clearly set forth in Prefaces, Supplements, and Essays the description of his style, and a few fragments of quotation may serve to recall the tenor of his well-known argument. He wanted to deal with "manners connected with the permanent objects of nature and partaking of the simplicity of those objects" (*Early Letters,* p. 221). He wanted to increase our knowledge of human nature "by shewing that our best qualities are possessed by men whom we are too apt to consider, not with reference to points in which they resemble us, but to those in which they manifestly differ from us" (*Early Letters,* p. 260); he was more interested in likeness than in distinction. "There is scarcely one of my Poems which does not aim to direct the attention to some moral sentiment, or to some general principle, or law of thought, or of our intellectual constitution" (*Letters: Middle Years,* pp. 128–129). "I have endeavoured to dwell with truth upon those points of human nature in which all men resemble each other, rather than on those accidents of manners and character produced by times and circumstances" (*Letters: Later Years,* p. 127). And, ". . . our business is not so much with objects as with the law under which they are contemplated" (*ibid.,* p. 184).

These beliefs and intentions made for the special relation of observation to generalization which was Wordsworth's own. In his note on the early "Evening Walk" he reports his "consciousness of the infinite variety of natural appearances which had been unnoticed by the poets of any age or country, so far as I was acquainted them"; he states of the poem, "There is not an image in it which I have not observed"; yet he states also that "the plan of it has not been confined to a particular walk or an individual place,—a proof (of which I was unconscious at the time) of my unwillingness to submit the poetic spirit to the chains of fact and real circumstance." In the note to a much later poem, "This Lawn a Carpet," 1829, he develops the stress on the combination: the need for fact as well as generality: "Admiration and love, to which all knowledge truly vital must tend, are felt by men of real genius in proportion as their discoveries in natural Philosophy are enlarged; and the beauty in form of a plant or an animal is not made less but more apparent as a whole by more accurate insight into its constituent proportions and powers." So Wordsworth articulates the tendencies of his era, to know more facts, and to draw wider inferences from them, and above all to feel more deeply with and about them, all directly and explicitly.

Such an attitude, such a sense of straightforward poetic power, gives us no hint of that fictionalizing which for many throughout history had been the essence of poetry. Aristotle named metaphor as the key creative device of poetic style; Wordsworth says almost nothing about metaphor except to warn against some sorts like personification. Genre and device proper to genre have little meaning for him; one notes that he makes his own groupings of poems in his own terms, the sorts of affections they deal with. And one notes that his recurrent names for the parts of poetizing, assuming some metrical form, are "thought, feeling, image"—the names not of device but of subject, and all in terms of human response. The image, the record of sight, sound, or impression; the feeling, an emotional association; the thought, a resultant and influential complex—these are the general human, and thus the poetic, essences for Wordsworth. Therefore all the devices of trope and generic propriety and metrical irony and so on, though present in his verse by long convention, are secondary, often as if accidental, and not usually even essential to the frame of the whole.

Consider as an example of such characteristic directness the poem "Written in Very Early Youth"—so much like what Wordsworth would write all his life:

> Calm is all nature as a resting wheel.
> The kine are couched upon the dewy grass;
> The horse alone, seen dimly as I pass,
> Is cropping audibly his later meal:
> Dark is the ground; a slumber seems to steal
> O'er vale, and mountain, and the starless sky.
> Now, in this blank of things, a harmony,
> Home-felt, and home-created, comes to heal
> That grief for which the senses still supply
> Fresh food; for only then, when memory
> Is hushed, am I at rest. My Friends! restrain
> Those busy cares that would allay my pain;
> Oh! leave me to myself, nor let me feel
> The officious touch that makes me droop again.

The theme here is the need for human harmony with the calmness of nature; it is conveyed directly through all the major substance, the selection and spread of natural examples in the octave, the threat of the obverse in the sestet, and the human response in *heal* and *rest.* Is there essential trope? Not the odd *wheel,* which moves no further, nor the *food,* which works very abstractly. Rather, the concept which lies behind the description, not as poetic ornament at all, but as belief. "Now, in this blank of things, a harmony / Home-felt, and home-created, comes to heal" we may take as figurative language in terms of our belief, but for Wordsworth it was a direct reporting of how he felt, how sensitive human beings would feel, in such a situation. "Blank" means "blank for him," and "to heal" is literal. As he says explicitly, objects should be reported not as they are but as they seem (*Prose,* 1815, II, 226), and it is the seeming that is literally reported.

In one sense, then, one could call Wordsworth's poetry a single vast metaphor of natural-human-divine harmony in terms of *breath, stream, spirit, power, flow, feeling, love, soul, light.* The primary terms of receptive emotion and descriptive concept work together toward this metaphor, and it infuses every single poem. For this very reason of pervasiveness, however, it is not to be taken as a literary device, but rather as a philosophical view, a conditioning of reality as the statement "The sun rises in the east" is a conditioning. Within this frame, Wordsworth's literalness magnificently operates. His by-the-way figurativeness seems less controlled, more accidental and unintegrated with the whole of the imagery, as is the *wheel* above, or nature as both *anchor* and *nurse* in one line of *Tintern Abbey.* Few poems are as thoroughly worked out in figures as "Hopes, what are they?—Beads of morning" in the 1818 "Inscriptions." Few on the other hand are as objectively descriptive, without spiritual interfusion, as the "Waterfowl" of 1812. Most make a literal general study of reflection like the poem of "Early Youth," and like the late Tours, or, in between, the *Prelude* with its great unfinished work, and such small characteristic pieces as "My Heart Leaps Up" and the poems on flowers. Thus directly Wordsworth thought art should function, as he wrote in 1811, "Upon the Sight of a Beautiful Picture":

> Praised be the Art whose subtle power could stay
> Yon cloud, and fix it in that glorious shape;

Nor would permit the thin smoke to escape,
Nor those bright sunbeams to forsake the day;
Which stopped that band of travellers on their way,
Ere they were lost within the shady wood;
And showed the Bark upon the glassy flood
For ever anchored in her sheltering bay.
Soul-soothing Art! whom Morning, Noontide, Even,
Do serve with all their changeful pageantry;
Thou, with ambition modest yet sublime,
Here, for the sight of mortal man, hast given
To one brief moment caught from fleeting time
The appropriate calm of blest eternity.

Thus art symbolizes, by preserving the timeless moment, and symbol like metaphor is, for Wordsworth, implied in the whole structure of the relation of time to eternity, not a literary device to be used in the indirection of idea.

It has often been said, and my own studies of statement of feeling have shown in one set of materials at least, that Wordsworth became in later years more fond of art, more "literary," and therefore more explicitly a user of figure and symbol as modes of statement. It is true that his later work used less of fine original abstraction and more of the personification, attribution, metaphysical metaphor which he had at first mistrusted, and that some of the result seemed mechanical rather than natural. But such poems as "Papal Abuses" or "Mutability" from the Ecclesiastical Sonnets should remind us of the power that Wordsworth sometimes gained from such artfulness, his ability to subordinate a rich trope to lofty statement. The last River Duddon poem may serve as example:

I thought of Thee, my partner and my guide,
As being past away.—Vain sympathies!

For, backward, Duddon! as I cast my eyes,
I see what was, and is, and will abide;
Still glides the Stream, and shall forever glide;
The Form remains, the Function never dies;
While we, the brave, the mighty, and the wise,
We Men, who in our morn of youth defied
The elements, must vanish;—be it so!
Enough, if something from our hands have power
To live, and act, and serve the future hour;
And if, as toward the silent tomb we go,
Through love, through hope, and faith's transcendent dower,
We feel that we are greater than we know.

The Form and Function, the morning of youth and transcendent dower, all are absorbed into the imagery of transience and persistence and into the cumulative abstraction of the ending.

Wordsworth offers us, then, a style of poetry to which modern poets are unaccustomed. In the hundred years since his laureateship, endings have become concrete and implicative, exclamations have been subdued, the human situation has become an instant of time, image has become symbol, and explication has become antipoetic. Nevertheless it seems to me possible to admire Wordsworth's complex in its own nineteenth-century terms, the explicit association of natural particularity with general human truth in a meditative pentameter and a vocabulary of pleasure. Wordsworth had his own version of this complex, more subtle, more understated, more "silent" as Miss Darbishire and others have made plain, at once joyful and calm, and steadily more direct, than either the pedestrians from Campbell to Lowell or the inventors from Blake to Poe would have cared to manage. This deliberation we have turned away from we may well turn back to, though at the moment few of Wordsworth's key terms or measures are primary for us, except perhaps the abstract *truth* and *mind* of a few didactic poets like Auden, an echo of smooth metrics, and the enduring idea of humanity.

Probably in the realm of idea we must most question Wordsworth's import for us. As his recent critics have pointed out, he has a very great deal to say about nature, a great deal of description, attribution, and personification, to which we are numb. What he has worked out to tell us, we have long learned and do not want to hear again. Grant, if we may, the possible renewal of his familiarly literal and explicative style, we must ask what attitude or theme of value can be conveyed through such a style. We tend to favor irony as attitude, and conflict as theme, and drama as mode. Wordsworth said rather that the poet might well be predominant over the dramatist: "then let him see if there are no victories in the world of spirit, no changes, no commotions, no revolutions there, no fluxes and refluxes of the thoughts which may be made interesting by modest combination with the stiller actions of the bodily frame" (*Letters: Middle Years,* p. 198).

And here he provides us with themes we can use philosophically as well as dramatically, downrightly as well as ironically—the victories, changes, commotions, revolutions in the world of spirit. Our Nature need not be his and cannot be his, but our human nature has still its commotions and victories, about which we in our poetry are as yet deeply unlearned. Miss Darbishire and others have told us that "belief in the greatness of the human mind is at the very center of Wordsworth's thought" (*The Poet Wordsworth,* p. 139), and indeed this is what the sympathetic reviews were saying in the early decades (for example, *Blackwood's* in 1822—cf. *Estimate . . . by His Contemporaries,* ed. Elsie Smith, p. 344). It is a belief we may well accept. The powers of sense, reason, intuition—as *The Excursion* says, of hope, faith, and love—are powers still our concern, as are equally the early themes of revolution, the late of institution, and the whole of science.

Relationship is what matters for Wordsworth, and in this theme he is our kin. But we are still tentative and oblique about the relationships we celebrate, and are not to be hurried. Douglas Bush thinks that because Wordsworth's prophecy for science has not come true, it will not. But it seems to me the very future toward which we move, the "if" of the second Preface: "If the time should ever come when what is now called science, thus familiarised to men, shall be ready to put on, as it were, a form of flesh and blood, the Poet will lend his divine spirit to aid the transfiguration and will welcome the Being thus produced, as a dear and genuine inmate of the household of man." This domesticity does not seem to me too explicit for us, nor too plain in sentiment.

As for politics, there the poetic again can make good sense, ecclesiastical and civil, and the exclamatory literal pentameter say what needs ever directly to be said:

> Toussaint, the most unhappy man of men!
> Whether the whistling Rustic tend his plough
> Within thy hearing, or thy head be now
> Pillowed in some deep dungeon's earless den;—
> O miserable Chieftain! where and when
> Wilt thou find patience! Yet die not; do thou
> Wear rather in thy bonds a cheerful brow:
> Though fallen thyself, never to rise again,
> Live, and take comfort. Thou hast left behind
> Powers that will work for thee; earth, air, and skies;
> There's not a breathing of the common wind
> That will forget thee; thou hast great allies;
> Thy friends are exultations, agonies,
> And love, and man's unconquerable mind.

Such a theme may prevail not only for the individual psychology of the *Prelude* and the sober institutionalizing of the mid-century sonnets, but for twentieth-century poetry to come.

As for the art, that we come back to as the be-all of what the poet has to tell—it is for Wordsworth, as he has said, a force for preserving and making serene what knowledge of life might otherwise be rough, transitory, and obscure. "Language, if it do not uphold, and feed, and leave in quiet, like the power of gravitation or the air we breathe, is a counter-spirit, unremittingly and noiselessly at work, to subvert, to lay waste, to vitiate, and to dissolve" ("Essay on Epitaphs").

The art for Wordsworth speaks in sentence and line, in cumulating phrase, in harmony of accent, and in literal statement, "sympathy with man's substantial griefs," "a blazing intellectual deity," "the dignities of plain occurrence," and "clear guidance . . . to the mind's excursive power." These in their accord of accent, emphasis, and understanding represent the aimed-for power of language which should uphold, and feed, and leave in quiet. Not variety of tone, complexity of structure, brilliance of metaphor are primary to his art, but rather the process which leads to concord of thought, feelings, images, the process which made all the poems one poem.

The power of the Wordsworthian mode for our day is the mind's excursive power, the change and commotion in the world of spirit. In its harmonious regularity and cumulative stress it demands meditation; in its accords, sympathy; in its balanced literalness, a steady observation. All these are difficult for us. An age of symbol, passion, and irony is not much good at a common view or a general concern or even a strong abstract statement in a determined meter. But we can learn. And Wordsworth's can be the poetry not only from which, but toward which, we proceed.

CHAPTER NINE

THE CLASSICAL MODE OF THE LATE NINETEENTH CENTURY

THE POETRY of the late nineteenth century, often called decadent, was structurally not only a falling off from old sublimities, but also a building up, a return from romantic extremes to poise and equilibrium with the renewed aid of classical models. As B. Ifor Evans has suggested in his survey of the era (*English Poetry in the Later Nineteenth Century,* London, 1936, p. 26), Swinburne's *Poems and Ballads* "made the year 1866 a turning-point in poetical history," for Swinburne, as distinguished from the Pre-Raphaelites of 1850, was concerned with a new need for smoothness and modulation as the century began to draw toward its close. Just as Sackville had begun to lead the Tudors, and Waller the Stuarts, and Goldsmith the eighteenth-century Georgians to a reconsideration of the balanced mode, so the young Pre-Raphaelite chose not to follow the implicative ballad structures of the brotherhood, neither one extreme in Browning nor another in

Tennyson, but rather to seek out and settle into a more harmonious and on-running explication, of Wordsworth's and Arnold's sort. In this middle way also such confrères as Bridges, Hopkins, Patmore, Francis Thompson, and Stephen Phillips proceeded, in contrast to the elaborated extremes of Wilde and Henley on the one hand or the understated extremes of Hardy and Housman on the other.

If we do not naturally wish to think of Swinburne and Phillips together with Hopkins and Bridges, as they themselves did not, yet we may remember that oppositions sometimes seem strongest within a realm of close agreement. Greek poetry was the resource of these poets, as they drew away from the brusque balladry; Hellenism was their tone, after Arnold and Pater; and Hellenism meant to all of them in their various ways that very molding of surface, flowing of line, force of continuity, language of substantial vision which we may see shared in their work. Wilde's decadence and Housman's decadence were something else again, to be distinguished as the two exceptional extremes of the era. The fullest force of their generation was devoted to effecting, as in other late-century generations, some sort of new integration of materials and structures, as if, perhaps, the very consciousness of the century's culmination pulled them back from exploring to an attempt at stasis.

Wordsworth and Shelley, as distinguished from the other early romantics, had made this attempt almost a century before, along with Southey, Rogers, Crabbe, and Burns; and some mid-century poets like Longfellow, Poe, and Arnold had maintained the poise against the strong ballad predication of Coleridge, Byron, Browning, and most of the Pre-Raphaelites. Perhaps it was the power of "Wordsworthianism," enforced by Arnold's pleas as well as practice, that gradually prevailed. At any rate, the young experimenters began abandoning rough sound, dialogue, argument, action, implication, in favor of a discourse fuller, smoother, richer, somewhat more distant.

The classical vocabulary renewed its strength along with smooth line and balanced structure. *Bright air, soft sky, long way,* the verbs of *growing, looking, seeming,* and the bodily forms of *breast, face, head, foot* helped to reëstablish the tone and form of human sense and measure characteristic of Wordsworth as of Dryden. The new words characteristic of the period were *young, child, dream, face, foot, shadow, summer, woman, wind;* in these was the temporal essence of the poetry as a whole, its quality of feminine sensibility which has been called decadent. Of these words only *dream* and *shadow* were newly romantic, or in the Pre-Raphaelite tradition. The rest were all part of the traditional classical poetic: the figures of youth, child, woman, bodily set forth in natural setting and season, with a minimum of active motion and no defining verbs. We have seen this bright beauty and feminine figure as early as the aureate work of Hawes and Dunbar, again in Shakespeare's sonnets and Crashaw's devotions, flowering for Waller, Marvell, Dryden, and their era, then for Goldsmith, Southey, and Rogers, now finally in the culmination of nineteenth-century aesthetic.

What does such poetry sound like, in its harmonious anatomizing? Arnold's "To a Gypsy Child" is a good early example, beginning with balanced questions and apostrophes, developing explicitly, filling out each line with modulation of sound, emotional but reasonable and normative, building a bodily impression.

> Who taught this pleading to unpractis'd eyes?
> Who hid such import in an infant's gloom?
> Who lent thee, child, this meditative guise?
> What clouds thy forehead, and foredates thy doom?
>
> Lo! sails that gleam a moment and are gone;
> The swinging waters, and the cluster'd pier.
> Not idly Earth and Ocean labour on,
> Nor idly do these sea-birds hover near.

But thou, whom superfluity of joy
Wafts not from thine own thoughts, nor longings vain,
Nor weariness, the full-fed soul's annoy;
Remaining in thy hunger and thy pain:

Thou, drugging pain by patience; half averse
From thine own mother's breast, that knows not thee;
With eyes that sought thine eyes thou didst converse,
And that soul-searching vision fell on me.

Glooms that go deep as thine I have not known:
Moods of fantastic sadness, nothing worth.
Thy sorrow and thy calmness are thine own:
Glooms that enhance and glorify this earth.

The balance of clause with phrase in these stanzas is quite exact, like the setting over of line against line, noun against noun, while the sounds move in opening and developing pattern, and the thoughts too are open and rounded.

Much of Swinburne reads in like fashion, as for example the beginning of "In the Bay," with its half molding of nature into person, its *watery resonance, folded fleet, sea's breast, soft sweep, disrobed* and *disentrammelled, ardent light,* and the full shaping of the stanzaic lines:

I

Beyond the hollow sunset, ere a star
Take heart in heaven from eastward, while the west,
Fulfilled of watery resonance and rest,
Is as a port with clouds for harbour bar
To fold the fleet in of the winds from far
That stir no plume now of the bland sea's breast;

II

Above the soft sweep of the breathless bay
Southwestward, far past flight of night and day,
Lower than the sunken sunset sinks, and higher
Than dawn can freak the front of heaven with fire,
My thought with eyes and wings made wide makes way
To find the place of souls that I desire.

III

If any place for any soul there be,
Disrobed and disentrammelled; if the might,
The fire and force that filled with ardent light
The souls whose shadow is half the light we see,
Survive and be suppressed not of the night;
This hour should show what all day hid from me. . . .

Not only the mellifluous and embodying vocabulary is characteristic of classicism, along with the balanced phrasal and clausal structures, but also the smaller inner patterns, of assonance, and of such antitheses as *east . . . west, lower . . . higher, any place . . . any soul, shadow . . . light, show . . . hid,* carefully fitted to the rounding of their periods.

For all Hopkins' just antipathies to Swinburne, the two are not wholly alien. They write in the same time with many of the same concerns: for one, a full-bodied classical verse. Swinburne shapes a pale material and Hopkins a vivid one, but both are devoted to the means of shaping, in linear plasticity representing a kind of visual plasticity. In the midst of the idiosyncratic terms and structures of "Hurrahing in Harvest," note for example the familiar classical vocabulary of explicit *summer, beauty, arise, looks, beholder, feet,* and the bodily form of "meal-drift moulded ever," "of realer, of rounder replies," "world-wielding shoulder," "as a stallion stalwart," and "The heart rears wings," and the structural balances of *now . . . now, around . . . above, walk . . . lift up, here . . . wanting, shoulder . . . feet.* The balances and assonances cut across the lines and are thereby even more formally powerful.

Summer ends now; now, barbarous in beauty, the stooks arise
  Around; up above, what wind-walks! what lovely behaviour
  Of silk-sack clouds! has wilder, wilful-wavier
Meal-drift moulded ever and melted across skies?

I walk, I lift up, I lift up heart, eyes,
  Down all that glory in the heavens to glean our Saviour;
  And, éyes, heárt, what looks, what lips yet gave you a
Rapturous love's greeting of realer, of rounder replies?

And the azurous hung hills are his world-wielding shoulder
  Majestic—as a stallion stalwart, very-violet-sweet!—
These things, these things were here and but the beholder
  Wanting; which two when they once meet,
The heart réars wíngs bold and bolder
  And hurls for him, O half hurls earth for him off under his feet.

The possible blend between Hopkins' intensity and Swinburne's tones of resignation is visible in many of Francis Thompson's poems or in such a work as Dowson's "Nuns of the Perpetual Adoration," the last stanzas of which proceed as follows:

They saw the glory of the world displayed;
  They saw the bitter of it, and the sweet;
They knew the roses of the world should fade,
  And be trod under by the hurrying feet.

Therefore they rather put away desire,
  And crossed their hands and came to sanctuary

And veiled their heads and put on coarse attire:
  Because their comeliness was vanity.

And there they rest; they have serene insight
  Of the illuminating dawn to be:
Mary's sweet Star dispels for them the night,
  The proper darkness of humanity.

Calm, sad, secure; with faces worn and mild:
  Surely their choice of vigil is the best?
Yea! for our roses fade, the world is wild;
  But there, beside the altar, there, is rest.

As Thompson has said for these passionate late-century classical poets, "O world invisible, we view thee, / O world intangible, we touch thee, . . ." and, "Yea, in the night, my Soul, my daughter, / Cry,—clinging Heaven by the hems." Their world, for all its cloudy mystery, took the form of human embodiment, and in this form preserved its heritage of aesthetic stability.

How different was the romantic ballad mode against which they had settled may be seen in a glance at their contemporaries Kipling or Hardy or Meredith—or Housman:

"Is my team ploughing,
  That I was used to drive
And hear the harness jingle
  When I was man alive?"

Ay, the horses trample,
  The harness jingles now;
No change though you lie under
  The land you used to plough.

"Is football playing
 Along the river shore,
With lads to chase the leather,
 Now I stand up no more?" . . .

Hardy's "I Look into My Glass" is as active and immediate, with the clauses counting, and the modifications subordinate:

I look into my glass,
And view my wasting skin,
And say, "Would God it came to pass
My heart had shrunk as thin!"

For then, I, undistrest
By hearts grown cold to me,
Could lonely wait my endless rest
With equanimity.

But Time, to make me grieve,
Part steals, lets part abide;
And shakes this fragile frame at eve
With throbbings of noontide.

This is romantic verse which is close to metaphysical, the nineteenth-century version of Herbert or Cowley, the late-century version of Coleridge or Browning. Rather than a classically externalized landscape with figures, we have here all inwardness, but inwardness related to macrocosm in its concepts of God, death, and time, and made dramatic and colloquial in the interrelationship.

At the other extreme, opposite to such active clausal verse which was the nineteenth century's main mode, was the minor mode, descended from the phrasal eighteenth century, of Keats, Whitman, Wilde, Henley, the freer exploring and rich cumulative line, as of Henley's "London Voluntaries," for example:

St. Margaret's bells,
Quiring their innocent, old-world canticles,
Sing in the storied air,
All rosy-and-golden, as with memories
Of woods at evensong, and sands and seas
Disconsolate for that the night is nigh.
O, the low, lingering lights! The large last gleam
(Hark! how those brazen choristers cry and call!)
Touching these solemn ancientries, and there,
The silent River ranging tide-mark high
And the callow, grey-faced Hospital,
With the strange glimmer and glamour of a dream!
The Sabbath peace is in the slumbrous trees,
And from the wistful, the fast-widowing sky
(Hark! how those plangent comforters call and cry!)
Falls as in August plots late roseleaves fall. . . .

In such lines, the phrasal modifications and inconclusive periods are the heart of the structure.

One may question whether these structural differences, easily enough visible in selected passages at a temporal distance, were in any way pertinent to critical discriminations in the poets' own time. Linguistic analysis takes us beneath the level of conscious poetic practice, and so too, perhaps, beneath the level of conscious judgment. Surely, we may say, it is a mere artifice of discrimination which may divide Coleridge and the Pre-Raphaelites from Keats and Wilde and Whitman, or join Hopkins with Arnold and Swinburne as classicists of the late century's middle way. Yet in many respects the common-sense judgments of the times were in accord with just such technical discriminations. For example, Byron and Keats were treated as poets of opposing schools, with Wordsworth as a sort of moderator. Byron was clearly called romantic, a clausal poet as we would call him; Wordsworth was often seen as classical, and called himself so; Keats, at the phrasal extreme drawn from the eighteenth century, inherited no name but pre-romantic and in turn handed on this lack of title to Tennyson, to Henley, to Pound. In such lack lay the only confusion: two structural extremes were both called romantic, as distinguished from the moderate classic; but always these extremes, even without separate titles, were seen in opposition, Tennyson to Browning, as Keats to Byron, and as Henley to Hardy, as Pound to Frost, with Arnold, with Wordsworth, with Bridges, with Eliot or Stevens as mediators.

Chronologically, the first two-thirds of the nineteenth century was strongly clausal, romantic, Pre-Raphaelite, metaphysical, active, whatever term one will choose; the last third settled into the more balanced classical mode. Even of this motion, as of their major allegiances, the poets were aware. Indeed, their term "decadence" is a technical awareness from a special point of view. To those nostalgic for the "art," the "beauty," of the eighteenth century, the mere balanced style was indeed a "falling off"; though more immediately it was a building up from nineteenth-century "barbarities."

We may remember that Hazlitt, writing in the *Edinburgh Review* in 1816, explained that "the most obvious distinction between the two styles, the classic and the romantic, is, that the one is conversant with objects that are grand and beautiful in themselves, or in consequence of obvious and universal associations, the other, with those that are interesting only by force of circumstance or imagination." Consider what such a distinction implies for language structure: for the classic, modifying phrases and epithets, the universal qualities, the *an sich* which we find again in Arnold and in Art for Art; for the romantic, verbs and clauses, active circumstance and imagined situation, as in the created world of the ballad, the constructed world of the metaphysical argument.

All poetry is apt to present truth, but if we are told it is "universal," it will probably be a more classical sort than the truth of romantic "fact" and "circumstance." So, recognizing Shelley to be a balanced poet like Wordsworth, we are not surprised when Carlos Baker writes (in *Shelley's Major Poetry,* Princeton, 1948, p. 271): "The ultimately classical quality of his achievement is owing in part to his preoccupation with psychological experiences at once universal and primary, and in part also to his determination to reveal, and thus to make vitally significant to human life, his vision of the cosmic law." Nor are we surprised at the loyalty of Swinburne to Shelley, as to Wordsworth, Arnold, Poe, and Pater, as against the romantic "Brownings and other blatant creatures begotten on the slime of the modern chaos" (*Letters of Swinburne,* ed. Gosse, 1919, p. 20). Swinburne, himself in the middle, distinguished between the sublimity of Milton and other "gods" on the right, the energy of Jonson and Byron and other "giants" on the left (*Letters,* p. 174, and essay on Jonson). Arnold, in other terms of distinction, contrasted the energy of Hebraism with the sweetness of Hellenism. J. B. Selkirk in 1878 wrote of the alternate heating and cooling process in the history of poetry, the cool being the classicism of his own day (*Ethics and Aesthetics of Modern Poetry,* p. 225). Most of the writers as critics, indeed, seemed conscious of some antagonism of styles, and some, even, of the sequence of three styles, from eighteenth-century loftiness to romantic rebellion to "decadent" moderation.

Browning, for example, recognized the extreme of style in Milton and Keats, calling them "the super-human poet-pair," and seeing Tennyson as in their sublime tradition (George Ford, *Keats and the Victorians,* 1944, p. 10). Arnold was seen to be more plain, Virgilian, not "loading every rift with ore" (p. 77). R. H. Horne (in *A New Spirit of the Age,* 1844) had also stressed the sublimity of Keats and Tennyson, the "divine mysteries of our existence"; and Elizabeth Barrett Browning had written that she heard in Tennyson's *Arthur* "a noble full orbicular whole in complete passages, which always struck me as the mystery of music and great peculiarity of Tennyson's versification." Tennyson himself, in the *Memoir* by his son, acknowledged his early debt to the sublimity of James Thomson, granted his lack of classical "middle-distance," and said sublimely, "To me often the far-off world seems nearer than the present . . . rolling round its green hills and paradises to the harmony of more steadfast laws" (*Memoir,* p. 171). Exactly, both spiritually and structurally, Huxley called him the modern Lucretius, not a "classicist" among classical poets (Harold Nicholson, *Tennyson,* p. 11). It was such aesthetic distance, such lack of solidity, that poets like Arnold, Austin, and Sturge Moore called subjective or feminine or trivial, as the 'nineties were in strong rebellion against it. Not a strong mode in the nineteenth century, it nevertheless bore the nostalgic power of the full eighteenth-century tradition, so that all other ways seemed in some degree a decline and decadence.

The most vigorous mode of the century was the romantic Pre-Raphaelite: the search for foreground, for human fact and act. The active psychological drama of Landor, Coleridge, and Byron was renewed by Rossetti, Morris, and Meredith in their mid-century years, in stages of reaction against the grand manner. As Laurance Housman later wrote, theirs was an endeavor "to express romance in terms of nature, with great intensity of individual feeling, and with a strong sense of character" (David Dickason, *The Daring Young Men,* Indiana, 1953, p. 21). Thus they began with "bare, stark-naked, and literal facts, tangible as a blow from a hammer" (Dickason, p. 58), and cried, "It is the absolute facts of everything that we are fighting for, and not for smoothness, not for execution, but for truth and reality" (Dickason, p. 85). Economy and toughness were criteria. Byron's "muscularity" was an important heritage for Rossetti and Morris, and Browning the only modern to be hailed. Patmore in 1861 wrote to Rossetti, "How I envy the iron and the electric nerve that appears everywhere in your poetic diction!" (*Family Letters,* ed. William Rossetti, 1895, p. 215). Opponents of such "nerve" called it barbarism, as they called it in Browning, as once in the "sinewy" work of Donne.

Always the close dramatic colloquial and psychological conflict seems to have been the concern of the romantics as they were critically recognized. As Hazlitt said, they created interest by situation. They dealt less with objects than with people, less with descriptive style than with spoken. As Meredith wrote in 1883: ". . . thought is tough, and dealing with thought produces toughness. Or when strong emotion is in tide against the active mind, there is perforce confusion." (*Letters,* 1912, p. 399.) Browning's was the same concern. As De Vane tells us (*Handbook,* 1935), "He is now seen to have been a pioneer and a revolutionist in the art of the new psychological poetry, a century before his time." And Browning himself makes very clear to us the difference between his own active extreme and Tennyson's atmospheric one, when he suggests in a letter of 1870 how both would treat an idyll of an unfaithful knight (*Handbook,* p. 384): "I should judge the conflict in the knight's soul the proper subject to describe; Tennyson thinks he should describe the castle, and the effect of the moon on its towers, and anything *but* the soul."

In the 1870's, moon and tower at least partly won out over conflict. The late-century poets were tired of both Browning and Tennyson; they sought a more moderate observation and contemplation. Even so early as 1837, after the first period of romantic conflict, the *Edinburgh Review* was glad that the period of "Sturm und Drang" seemed over, for "contemplation is visibly assuming the ascendancy over wild and irregular action; and the sources of emotion are sought less in the low, the startling, and the transitory, than in the elevated, the calm, and the enduring" (Nicholson, *Tennyson,* p. 25). Using Hazlitt's very distinction, the *Review* bid for classicism as against romanticism, and by the 1870's won its bid.

Peacock wrote in his *Memories of Shelley* (p. 167): "I now understand why the Greeks were such great poets; and, above all, I can account, it seems to me, for the harmony, the unity, the perfection, the uniform excellence of all their works of art. They lived in a perpetual commerce with external nature, and nourished themselves upon the spirit of its forms. Their theatres were all open to the mountains and the sky. Their columns, the ideal types of a sacred forest, with its roof of interwoven tracery, admitted the light and wind; the odour and freshness of the country penetrated the cities."

John Stuart Mill wrote in his *Autobiography* (Collier, 1909, p. 98): "I needed to be made to feel that there was real permanent happiness in tranquil contemplation. Wordsworth taught me this, not only without turning away from, but with greatly increased interest in, the common feeling and common destinies of human beings."

Arnold contrasted the Greek way of treating nature with the conventional and the Celtic ways, by stressing Greek lightness and brightness, the very terms we have seen to be characteristic of English "balanced" poetry throughout its history. Greek literature liberates for us, said Arnold in his essay "On the Modern Element in Literature," 1869, "that harmonious acquiescence of mind which we feel in contemplating a grand spectacle that is intelligible to us."

So spoke Robert Bridges, Hopkins, Swinburne, Gosse when, as Jerome Buckley explained in his recent *Victorian Temper,* "taste simplified" for this last generation. The new French Symbolists, moving from Parnassianism, concurred in the change and both praised and were praised by the English generation. Gautier's words were greeted—"I am a man for whom the visible world exists," and "the perfection of form is virtue." Baudelaire's lines were seen to be "smooth and deliberate with the classic curve" (Ruth Temple, *The Critic's Alchemy,* 1953, p. 141). Swinburne and Shelley were praised for "ample periods" and "plastic form" (Temple, p. 112). The real secret of Whistler was said to be "that he does not try to catch the accident when an aspect becomes effective, but the instant when it becomes characteristically beautiful" (Temple, p. 155).

Fin-de-siècle liking for the emotional and musical power of Baudelaire and Mallarmé and Milton, as well as for Gautier and Wordsworth, shows how strong was the pull back to eighteenth-century sublimity away from romantic barbarism. Only a few extremists like Whitman, Wilde, and Henley managed the re-creation of a new Pindaric mode; but many tended to praise older examples. Drawn from one extreme toward another, they seemed to move halfway, to a middle position. Hopkins, for example, often sounded extremely Miltonic, Keatsian, Greek in its most un-Roman sense of unreasoned power. He abjured English particles and connectives, and even much clear classical syntax, in order to achieve the presentative power of Greek: one sentence as one word (W. H. Gardner, *Hopkins,* Yale, 1948, I, 49, 122, 126), so that Gardner was able to say, "In its prime intention and general method, Hopkins' total complex of style is Classic rather than Romantic," and "no English verse, in its diction and movement, conveys the 'feel' of Greek melic poetry so well as that of Hopkins" (I, 196; II, 33). Phillips, also, the most popular of late-century poets, aimed for the Miltonic and achieved something more moderate. The term "Georgian" as we use it today for the turn-of-the-century spirit in poetry, smooth, rural, shapely, emotional, intense, is indeed suitable for many of the *fin-de-siècle,* not only for their king to be, but for their renewal of the golden mean in its Virgilian Georgic mode, and for their interest in the sublimity of the eighteenth-century Georgians. Arthur Symons in his *Romantic Movement in English Poetry* (p. 12) said, as Cleanth Brooks said later in *Modern Poetry and the Tradition,* that the poetry of the eighteenth century has no fundamental relation with the rest of English poetry; he was disturbed by an extreme of style not clearly identified and not clearly labeled in relation to classicism and romanticism, his own era's terms; yet the fascination was clear in much of his own work. While Wordsworth's classicism withdrew from the heights of the sublime, Symons wrote for an age moving toward the sublime, away from the rough and dramatic economies of romanticism. So we see a new sort of balance, but one which draws again on the age-old resources of classical substance and form.

Intense was a key term of value for the late nineteenth century. It might imply any mode—the intense action or argument of the clausal romantic, or the intense ecstasy of the sublime as Longinus meant it, or the intensity of focus in between. At least we know that for Mill's father, as a Hartleian, "the intense" was "a bye-word of scornful disapprobation" (Mill, *Autobiography,* p. 377), while by the 1860's intensity and refinement were favorably related to perception of the *Ding an sich.* By 1885, Andrew Lang said, "Intense is the adjective dearest to me" (Ford, *op. cit.,* p. 118). Walter Hamilton in 1882 (*op. cit.,* pp. 31, 36) related intensity to Wagner and the aesthetes, to superlatives rather than refinements; and E. S. Dallas related it to lyricism. The criterion of individual intensity which Hazlitt and Keats had drawn from Longinus, Arnold opposed as too far from center (Lionel Trilling, *Arnold,* p. 113). Yet by the time of T. E. Hulme, intensity had become a part of classic concentration. All these variations imply one likeness: an *an sich* focus. If on an individual person, then perhaps intensity of drama or rhapsody; if on an object, then classical shape and clarity, and this latter was the increasing focus of nineteenth-century classicism as it culminated in Hulme, Eliot, and Imagism.

Classical clarity of outline and objective intensity had to cope with the countermove of the nineteenth-century Symbolists toward "implication" and "music," away from "statement" and "picture." The increasing vocabulary of cloud and shadow, the increasing freedom and implicativeness of versification, the increasing openness of sentence structures, with their endings in three dots... , all moved toward the effects of sublimity, away from the familiar forms of classicism. Yet in one word, *presentation,* may be suggested the nature of the compromise which the Imagists made, which, in their various ways, Swinburne, Bridges, Hulme, Valéry, Yeats, and Eliot, made. Presentation kept to its classical shapes, forms, objects, and objectivities, but cut down discursive descriptions; narrowed from scenes to smaller items; stressed sound as presentative, that is, as onomatopoetic; and emphasized the hard, the clear, the definite, the exact, the limited, as Hulme and Pound prescribed, preserving the sense of the whole. What Erich Auerbach has described in his *Mimesis* as classical—external, direct presentation of phenomena, without gaps and blurs, in a local and temporal present which is absolute—is true of much Georgian and much Imagist poetry. There is focus rather than procession of figures, and this is the compromise that *intensity* has called for, against the long pull of Longinus, Ramus, Milton, Keats, Mallarmé, Pound upon the scenic world of classicism toward something higher, deeper, and beyond the *an sich* of mimetic observation.

The office of the new critics in the twentieth century has been mainly to foster and formulate the standards for dramatic, metaphysical, and romantic, predicative poetry, renewed by Donne's renewal in 1912, from Hardy and Housman and Meredith, and carried on in our time by Robinson, Frost, Auden, Warren, and many of the younger discursive poets. These are at the center of theory in our generation. But along with these have moved steadily the theorists of classicism as it may proceed again in the direction of Longinus, from pure presentation to dream and rhapsody through symbol, so that we may come round to the Miltonic once more.

Traditionally we have had three styles discriminated: high, middle, and low: with the shifting extremes in tragedy and comedy, or drama and description, or sublime and pathetic, or *I am that* and *that is I* in the terms of Dallas, or melopoeic and logopoeic in the terms of Pound. The middle ground has maintained a relative stability as the extremes have altered: the beautiful, the observed, the objective, the *that is that* of Dallas, the phanopoeic of Pound: the natural human world as classical balance between spirit and flesh or heaven and hell: the Virgilian world. While the Longinian and Lucretian and

Pindaric world is sublime and cosmic, spiritual in the Christian sense, and ethical in terms of individual sincerities, the medieval, metaphysical, and romantic world is active and interactive, a complex of facts and propositions, of truth and falsity. The Virgilian aesthetic world lies between these two, sharing the sensibility of the first and the humanity of the second, and more observing than either.

Even the central vocabularies of these styles bear out the traditional discriminations, as we relate the simple modes we have distinguished to the larger matters of theme and attitude. What we have called the active clausal mode, the native English predication of Chaucer, Wyatt, the metaphysical poets, and the romantics including Hardy, Frost, and Auden, uses characteristically a terminology of cognition and interaction: words like *cruel, poor, true, wise, blood, death, earth, fire, pain, thing, word,* and the verbs, *bring, live, keep, take, think*. Such poetry is dramatic, admits conflicts and the difficulties of life, recognizes the low, even the hell, which may be on earth. It is the poetry of Donne, of Coleridge, of Browning, of Hardy. At the opposite extreme is the soaring, the sublime, not only of the eighteenth century but of Sylvester and Milton before and Keats, Tennyson, Whitman, Crane and Thomas after; this mode which we have technically distinguished as phrasal uses a central vocabulary of cosmic reach: *air, dark, divine, golden, high, deep, rise, fall, sea, wind, light, cloud, flower, star, voice,* and *silent:* the poetry of suggestion, implication, music, and divinity, in the mode not only of Milton but of much modern Symbolism.

Between these two extremes persists the classical mode as a steady part of the classical style in English: the balance of phrasal and clausal structures, the molding and limiting of line patterns, the central vocabulary of human form in natural landscape: *breast, head, foot, grow, lie, look, seem, name, fate, soft, sky, hour, year, green, scene, long, way, nature.* Of the three vocabularies, this is the closest to aesthetic sense, as it is to Virgilian and Ovidian models. It speaks for Spenser and Shakespeare, then a century later for Marvell and Dryden, then for Goldsmith, Crabbe, and Wordsworth, then for Swinburne, Hopkins, Bridges, and for Stevens and Eliot. In each century the contexts differ and the tones differ, depending upon the forces from which the balance has been won, but some of the basic materials in sound and sense persist and steadily recur as the structural mode recurs.

In the nineteenth and early twentieth centuries, the context for the classical mode has been the variations upon Imagism as between the metaphysical and the symbolic and surreal. The phanopoetic or presentative force of the image has its inheritance from the classical *ut pictura poesis* and its whole recurrent tradition, as distinguished from *ut musica* and what one might call the metaphysical *ut verba.* At the same time, the whole nineteenth century has moved toward a poetic vocabulary much more strongly sensuous and aesthetic than ever before, and much more tinged with the shadowy implicativeness of the sublime. Therefore in our own modern version of the classic vocabulary some of the more general terms like *fate, scene,* and *nature* have been lost; and to the *woman's face* and *foot,* the *green* and *golden summer* of the present classical mode have been added the shades of sublimity in *sea,* and *shadow, wind, water,* and *dream,* and one metaphysical *nothing.* As a whole, temporal contexts are perhaps stronger than modal. But the modes, carrying their characteristic tones and attitudes in characteristic technical forms of substance and sentence structure, are the forces of conservation and recurrence. Especially the classical mode, in its recurrent mediation between extremes, and in its own integrity of perspective, has reminded us again, in the last century and our own, of the power of the human form, the natural scene, the observing sense, the middle distance.

CHAPTER TEN

HOPKINS: THE SWEET AND LOVELY LANGUAGE

Two POETS who very differently exemplify this classical middle distance are Gerard Manley Hopkins and William Butler Yeats. Both praise Dryden as a master; both like that achievement of balance between the forces of colloquialism and the forces of ceremony. Yet Hopkins seems consciously to work with sound and structure, easily to assume the richness of the classical and even the sublime traditions; while Yeats assumes sound easily, and consciously struggles with the forces of abstraction. In the following description of Hopkins I stress his difference from Donne, the Pre-Raphaelites, and Browning, and his likeness to the sublime mode, as well as the balanced, because his vocabulary of intense feeling pulls always, away from predication, in the sublime direction.

Gerard Manley Hopkins was a champion and great master of epithet. He expected poetry, including his poetry, to catch and convey vividly what eye saw and heart felt. *Vivid* was a word he liked to use in his letters, and he used it often with *imagery,* in praise. He denied the validity of Lessing's old distinction between painting and poetry: "'Vermilion, saffron, white' is a brilliant stroke (that is a lie, so to speak, of Lessing's that pictures ought not to be painted in verse, a damned lie—so to speak)" (*Corresp. with Dixon,* XVI). He demanded for poetry the colorful, descriptive, elaborate, and in this demand agreed with Spenser, the first master of his mode.

Many who like Hopkins' poetry like to have it made up at its best of their own wishes, some Donne, some Anglo-Saxon, some Dryden for whom Hopkins stated his admiration outright, preferably metaphysical traits wherever possible, and a little of the gloss, glow, and affection of the poetic lingo of Keats's century, in which Hopkins lived. I suggest no alteration in these recognitions, but a change in their proportion. As for the Anglo-Saxon, Terence Heywood has shown how late he came to its study (*Poetry,* LIV, 209–218); as for the metaphysicals, much of what he shared with them he shared with Milton also, in a bond which he himself stressed; and as for Keats, Hopkins never did get over him. Why should he have, except for our tender sakes? The *Letters* and *Notebooks* discuss poetry in nineteenth-century terms, and those were partly Keats's terms. Tennyson and Morris disappointed; Swinburne and Browning disgusted; Keats, Barnes, Dixon, sometimes the Pre-Raphaelites, pleased; but in pleasure or displeasure, this was the field of Hopkins' acquaintance and reference. And his strongest words of praise and awe, as well as some of blame, were for Milton and Keats (*Letters to . . . Bridges,* XXX; *Corresp. with Dixon,* II).

In large part the regular substance and pattern of his diction has not only that magnitude of idiosyncrasy which we tend immediately to recognize, but also the constancy of classical descriptive tradition which we tend to pass over without recognition. In Hopkins, as in any poet of whom we are fond, we are quicker to trace traits peculiar or pleasant to us than to identify the large portion of traits assumed and accepted without stress but with thorough ease by the poet. So the sheer quantity, the repeated form and function, the regular presence, of Hopkins' descriptive adjectives through all the variations of his poetry help clarify some of his perhaps partly unconscious assumptions about poetic quality, and suggest his alliance to the painter poets, with their balanced forms.

Hopkins' most frequent adjectives, those he used ten times or more apiece in the fourteen hundred lines which the Oxford edition presents as completed work as distinguished from fragments, are adjectives of sense and lively response. *Sweet* was his favorite, his world was *sweet:* flowers, soul, skill, heaven, earth's being, a stallion, spells, wood, scene, notes, sending, ending, air, hopes, scions, looks, landscape, reprieve, alms, gift, fires, scarless sky, and a dozen more, were *sweet.* A dozen more were *lovely* and a dozen *dear;* freshness, aspens, charity, dogged man, concern, daystar, chance, father and mother, and more, *dear;* starlight, Death, Providence, weeds, fire, behaviour, woods, manly mould, Christ, dale, lads, mile, men's selves, "Holiest, loveliest, bravest." These are terms, especially in their contexts, of aesthetic feeling and affectionate response. They serve to make abstracts more sensible and concretes more personal. They give *skill* or *reprieve* a taste and fragrance; they are friendly toward *freshness;* they love and find lovelike *Providence* and starlight as well; and together they provide the constant poetic line of early poems, *Deutschland,* late great sonnets alike.

Sweet, dear, and *lovely* do not bear a strict Hopkins label. They sound quite like the nineteenth century and perhaps, except for *lovely,* like the sixteenth. Neither is the natural world they modify, the nouns of *earth, wood, fire, sky, cloud, air,* and *aspen,* in any way idiosyncratic or peculiar; in fact it is the very world Ruskin writes about as modern in *Modern Painters,* the "inscape" and "instress," in Hopkins' terms, of natural objects closely admired by the devout painter's eye. Nor are *soul* and *skill, charity* and *concern, chance* and *death,* abstractions new to the poetic scene; they are common to many centuries and have been sensibly qualified by many. Here runs through Hopkins' poetry the vigor of tradition in fact and epithet.

Other of his major adjectives are equally traditional. *Good* and *bad* are Elizabethan and later; weather and nature and man himself are *bad,* and gift, being, and beauty *good,* for Hopkins. *Bright* and *dark* are, on the other hand, observer's epithets; for Hopkins' sun and cloud were *bright,* but also wing, borough, paling, sandal—this last a special application.

Of the other major epithets one is sublime, *wild:* waters, meal-drift, hoarlight, air, in Hopkins' special stamp. Others are colors, his distinctively, *black* west and bough, *grey* lawn and drayhorse, *blue* days, heavens, embers, for samples. And finally, *fresh* is distinctively his, sounding more like him even than *lovely. Fresh* crust and youth and thought and wind and windfalls. What's fresh seems sweet, says Hopkins and so he adds to the poetic vocabulary of praise.

A substantial part of the language of his poetry is, then, language shared, and shared more with the descriptive painter-poets than with the metaphysicals. His dozen most frequent epithets, appearing in all a hundred and fifty times or so, bulk large and speak in rich tone, modifying a familiar nature closely perceived. In them Hopkins appears a sensitive, an enthusiastic, a properly individualistic Pre-Raphaelite participating, against his other conscience, in the tradition of Keats. So, too, less frequent adjectives represent him: *kind, fond, sheer, poor, tender, low, high, bold, proud.* These are terms of attitude and quality much more than are the *fair, good, great, new, old, true* terms of the Elizabethans and the school of Donne. From the Elizabethans Hopkins kept just those epithets which, like *sweet* and *good,* most conveyed attitude; from the eighteenth-century stress of Collins and Goldsmith he kept his *fond, tender,* and *kind,* and his qualities of colors, of *low* and *high, dark* and *bright,* to which his own *lovely, sheer, fresh* contributed their individual version of sense and scene. Qualified by these, Hopkins' metaphysical traits, like his metrical inventions, were smoothed and controlled in the direction of descriptive value in its inherited balanced pattern.

By a sort of silence Hopkins helps explain the force of his inheritance in vocabulary. He expressed little formulated theory on the subject. True, he wrote of the diction of Parnassianism, he liked or disliked certain phrases, he explained some technical uses of his own, he believed that the language of poetry should be "the current language heightened" (*Bridges,* LXII); but for every merest passing reference to phrasing there are a dozen heartfelt studyings over rhythm and meter. In sound lay Hopkins' revolutionary preoccupations. In the jolt more than the sense of his speech grew his new poetic world. And message after message, note after note, puzzled over and expounded and pieced together this new world in creation. He was well enough content with vocabulary; he had all his contemporaries' ways and means in it, and did not need to raise any issues. So in the Index to the *Correspondence with Dixon,* where there is more than a column of references under "Music," and another under "Versification," only one or two items are to be mustered for any topic of diction or vocabulary.

One item, listed under "Wordpainting" and praising the novelists of his day, puts Hopkins squarely in the main line of descriptive masters: "Wordpainting is, in the verbal arts, the great success of our day. Every age in art has its secret and its success, where even second rate men are masters. . . . These successes are due to steady practice, to the continued action of a school: one man cannot compass them. And wordpainting is in our age a real mastery and the second rate men of this age often beat at it the first rate of past ages. And this I shall not be bullied out of." (*Bridges,* CLV.) He blamed those of his time who were too subtle for word painting; he praised the novelists for using it so well.

Like the "aureate" poets of the sixteenth century, including Spenser, and like the classical poets of late seventeenth and eighteenth centuries, Hopkins valued the "scope" in poetry, the shape and scene, the qualified and epitheted view.

A gentle knight was pricking on the plaine,
Ycladd in mightie armes and silver shielde,
Wherein old dints of deepe woundes did remaine,
The cruell markes of many a bloody fielde. . . .

Yet once more, O ye Laurels, and once more
Ye Myrtles brown, with Ivy never sere,
I come to pluck your Berries harsh and crude,
And with forc'd fingers rude,
Shatter your leaves before the mellowing year. . . .

Farewell, for clearer Ken design'd,
The dim-discover'd Tracts of Mind:
Truths which, from Action's Paths retir'd,
My silent Search in vain requir'd! . . .

St. Agnes' Eve—Ah, bitter chill it was!
The owl, for all his feathers, was a-cold;
The hare limp'd trembling through the frozen grass,
And silent was the flock in woolly fold. . . .

The fine delight that fathers thought; the strong
Spur, live and lancing like the blowpipe flame,
Breathes once and, quenchèd faster than it came,
Leaves yet the mind a mother of immortal song.

The regular modification in these stanzas, the *mightie armes and silver shielde, Myrtles brown, with Ivy never sere, dim-discover'd Tracts, silent flock in woolly fold, fine delight* and *strong Spur,* is a way of thought in poetry which is in clear contrast to the mode, for example, of Donne, of

> I wonder by my troth, what thou, and I
> Did, til we lov'd, were we not wean'd till then?
> But suck'd on countrey pleasures, childishly?
> Or snorted we in the seaven sleepers den?

Not only are there fewer adjectives in Donne's four lines; the adjectives are not wordpainting; and the sound-and-sense structure of the writing is not set up in the expectation of a regular descriptive need. I use the contrast not as a random one, of course, but as a representative one. Not that four lines full of adjectives are never to be found in Donne and his kind, not that the painting poets never lay down their colors to converse; but simply that generalization about the details of the major sorts of poetry is illustrated in these selections.

As Hopkins participated in the classical mode of composition, he shared also in its major vocabulary. While the main epithets of the metaphysical poets and their inheritors in the nineteenth century, like Browning, whose work Hopkins disliked, were terms of standards and human relations, *bad, good, fair, great, new, old, true,* classical vocabulary was, like Hopkins', sensibly and emotionally descriptive. *Dear, sweet,* and *gentle, high,* and *sad, black,* and *deep,* are words which Spenser stressed. *Happy, high,* and *sweet,* with a good deal of *bright* and *dark,* are Milton's too. With an addition of sublimity the major epithets of Collins are *deep, fair, gentle, green, sad, soft, sweet, wild;* and of Keats, *bright, fair, golden, good, great, green, high, little, old, soft, sweet.* Of Hopkins, now we may recognize, of *sweet, dear, lovely, wild, black, grey, blue, fresh, good, bad, bright, dark,* the tone is the same. Such are the great, lovingly used, and most abundantly used, adjectives of poetry of the classical school and of its maturity at the turn into the nineteenth century. Term by term can be seen the major modern vocabulary building, from the *high* and *deep, gentle* and *sweet* discriminations of Spenser, through Collins' strong adjectival stress and his addition of color and wildness, to the whole "school's" acceptance, in the names of Wordsworth, Shelley, Keats, and Poe, of a central core of sublime terms, the *bright* and *dark, deep* and *high,* and *wild* variety.

To this school of the vitality of the sensed and visible natural world, Hopkins went, and was at home without theory. He did not write in letters, and would not have been aware, so easy was his acceptance, that of the dozen main epithets he used so much through his whole life, all but three or four he shared with certain allied predecessors, the negative *bad* with Donne and Milton, and the rest with Keats and his earlier kin. Even his own contributions in abundance and emphasis, his *fresh* and *lovely* and his color discriminations, maintained the tradition of these poetic friends. Moreover, he did not radically change the contexts of these terms. His flowers and woods, charities and concerns, in their mixture of abstracts into the scenic world were not far from Keats's copes and roses, bequests and essences, or even from Milton's groves and converses, though Milton's world was on the whole a far more cosmically ordered one, with its vocabulary of circles, processions, and realms, as Collins' too was more processional. Painting, by Hopkins' time, was still of landscape with thoughts, but of a closer and more personal scene. Wood dove, falcon, drayhorse, were distinguished, and with the classical Boreas on the one hand, the shapes and colors of leaves on the other. Indeed, the differences in what painting poets saw to paint may be noted even more clearly in their prose than in their poetry; Keats and Hopkins, like Ruskin, in the tendency of their time, found more minute natural detail to see.

There is likeness, too, in the devices by which the adjective users record the details of their observation and response, whether cosmic or pastoral, processional or individual. Characteristic of Hopkins and of Milton, Collins, and Keats, as distinguished say from Wyatt, Donne, or

Pope, is strong use, up to a third of all adjective forms, of participles as adjectives. "With forc'd fingers rude," "for clearer Ken design'd," "The hare limp'd trembling," the "Spur, live and lancing" are examples. The larger portion are past forms, and they serve to catch and fix motion and quality into a more permanent state; they work, then, in a way counter to action and motion. Where Hopkins is short on straight active verb forms, despite the general impression of many readers, he is strong in these crystallizing elements. Of the most vigorous of the present participial forms (and his *hurling, riding, heaving, calling, swirling, poising, rolling, racing, wrestling, echoing, soaring* are assuredly more lively than Keats's *glowing, breathing, dreaming, dying, aching, blazing, wand'ring, whisp'ring,* for example, though the two share visual terms like *dazzling*) even the most active participles are yet more statements of quality than of action.

The past forms are intensely qualitative. Few are common or repeated. *Laced, hung, lost, fallen, wept* are repeated a few times. But a great amount of invention and compounding comes for Hopkins in these forms, just as it did for Milton, Collins, and Keats. Keats had doubled Collins' compound epithets; Hopkins in turn doubled Keats's. His inventiveness worked here again in the main line which the adjectival poets had established. Keats's *carved, wing'd, hid, faded, unseen, moss'd* became Hopkins' *carved, winged, dogged, cursed, freckled, fetched, plumed,* in all a somewhat rarer lot; and Keats's *eager-eyed, hot-blooded, half-anguished, deep-loved, purple-stained, wild-ridged* became Hopkins' more complicated and special *carrier-witted, scroll-leaved, whirl-wind-swivelled, else-minded, heart-forsook, care-coiled, bell-swarmed, dapple-dawn-drawn, no-man-fathomed, five-lived, rarest-veined.* The change is not one, as far as I can see, toward greater metaphysical far-fetchedness, but rather is an intensification of quality statement, an emphasis on the special perceivable nature of things, the physical sense of whirlwind, leaf, care, bell qualities. Emphasis is just what Hopkins said, in his early essay on "Poetic

Diction," the accented past participle is good for. Poetry needs more emphasis of all sorts, he said there, more eighteenth-century liveliness, more nineteenth-century vividness, to make mere flat "Parnassian" descriptiveness come alive. The accented past participle does have a life-giving quality when chosen thus in substitute for adjective, rather than for verb; the very choice shows the direction from which Hopkins felt himself to be working. "'O well wept' should be written asunder, not 'wellwept.' It means 'you do well to weep' and is framed like 'well caught' or 'well run' at a cricketmatch" (*Bridges,* XLI). Here is the life in the structure for Hopkins, and a life from spoken language it is. But a little later, writing on the need for reshaping English compounds to poetic use, Hopkins contrasted *potato* as an ugly and laughable word to *earthapple* as a stately one (*Bridges,* XCIV). This is the life in the sense stress for Hopkins; the compound can give the fuller sense quality, the rhetorical "colors" of the thing, as Aristotle had long recommended and as Spenser, Milton, Shelley, and Keats had mainly contrived in English poetry to show.

The *flint-flake, white-fiery, lovely-dumb, piece-bright, lull-off, silk-sack, very-violet-sweet,* and later more infrequent *wet-fresh, age-old, rope-over* epithetical compounds without verb forms, which amount to nearly half the number, bear out Hopkins' need of specifying quality as closely as hyphens could do it. Adjective or adverb plus noun or adjective do the attributing. From the thing its quality is drawn by punctuation, as if there in the making. So most commonly the meaning of *with* or *like* is assumed in the participle forms, in *crimson-cresseted* or *black-leaved* for example.

So also the *y* forms of the adjective, characteristic of the painter-poets, gave Hopkins great scope in quality making, by condensing and assuming *like*. He used more of these forms than any other poet I know; not only the *starry, mazy, airy, glassy, watery, wintry, vaulty, wiry* familiar from Keats and the eighteenth century, but the *roundy, branchy, beadbonny, fretty, barrowy* which sound less familiar. His word-making force was a force toward analogy and especially sense analogy, thereby to catch the inner landscape in the outer. His prose epitheting worked the same way. "I am, so far as I know, permanently here, but permanence with us is ginger-bread permanence; cobweb, soapsud, and frost-feather permanence" (*Bridges,* XLIII). This is far from the metaphysical searching of microcosmic relationships; it is the crumbling, spattering, and weighing of the feeling. "Feathery rows of young corn," wrote Hopkins as a note to himself (*Notebooks,* p. 41). "Ruddy, furred and branchy tops of the elms backed by rolling cloud." And of a sunset: "Above the green in turn appeared a red glow, broader and burlier in make; it was softly brindled, and in the ribs or bars the color was rosier, in the channels where the blue of the sky shone through it was a mallow colour" (*Dixon,* App. II). Hopkins, like Ruskin, was a notebook sketcher and painter, by nature as by convention a wordpainter. When he was in a hurry and had little to say of the day which was closing, if it were fine he often wrote *Fine* in his Journal, but often *Bright.*

The terms and devices of the painting poets were satisfying, then, to Hopkins; satisfying at least as we see satisfaction in constant use and agreement, be it in explicit defense or only in taking for granted. The epithets and forms most often recurring, in poem after poem, early and late, are the epithets and forms of Keats and his line, the words of thought in scene, the relatively few active verbs and negatives and small undecorative conversational words, the discriminating compounds and the crystallizing participles, the catching and rendering the qualities of things, the vivid images. "I want Harry Ploughman to be a vivid figure before the mind's eye; if he is not that the sonnet fails" (*Bridges,* CLV).

One would quickly say that Hopkins' poetry is much more than these matters of modification, and I should agree, but as it is more, it is also these. These he did not puzzle over, but these were the assumptions past which his puzzles, of meter, of grammatical compression and lyrical intensity, went. In every poem simple descriptiveness in nineteenth-century terms underlay the complexities, as in "To what serves Mortal Beauty?" the *flung, prouder form, lovely lads, wet-fresh windfalls, swarmed Rome, dear chance, barren stone, love's worthiest, World's loveliest, sweet gift, better beauty* underlay in all confidence of accepted poetical substance the packed accents, broken rhyme words, repetitions and ellipses, and gnomic meanings.

To what serves mortal beauty—dangerous; does set danc-
ing blood—the O-seal-that-so feature, flung prouder form
Than Purcell tune lets tread to? See: it does this: keeps warm
Men's wits to the things that are; what good means—where a glance
Master more may than gaze, gaze out of countenance.
Those lovely lads once, wet-fresh windfalls of war's storm,
How then should Gregory, a father, have gleanèd else from swarm-
ed Rome? But God to a nation dealt that day's dear chance.
  To man, that needs would worship block or barren stone,
Our law says: Love what are love's worthiest, were all known;
World's loveliest—men's selves. Self flashes off frame and face.
What do then? how meet beauty? Merely meet it; own
Home at heart, heaven's sweet gift; then leave, let that alone.
Yea, wish that though, wish all, God's better beauty, grace.

Here, far less obviously than in "The dappled die-away / Cheek and wimpled lip, / The gold-wisp, the airy-grey / Eye, all in fellowship" sort of poem, but still with apparent force, the descriptive standards work and persist.

It takes a whole poem to convey Hopkins' individual nature, because it is the dynamics that is his. Cut crosswise, as by an index of first lines, the poetry immediately shows its alliances as strongly as its special traits. In the longest group, under "T," simple statement works most often with the regular descriptive epithets, *best* and *bare, fine* and *fresh* and *massy, strong* and *darksome;* and the participles. First lines:

The best ideal is the true
The boughs, the boughs are bare enough
'The child is father to the man'
The dappled die-away
Thee, God, I come from, to thee go
The Eurydice—it concerned thee, O Lord:
The fine delight that fathers thought; the strong
The furl of fresh-leaved dogrose down
There is a massy pile above the waste
'The Rose in a mystery'—where is it found?
The sea took pity: it interposed with doom:
The shepherd's brow, fronting forked lightning, owns
The times are nightfall, look, their light grows less;
The world is charged with the grandeur of God.
This darksome burn, horseback brown,
Thou art indeed just, Lord, if I contend
Though no high-hung bells or din
Thou mastering me
Thou that on sin's wages starvest,
To him who ever thought with love of me
Tom—garlanded with squat and surly steel
To seem the stranger lies my lot, my life
Towery city and branchy between towers;
To what serves mortal beauty—dangerous; does set danc-

Some of the most eccentric single lines, ones that leap out as Hopkins, are ones that spring from adjective center: "Cloud-puffball, torn tufts, tossed pillows flaunt forth, then chevy on an air," "Earth, sweet Earth, sweet landscape, with leavès throng," "Earnest, earthless, equal, attuneable, vaulty, voluminous, . . . stupendous," "Hard as hurdle arms, with a broth of goldish flue," "Have fair fallen, O fair, fair have fallen, so dear," "Wild air, world-mothering air."

What Hopkins' inventive rhetoric of structure did for his rich epithet substance was to richen it further. His *sweet, lovely, dear, wild, fresh, good, bad, black* and *grey, bright* and *dark,* he exaggerated and specialized in the ways they had already been exaggerated and specialized, but more so: by repetition and exclamation, by compounding and the piling up of vigorous participial modification, by color, variety, and affectionately detailed application. What Lionel Trilling described as opposed by Matthew Arnold in his era (*Arnold,* p. 149), Hopkins maintained: intense piety, rushing to meet life, violence of imagery, multitudinousness; but he gave it a moderating shape. The language of this intensity Hopkins did not have to invent; as a reader he had learned and liked it; he had simply to elaborate and to use it. The vocabulary and technique of epithet which he shared with Spenser, Keats, and the painter-poets made him see afresh, and then were lent to a deeper hearing afresh.

What I have noted here about Hopkins' language is partly counter to the warnings of F. R. Leavis, that "Hopkins belongs with Shakespeare, Donne, Eliot and the later Yeats as opposed to Spenser, Milton and Tennyson" (*New Bearings,* p. 171); of Terence Heywood, that "critics have fortunately given up likening Hopkins to Milton," because he "is *not* in the Spenser- Milton-Tennyson tradition" (*Poetry,* 54: 271–9); and of E. E. Phare, that "His likeness to Keats is largely potential and a matter of conjecture" (p. 41). Certainly these warnings are wise if one is to look for the lone master in Hopkins. But he himself was devoted to schools and to schooling, the successes "due to steady practice, to the continued action of a school: one man cannot compass them." When he described the romantic and the Lake schools he wrote to Dixon (XXII), "I suppose the same models, the same masters, the same tastes, the same keepings, above all, make the school." In respect to tastes and masters the epithet keepings of Hopkins should well, I think, be considered; for the master is great in his school.

CHAPTER ELEVEN

THE CLASSICAL MODE OF YEATS

MUCH argument has been expended upon the stages of Yeats's poetic development, and "early," "middle," and "late" Yeats have been variously distinguished. Most recently, in *W. B. Yeats, Self-Critic,* Thomas Parkinson has made clear how crucial were the early-century years of the Abbey Theater for the developing active style of which the poet himself was consciously proud; in *The Identity of Yeats,* Richard Ellman has emphasized the persistence of themes and symbols through all the stages of change; and the general view is of a style growing steadily in strength and power from about 1900 to 1930 or later, as Yeats grew away from his first adjectival and misty romanticism toward the vigor and idiosyncrasy of his maturity and late years.

A study of his modes of language reveals a pattern more specifically traceable in development than this general one, and significant as it coincides with Yeats's own line of developing comments upon his work and belief. While mode is only a part of style, it is useful because easily discriminable and precisely identifiable within the great complexities of the poet's art. Yeats, as we might guess, used two modes rather than one, the relation between them being a main theme of his own critical musings. In the 1880's and 1890's he wrote mainly a balanced mode, just as his contemporaries were doing. In the 1900's and 1910's he changed to a predicative mode, just as his contemporaries were doing; as he said in the Oxford *Modern Verse,* about 1900 "everybody got down off his stilts." In the 1920's and 1930's he returned with great success in such volumes as *Michael Robartes, The Tower,* and *The Winding Stair,* and in later distinguished single poems, to his first balanced and classical mode, a return more characteristic of himself than of his era.

While critics have all distinguished the first stylistic change, toward predication, away from adjectival modification—and indeed this change was one of the most persistent preoccupations of Yeats's prose reveries,—they have assumed that it continued throughout his life, with a general tendency toward fewer and fewer adjectives, toward more action and clarity as he grew older. But one might well keep an eye open for cycles in the style of a man who believed in cycles, and for "rebirth" in the verse of a man who said he felt it; even for the balances of classicism in a poet who began to praise the classical in history as he began again to write it in verse.

Yeats indeed set his own dates for his own stages. In his *Autobiography,* "Dramatis Personae," v, he wrote, "When I went to Coole the curtain had fallen upon the first act of my drama"; later in IX, "For twenty years I spent two or three months there every year." The first of these dates was 1896, when he was about thirty years old; the second then, 1916, just before his marriage and the establishment of his own home at Toor Ballylee. These are the dates, also, which most clearly mark the technical changes of poetic mode.

By 1896 he had written the poems of *Crossways* and *The Rose* and many of *The Wind among the Reeds,* the majority of which were balanced, using clausal statement and phrasal qualification just about equally. Of course, as we know, he was trying many styles, so that there are poems both of extreme modification like the "Happy Shepherd" and some of the Lover's poems in *The Rose,* and of extreme predication like most of the ballads. But the middle ground dominates, from "The Sad Shepherd" and "King Goll," through "Innisfree" which seemed to Yeats, as he wrote in the *Autobiography,* "Four Years," xv, "my first lyric with anything in its rhythm of my own music," to the elaborations of "The Everlasting Voices," "The Unappeasable Host," and "The Elemental Powers." In even a brief poem like "The Rose of Peace," we may see the poise of idea, the reconcilation, behind the balanced structures, as the adjectives, mostly heavenly, *divine, white, gentle, brooding, rosy,* and others, give motive to the actions like *look, forget, go, bow, tell, bid, make,* of heaven and earth alike:

If Michael, leader of God's host
When Heaven and Hell are met,
Looked down on you from Heaven's door-post
He would his deeds forget.

Brooding no more upon God's wars
In his Divine homestead,
He would go weave out of the stars
A chaplet for your head.

And all folk seeing him bow down,
And white stars tell your praise,
Would come at last to God's great town,
Led on by gentle ways;

And God would bid His warfare cease,
Saying all things were well;
And softly make a rosy peace,
A peace of Heaven with Hell.

The adjectives slow the action and end the war, these being their functions often in the early volumes.

Specifically, the adjectives which predominate in *Crossways* and *Rose* are the famous *dim,* for which Yeats has been blamed, and blamed himself when he wrote in the Preface to *Poems 1899–1905* of the manful energy of drama in contrast to "those outlines of poetry that are blurred with desire and vain regret"; the colors *green* and *red,* which Yeats called "dull" and "overcharged" and blamed on Shelley and the romantics in both "Reveries," XVII, and "Ideas of Good and Evil"; and *gay, little, old,* which he used affectionately, *old* to dominate every volume to come. The substantial world these adjectives modified was the natural world of the romantics: *leaf, night, sea, star, sorrow,* with support of *bird, hill, moon, sky, tree, wood, water*. Distinguishing verbs were not powerful: *seek, sigh,* and *fall;* no wonder Yeats expressed desire for more energy than these conveyed, though he stressed also the traditional *know* and *make;* his resolutions were in danger of being made more from inertia than from conflict solved.

He worried, too, that his sound was too easy and smooth; in "Reveries," XVII, he reported the "loosening" of his meters after *Oisin;* we can see in "Innisfree" what he meant, the freeing and delaying spondees of *go now, build there, heart's core,* and their like. He found too easy his solutions of poise and balance in foot as in epithet, and was troubled by what he felt to be their effeminacy, their vagueness and generality of effect. Spenser, Shelley, Blake, the chief poets of his acquaintance at that time, his friends in the Rhymers Club, and Mallarmé from whom he remembered influence in "The Tragic

Generation," xi, all were poets who would sponsor such elaboration of implication, and would do little to help Yeats break away to something more dramatic. Morris and the Pre-Raphaelites might help, but it was probably Lady Gregory, even before the years of the theater, who saved the day with her folk language, her prose, and lingo. The simple active joggings of the early ballads began to merge with the more aesthetic verse and the slower line, at first merely in the sequential form of "The Song of Wandering Aengus":

> I went out to the hazel wood,
> Because a fire was in my head,
> And cut and peeled a hazel wand,
> And hooked a berry to a thread; . . .

but increasingly with the complexity of such a poem of thought as "To Ireland in the Coming Times" and such a masterly predication as "He Thinks of Those Who Have Spoken Evil of His Beloved"; so that a little later *The Seven Woods* of 1904 and *The Green Helmet* of 1910 took the more complex and predicative shape which most critics have noted, as in "The Folly of Being Comforted," and "Adam's Curse," and "The Fascination of What's Difficult." The first of these, as a good example, runs as follows, with the qualifications and modifications caught up fast into dramatic context, the constant small and neutral actions becoming a deeply implicative one at the end:

> One that is ever kind said yesterday:
> "Your well-belovèd's hair has threads of grey,
> And little shadows come about her eyes;
> Time can but make it easier to be wise,
> Though now it seems impossible, and so
> All that you need is patience."
> Heart cries, "No,
> I have not a crumb of comfort, not a grain,
> Time can but make her beauty over again:

Because of that great nobleness of hers
The fire that stirs about her, when she stirs,
Burns but more clearly. O she had these ways
When all the wild summer was in her gaze."

O heart! O heart! if she'd but turn her head,
You'd know the folly of being comforted.

In meager epithet, the first diminishments of kindness, *little, grey, easy* are answered by heart's *great* and *wild* and finally by no epithet at all; while the actions, on the other hand, build to the climax of "if she'd but turn her head, / You'd know," the complex subordination of which completes the earlier complexities of "though now it seems," and "can but make," and "stirs . . . when she stirs." The drama is in the implicative predication, as J. B. Yeats would have it, yet personal, as the will of his son would have it.

The vocabulary of this personal predicative poetry changed strongly from the earlier natural scene, the pictures and observations which Yeats had come to mistrust, to an emphasis upon human form. The terms were still of Pre-Raphaelite quality, in adjectives *pale, young, grey, golden,* in *dream* and *wind,* and the *breast, eye, hair, hand* of woman, and the structural verbs. Structure seemed for a while more rigorous than reference. But by the time of *Responsibilities* in 1914 and many of the *Wild Swans* poems, the human form had taken the shape of *friend* and *beggar,* with *blood* and *bone,* and active verbs *bring, give, keep* as if a poetry of more complex human relationship were being achieved. Here with this stark vocabulary we find expert predications: "And I took all the blame, out of all sense and reason, / Until I cried and trembled and rocked to and fro, / Riddled with light." Or, "A doll in the doll-maker's house / Looks at the cradle and bawls." Or, of the wild swans, "Their hearts have not grown old; / Passion or conquest, wander where they will, / Attend upon them still." Personal and passionate as these poems become, dramatic action sustains them and provides their structure of expression, the stage on which the author bespeaks his own will and subjectivity, the restlessness of his desire.

This is a mastery well recognized in Yeats, but there follows another, which has also been recognized, as "lyric" by Parkinson, as "classic" by Eliot and Ellman. In the mode which Robartes brings back, the balanced structure of deliberating language, a new vocabulary enters, in concepts like *mind* and *thing* which the younger Yeats had feared, in the commentary adjective *great,* in the active *find* and *seem.* At the same time, some of the earlier vocabulary returns: the adjectives from the past, *young* and *wild,* and the noun *night.* Innovation combines with renovation in vocabulary as in structure, as the poet calls back the *dark* and *wild* world of *woman, soul,* and *night,* with *mind* and *seeming.*

I have suggested that it was the character of Michael Robartes who brought back the classical mode to Yeats. His return brought back not only the night but also the forms of conscious debate, as with Aherne, between lover and saint; it made the oppositions explicit. As Ellman points out (*Identity,* p. 148), "Ego Dominus Tuus" in 1915 was the first poem to mention the tower, and it is one of the first also to clarify the classical style of debate.

HIC. On the grey sand beside the shallow stream
Under your old wind-beaten tower, where still
A lamp burns on beside the open book
That Michael Robartes left, you walk in the moon
And though you have passed the best of life still trace
Enthralled by the unconquerable delusion
Magical shapes.
ILLE. By the help of an image
I call to my own opposite, summon all

That I have handled least, least looked upon.
HIC. And I would find myself and not an image. . . .

Thus begins, or begins again in its fulfillment, the deliberative and explicit, conscious rhetorical style of Yeats. HIC argues for simple identity and love of life, as in Dante and Keats. ILLE sees the complexities in both, and argues for recognition of the anti-self along with the self: the result is a personal and meditative style.

It is in clear and conscious contrast to the highly predicative style of the preceding vigorous decades. The rationale for the predicative style Yeats had expressed well in a letter to his father summarizing the work of the decade from 1903 to 1913: "Of recent years instead of 'vision' meaning by vision the intense realization of a state of ecstatic emotions symbolized in a definite imagined pattern, I have tried for more self-portraiture, I have tried to make my work convincing with a speech so natural and dramatic that the hearer would feel the presence of a man thinking and feeling. There are always two types of poetry—Keats the type of vision, Burns a very obvious type of the other, too obvious indeed." (*Identity,* p. 129.) Relatively, Keats is the more adjectival and passive, Burns the more active of these two; and it is the lyric of active self that Yeats is asserting here in 1913, as he has succeeded in it for a decade and more. But by 1919 his return to Ballylee seems to return him also to his anti-self, and to a mellower debate, a fuller view, a more commentary and explicit style. The moon is now past the full for Yeats, and, as Aherne says of the soul in "The Phases of the Moon," "Before the full / It sought itself and afterwards the world." Or, in "Under Saturn":

You heard that labouring man who served my people. He said
Upon the open road, near to the Sligo quay—
No, no, not said, but cried it out—"You have come again,
And surely after twenty years it was time to come."

I am thinking of a child's vow sworn in vain
Never to leave that valley his fathers called their home.

So too in June, when thought of his young daughter occasioned a prayer, the prayer was for the early graces he had long abandoned, the ceremony as well as the artifice of poetry, for "How but in custom and in ceremony / Are innocence and beauty born?" It was as if Yeats returned in many ways to the more feminine side of his nature, in his wife, in his daughter, in his secure tower, in his youthful elaborations of myth, in his family countryside, in his Irish nation, in his very age, so that drama might be tempered in deliberation.

The consequent poems, the poems of *The Tower* and *The Winding Stair,* are held by many to be Yeats's best, and are called by many literally "classical." Yeats himself recognized the quality, though he did not call it so (Hone, p. 339). Eliot wrote (*Southern Review,* Winter, 1941) that he liked only these; being himself classical, he found the poetry before 1919 too Pre-Raphaelite. W. Y. Tindall in *The Permanence of Yeats* called the later poems classical. Archibald MacLeish in the *Yale Review* (Spring, 1938) praised the later poems for their "public" speech, and Yeats wrote to Dorothy Wellesley that, amazing as it might seem, he was pleased by the epithet (*Letters,* p. 179). Ellman in *The Identity of Yeats* praises the *Tower* and *Stair* poems most highly, for their myth at last rooted in earth (p. 148), their change from drama to ritual (p. 179), the outlook which is "in fact, close at all points to what Hulme describes as classicism" (p. 4).

The more the pity, then, that an old error concerning the lessening of adjective qualification in Yeats's work should have been perpetuated as cliché, because, in fact, the increase of qualification in these two most praised books is one of their most effectively defining characteristics. As we have seen, Yeats used the balanced mode, sometimes an even more adjectival one, when he tempered action with quality and manner, and the fierce, rebellious, what he called "salty" and "masculine," vigor of early century (Ellman, *Masks,* 1903, 1906) he here combined again with the "sweet," the "beauty," with which he had begun.

The Tower's opening poem, "Sailing to Byzantium," is a good example of the newly effective mode, both in its balance and in its explicit idea. The rich youthful world is expressed adjectivally: "Caught in that sensual music, all neglect / Monuments of unageing intellect." The aged man, on the other hand, is that tattered coat upon a stick which Yeats had challengingly asserted at the end of *Responsibilities* when he favored stylistic nakedness over embroidery, and which later he was to name as the worst of apparitions. Man needs embroidery, the singing of the soul; therefore he has come to accept the artifice, with the ceremony, of Byzantium. In this poem, the acceptance is celebrated, and it is again discussed in poem after poem of the *Tower* volume. The title poem, for example, complains again about the old man's troubled heart that needs more soul and more argument; and makes the argument; and makes the soul "Study in a learned school," till the wreck of body seem but the clouds of the sky. In "Meditations in Time of Civil War" he calls on the honeybees to build in the empty house of the stare. "Two Songs from a Play" asserts the fabulous dark in which man's own heart flares. "Among School Children" lets body and soul together leaf and sway; the dancer and the dance move as one in the poise of the rhetoric.

A poem of especially conscious blend and balance is "A Dialogue of Self and Soul" in the next volume, which reclarifies what was early said in the Robartes poems about self and anti-self and the tension of the two. Yeats's *self* he thought of as his heart, masculine, active, daytime, naked, a sword, laborious, sinful, blind, foolish, and passionate. His anti-self, or *soul,* he thought of as feminine, embroidery, dark, blood, life, innocence, body, beast, and daemon. So in "A Choice" he said he had to choose between "perfection of the life or of the work" . . . the day's vanity, the night's remorse; and in "Vacillation" he briefly summarized what he had debated in "Shepherd and Goatherd," "Ego Dominus Tuus," and elsewhere.

> The Soul. Seek out reality, leave things that seem.
> The Heart. What, be a singer born and lack a theme?
> The Soul. Isaiah's coal, what more can man desire?
> The Heart. Struck dumb in the simplicity of fire!
> The Soul. Look on that fire, salvation walks within.
> The Heart. What theme had Homer but original sin?

Most happy is the blend of these in the "Dialogue." The Soul offers, in the tower and in the ancestral dark, deliverance "from the crime of death and birth," and the Self, with Sato's sword as symbol of day set upon his knees, claims "A charter to commit the crime once more." The Soul asserts the heaven where man cannot tell the knower from the known, the dancer from the dance; the Self is ready to endure the earth again, and the blindman's ditch, to feel remorse, and then, even to take the part of the Soul, to cast out remorse! This is the earthly paradise, this the self-forgiveness, which Yeats as poet came to.

> So great a sweetness flows into the breast
> We must laugh and we must sing,
> We are blest by everything,
> Everything we look upon is blest.

Such reconcilation Yeats was not to keep until his death. The Crazy Jane poems, the "Woman Young and Old," and many of the Last Poems, preserve rather the stripped ballad technique of the early century, giving to Jane and other ladies not the old dreamed-of or satisfied elegance of body and night, but much of Yeats's own rebellion and restlessness. Nevertheless, the best-praised and most meditative poems of the late years, like "The Gyres," "The Statues," "The Circus Animals' Desertion," preserve the mode of *Tower* and *Stair* in their integration. "The Gyres" reminds that beauty dies of beauty, needs its opposite, and its coarse opposite will come round to beauty again. "The Statues" draws from Asiatic vague immensities and this filthy modern tide the "proper dark" of the Irish and its passionate hope of design. "The Circus Animals' Desertion" summarizes the stages of thought and style which we have been tracing here: first, the early "embroideries" of the animals—boy, chariot, lion, and woman, as woman and beast move together,—then the dissatisfactions of the bare heart; first, the heart and its dream in narrative, then the more classical soul and its dream in the 'nineties, then in the new century the active fight of Cuchulain and his dream; then, finally, both the ladder and the heart. The poem complains of "desertion," but its own poise of awareness suggests the live presence of woman and lion still in the heart. Even "Under Ben Bulben," Yeats's last poem, restless and imbalanced as it is, recognizes the possible moment of ease, the "profane perfection of mankind," and the survival of the horseman, that classic blend of beast and man, who looks on life and death alike.

Both of Yeats's styles served him late, as they had served him early. It was only, or mainly, in the *Helmet* and *Responsibilities* eras that the predicative mode strongly dominated the balanced, and this was the era, as Yeats himself was aware, of the strong and hatefully rebellious assertion of *anima hominis* over *anima mundi;* of his self over his soul, his nakedness over beauty, his loneliness over love. By 1919, it was a time redeemed. One may ask why we follow Yeats in stressing two styles, when he clearly wrote in all three, the rich adjectival mode as well as the other two. The answer is that he never wrote in this third way consistently or steadily enough to give its character to any single volume, or even group, of poems. This was the Keatsian mode, which Yeats tended to distrust and which he called *vision.* When he himself finally came to *A Vision,* he came in his poetry more moderately than Keats, though he did certainly move in his direction, the direction of body. Interestingly enough, throughout his whole work, the most adjectival and bodily poems are those treating of women, like the *Rose* poems, for example, or "Leda," or "To Dorothy Wellesley." About 1895, when Yeats "Mourns for the Change That Has Come upon Him," he writes in the active, pursuing voice of the hound that he has been changed to; then still in "Dejection" in 1915, though he mourns the same change, he does so in the mode of that which he desires, as if he were beginning to win back in style, as he was to do also in fact, the dark leopards and the wild witches of the moon. The subjects of the most adjectival poems are "beautiful" and "ignorant"; but at last, in the balanced poems, it is possible also to "labor to be beautiful," so that the work may perfect the life. The beautiful was never a dominant mode for Yeats, but persistent to a degree that finally made possible a compromise with the dominant active mode of predication, so the poet got some peace in this world, its classic happiness.

I do not mean to praise one mode over the other. Yeats's whole first great development at the turn of the century was a development, in stylistic terms, of predication; in his own personal terms, of restlessness, salt, hate, masculinity. We could not think of him without this development; indeed, we think of him primarily in its terms. Yet I would remind that, as readers of his theory might well expect, he circled back again, to pick up an earlier balanced mode, the grace of his youth, and to develop it in turn, into the classic poise which his age in part possessed. In stylistic terms, he found the poetry in adjectives again; in personal terms, he refound the poetry in the feminine and his own anti-self, the home which he had fled and to which he returned.

The contexts of the new and renewed vocabulary in *The Tower* show us how the terms fit together. The most distinguishing term, *great,* is applied to joy, glory, bog, dice, labyrinth, eyes, wings, Mother, Hector, bell, and affairs, as the poems progress; both colloquial and traditional uses are dominant, with a sense of marvel or praise. So too with *old*—the colloquial in bawn, lecher, neighbor, scarecrow, beggar, clothes, and sticks, the more lofty traditional, as in the term *ancient* also, for terraces, rooms, thorntrees, wrongs, and songs. *Wild* is associated with wonder, unpredictability, in nest, bird, infancy, divinity, sake; and *seem* also, with marvelous, unchanging, moonlight and sunlight, dragon, sheer miracle; while *mind* is a mind of vigor, burden, piety, perturbation, change, wandering, and peace, with the *mind's eye* doing the discerning. In other words, in *The Tower* Yeats has finally managed to join outer with inner, the eye with the mind, observation with ideas; to resolve this opposition which long had troubled him, or to set it forth explicitly. We remember how at first he had tried for "pictures," as versus abstractions; at later times, as in 1913 to his father, he had opposed observation by personal insight. In the Tower poems, beautiful sights are seen again, but with the eye of the mind, that is, meditatively and imaginatively, with wonder and praise.

Further, more conceptual oppositions are made explicit in the major vocabulary of this volume. *Old* and *young, night* and *day, moon* and *sun, body* and *mind, soul* and *heart, woman* and *man, take* and *give, come* and *go,* all are major terms, while only two or three of these are present as pairs in other volumes. It was the night side of these pairs that Yeats was coming to accept: the *old moon* and *night, body* and *soul,* and *woman,* and as he did so he more joyfully also asserted *youth, sun,* and *mind* along with their *wildness, child, dream, bird, song,* and the explicitly communicating verbs of *call, cry, sing,* and *tell.*

> I need some mind that, if the cannon sound,
> From every quarter of the world, can stay
> Wound in mind's pondering
> As mummies in the mummy-cloth are wound;
> Because I have a marvellous thing to say,
> A certain marvellous thing
> None but the living mock,
> Though not for sober ear;
> It may be all that hear
> Should laugh and weep an hour upon the clock.
> ("All Souls' Night")

The Tower ends with these damned and blessed antitheses, "Till meditation master all its parts," and *The Winding Stair* ends with the question we have been considering: "What made me live like these that seem / Self-born, born anew?" We have seen that in basic structure of language and in emphatic selection of terms, as well as in thematic explication, *Tower* and *Stair* were volumes of rebirth and renewal for Yeats, and we can be the happier that people like and praise them in particular, that the difficult integration is an effective one.

A corresponding integration in sound pattern should also be mentioned: the drawing together of two quite different meters and forms, one the bare ballad, the other the long-lined lyric. In the first three or four books these appeared separately, the one clearly predicative, the other clearly qualitative, but gradually they joined, into the strict but variable meters of *The Tower*. Perhaps as Yeats himself suggested, the clue of change lies in an early poem like "Innisfree," where the expectably adjectival line is slowed by spondaic rests, so that silence may take the place of a modification. Perhaps, then, the clue to the second change, back to a more intrinsic balance, is to be seen in such a poem of renewed tension as "No Second Troy," where the brisk verbs, *blame, filled, taught, hurled,* are succeeded by a slower speculation of epithets: "What could have made her peaceful . . . With beauty like a tightened bow . . . ?"

Given Yeats's poetic success in the clarification of antitheses, both in statement and in structure, and given also his explicit lifelong concern for the philosophy and symbolism of antithesis, may we not possibly discern a more integral connection between his prose and his verse, and consequently a clearer sense of the ideas behind the achievement of the Tower poems? The doubleness in Yeats has been commented upon in many ways, as we know, partly as a matter of temporal change at the turn of the century, when he gave up his "ceremonial" style, as F. R. Higgins and others have called it (cf. p. 148 of *Scattering Branches*), and when, as he himself said in the *Oxford Book of Modern*

Verse, "everybody got down off his stilts"; even as a later change from what T. S. Eliot called Pre-Raphaelite to what Ellman called classical. But partly also the doubleness was pervasive, as we have seen: not only the use of two modes, but their combining in both structure and concept. Yeats was early aware, as Lenox Robinson reported in *Scattering Branches,* that he composed to two tunes, and early set up symbols of contrast for himself: Wilde's idea of pose, Robartes' daring versus Aherne's restraint, "the war of spiritual with natural order" in *The Secret Rose,* the tumult of the sea versus the rhetoric of the platform in *The Book of Irish Verse,* the bird versus the market cart in *The Cutting of an Agate,* the two styles which, as Ellman reports in *The Man and the Masks,* he asked Fiona McLeod in 1895 to choose between. Further, as Ellman has adduced from unpublished letters in *The Identity of Yeats,* the sheer necessity of doubleness and conflict was clear to him, that "we need something in ourselves to batter down," that "all depends upon the completeness of the holding down, on the stifling of the beast underneath"; that "I find my peace by pitting my sole nature against something and the greater the tension the greater my self-knowledge" (*Identity,* pp. 8 ff.).

But we see that these later statements of opposition are quite different in realm of reference from bird and market cart, and we may wonder whether Yeats's sense is of any opposition *per se,* or of certain basic continuities of kind, perhaps with a clear change or consolidation between *Responsibilities* and *The Tower.* Since much of Yeats's prose is reminiscing after the fact, there is difficulty in tracing change; but the collection of materials in the *Autobiography,* of final date 1938, affords one excellent opportunity for contrast and comparison. The "Reveries over Childhood and Youth" and "Estrangement" are written before the end of 1914; "The Trembling of the Veil" and "The Bounty of Sweden" are written by or after 1922. If we follow along the oppositions and dichotomies set up by Yeats in these two main periods, we may learn the nature of any possible change between them.

From the point of view of 1914, Yeats portrays himself in the 1880's and 1890's as a sort of Hamlet, seeking the protection of Hamlet's role, against self-doubt. "For many years, Hamlet was an image of heroic self-possession for the poses of youth and childhood to copy, a combatant of the battle within myself" (p. 43). And "I was about to learn that if a man is to write lyric poetry he must be shaped by nature and art to some one out of half a dozen traditional poses, and be lover or saint, sage or sensualist, or mere mocker of all life; and that none but that stroke of luckless luck can open before him the accumulated experience of the world" (p. 77). Two of his early defenses were those of ancient beauty (p. 73) and psychical research (p. 79), both as explicit stands against his father's strong opinions. His father at breakfast would read passages from the poets, always from the poem's most passionate moment, never a passage of generalization or speculative interest. "He despised the formal beauty of Raphael . . . all our discussion was of style" (p. 58). Later, Yeats felt he had made the discovery that "personal utterance, which had almost ceased in English literature, could be as fine an escape from rhetoric and abstraction as drama itself. But my father would hear nothing but drama; personal utterance was only egotism. I knew it was not, but as yet did not know how to explain the difference. I tried from that on to write out of my emotions exactly as they came to me in life, not changing them to make them more beautiful." (P. 91.)

His well-known statement about change of style after *Oisin* is the better read in the light of these defenses: he opposes intense emotional color and expression; he seeks strength in design, a controlled or "cold" emotion, the old and implicative intensity of Pre-Raphaelitism, but centered in self. At times he mourns his failure: "All life weighed in the scales of my own life seems to me a preparation for something that never happens" (p. 94).

The diaries of 1909 support this same self-questioning. The artist is lonely, incomplete, selective, seeking a full arc of wholeness (pp. 393,

400). Yeats adopts a simple style and hunts truth into its thicket, and cries out against his life, in doubt whether work and poetry fit together, deliberating more and more upon Renaissance images, Christ and Caesar, and the greater traditional unities (pp. 402, 420, 445). We may remember that Yeats was warned by a seer to stay out of thickets and the sun, since water and the moon were more true to his nature than daily facts (p. 315). But in these years he has been endeavoring to understand himself in his roles, in active virtue and the thickets of labor, not in the moon's visions. He has chosen an active and masculine mode in order to be true to self in its world, to be direct and unelaborate. He has temporarily renounced the visions of Robartes and Aherne.

Most significantly, he says that he had planned a visionary *Légende des siècles* for the 1890's but Synge persuaded him "that we must renounce the deliberate creation of a kind of Holy City in the imagination, and express the individual" (p. 422). So that was his choice for two decades and until *Byzantium.*

Nevertheless, lingering in the mind of the diarist was his old and early love of wonder, and as he read more he gave it a new form: the form of the artist Apollo as distinguished from the natural Dionysus (Ellman, p. 92; Hone, p. 196), the form of subject and idea (*Autobiography,* p. 418): "I now see that the literary element in painting, the moral element in poetry, are the means whereby the two arts are accepted into the social order and become a part of life and not things of the study and the exhibition. Supreme art is a traditional statement of certain heroic and religious truths, passed on from age to age, modified by individual genius, but never abandoned." The strong classical morality of the Renaissance weakened, says Yeats, by the time it got to Arnold; but "the arts are about to restate the traditional morality." And (p. 440), "The act of appreciation of any great thing is an act of self-conquest."

In this passage from the 1909 diaries Yeats answers much of his own argument from the past and looks forward to what he will say over and over in the 1922 memoirs: that to seek the self, dramatically to express the self, is not to find it; rather it is to be found in the holy city, in classical tradition, in "appreciation of any great thing"; that it is passive as well as active, and painful ecstasy as well as joyful will. This, as we have seen, is the very theme of "Ego Dominus Tuus," the first Tower poem, and one of the first in the classical *Tower* mode: the search for anti-self as well as self, for night as well as day, for body and soul as well as mind and heart; the reclaiming, in other words, of those very traits of his earliest verse which Yeats had for a while rebelled against.

The 1922 "Trembling of the Veil" begins with a memory of William Morris which is most helpful in the relating of old states of mind to new. The poetry of Keats, Henley, Wilde had been too elaborate for Yeats; he welcomed the stronger tone of action in Morris as in Chaucer and in much of the Pre-Raphaelite tradition. In *The Earthly Paradise,* which he especially admired, are the wise old men, the city of Byzantium, the four winds and directions, and much other familiar material. Looking back upon it, what he sees for admiration is its relation to Morris, its quality of anti-self, of all that Morris himself was not (pp. 123–124):

"To-day I do not set his poetry very high, but for an odd altogether wonderful line, or thought; and yet, if some angel offered me the choice, I would choose to live his life, poetry and all, rather than my own or any other man's. A reproduction of his portrait by Watts hangs over my mantelpiece with Henley's, and those of other friends. Its grave wide-open eyes, like the eyes of some dreaming beast, remind me of the open eyes of Titian's 'Ariosto,' while the broad vigorous body suggests a mind that has no need of the intellect to remain sane, though it give itself to every phantasy: the dreamer of the middle ages. It is 'the fool of fairy . . . wide and wild as a hill,' the resolute European image that yet half remembers Buddha's motionless meditation, and has no trait in common with the wavering, lean image of hungry speculation, that cannot but because of certain Hamlets of our stage fill the mind's eye. . . .

"The dream world of Morris was as much the antithesis of daily life as with other men of genius, but he was never conscious of the antithesis and so knew nothing of intellectual suffering. . . . Instead of the language of Chaucer and Shakespeare, its warp fresh from field and market—if the woof were learned,—his age offered him a speech, exhausted from abstraction, that only returned to its full vitality when written learnedly and slowly.

"The roots of his antithetical dream were visible enough; a never idle man of great physical strength and extremely irascible—did he not fling a badly baked plum pudding through the window upon Christmas Day?—a man more joyous than any intellectual man of our world, he called himself 'the idle singer of an empty day,' created new forms of melancholy, and faint persons, like the knights and ladies of Burne-Jones, who are never, no not once in forty volumes, put out of temper. . . .

"He did not project like Henley or like Wilde, an image of himself, because having all his imagination set upon making and doing he had little self-knowledge. He imagined instead new conditions of making and doing; and in the teeth of those scientific generalizations that cowed my boyhood, I can see some like imagining in every great change, and believe that the first flying-fish first leaped, not because it sought 'adaptation' to the air, but out of horror of the sea."

Yeats's own first great change, to a hard style, was "out of horror of the sea," but, as a fish, he succeeded later in making sea as well as air his home. Despite the success, he begrudges the consciousness of the labor, and would be a Morris, his very opposite, a dreaming beast, a Buddha, a body and mind with no need of intellect to remain sane; indeed, no flying fish at all, but a natural inhabitant of the sea. So it is not Yeats, but Yeats's antiself, which by 1922 this Hamlet, this flying fish, is able and wishful to accept, in prose as he has in poetry. The

Tower and the Stair, the sea and the fish, the Buddha and the Hamlet, come together in the classical style, which accepts and meditates, if not reconciles, antitheses.

Yeats's comments on his early difficulties with style show his awareness of going beyond them. For example, he remembers in the 'nineties his love of generalization yet his shame at using it, because of his Pre-Raphaelite tradition in its special Irish and dramatic form. Remorse made the poetry sentimental, by barring intellect "which I considered impure" (p. 164). He, the bookman Ille, had then refused to read books, lest he be contaminated by ideas! Even in practical life, he says, he only gradually began to use "generalisations that have since become the foundation of all I have done, or shall do, in Ireland." This whole section XXI of the "Four Years" seems to me crucial for Yeats's thought, as it goes on to explain:

"As life goes on we discover that certain thoughts sustain us in defeat, or give us victory, whether over ourselves or others, and it is these thoughts, tested by passion, that we call convictions. Among subjective men (in all those, that is, who must spin a web out of their own bowels) the victory is an intellectual daily re-creation of all that exterior fate snatches away, and so that fate's antithesis; while what I have called 'the Mask' is an emotional antithesis to all that comes out of their internal nature. We begin to live when we have conceived life as tragedy."

Here Yeats is telling us of the great difference between *Responsibilities* and *The Tower:* that the earlier active and dramatic poetry was a poetry of self and mask, while the later meditative poetry is also of mind and fate, of both emotion and intellect, a fuller and profounder victory to be discerned and won. Tragedy helps carry us to that victory, beyond the joy and pain of self, the ecstasy of anti-self and of anti-fate. Says Yeats, "even now, after twenty or thirty years, I feel at times that I have not recovered my natural manner" (p. 201): that is, his deliberative manner before the dramatic assertion of self.

"I know now that revelation is from the self, but from that age-long memoried self, that shapes the elaborate shell of the mollusc . . ." (p. 233). Dante and Villon present such revelation, reborn by art from the vision of fate and evil. "They and their sort alone earn contemplation, for it is only when the intellect has wrought the whole of life to drama, to crisis, that we may live for contemplation and yet keep our intensity" (p. 235). This is the bringing together of the originally antithetic values, the classical centaur shape, the joining as in Commodus of animal and human beauty (p. 267), which Yeats returns to Pater to acknowledge (pp. 257 ff.), and which he describes also in the half animal, half divine statues of Mausolus and his Queen, "where the luminous circle is motionless and contains the entire popular life" (pp. 274 and 131). So Yeats allows for the Savage God of the future as he envisions it, for "All creation is from conflict, whether with our own mind or with that of others, and the historian who dreams of bloodless victory, wrongs the wounded veterans" (p. 476).

As a veteran, in the 1920's, Yeats is able to spell out in prose what he has learned also in poetry, the possibility that in conflict art may include both sides. Essence and accident, quality and deed, comment and action, stasis and motion, epithet and verb, may hold together in the centaur shape the hoof of Dionysus and the head of Apollo. The great difference in the oppositions as they are spelled out after 1915 is not only their wider context, of fate and classic circumstance, but also their asserted combination in the vision of art. We may remember that in "Ego Dominus Tuus" Yeats wrote:

> The rhetorician would deceive his neighbours,
> The sentimentalist himself; while art
> Is but a vision of reality.

These three lines name the three stages we have seen in his concern: first, a traditional rhetorical smoothness and the fear of it; second, self-expression without intellect, as he has earlier defined his dramatic years for us; and third, the effort at vision, to avoid both these partial deceits of world and self by seeing both as reality.

"Ireland after Parnell," III, in the *Autobiography* clarifies this same series of stages for Ireland and his friends: from public rhetoric to private personality to the joining of this sweet with this bitter. "If we were, as I had dreaded, declamatory, loose, and bragging, we were but the better fitted—that declared and measured—to create unyielding personality, manner at once cold and passionate, daring long premeditated act; and if bitter beyond all the people of the world, we might yet lie—that too declared and measured—nearest the honeyed comb:

> 'Like the clanguor of a bell
> Sweet and harsh, harsh and sweet, . . .' "

So does the subjective and metaphysical spider become also, by declaration and measure, the objective and classical bee. The bee builds in the house of the stare, and darkness of soul gains sweetness in the strong and bitter verse.

The edition of Yeats's *Letters* edited by Allan Wade (1954) confirms by many more by-the-way comments as well as by a number of full explanations Yeats's own sense of two main changes in his style, the first away from reverie toward dramatic action, the second back toward meditation in a richer and more complex form, with his return to Ballylee. Time and again his early letters assert the need for realism over fantasy: for example, pages 180, 219, 354, 397, 402, 434, 460, 462, 466, 469, with transitional doubts, as on pp. 534, 568, 588, and then, after 1916 the joyful recognitions of the new mode of feeling, as on pages 624, 626, 633, 643–647, wherein fantasy, weakness, the feminine, the dark and the sea, even ceremony, need not be hated and rejected, but may be thought upon and loved. The full strength of the first assertion of change came with the publication of the *Works* in 1907; after that were variations of doubt until the new full recognition of 1917. A sequence of quotations will serve to exemplify the sequence of change in attitude:

First, the much-quoted note to Lady Gregory in 1903 (p. 397): "I was never so full of new thoughts for verse, though all thoughts quite unlike the old ones. My work has got far more masculine. It has more salt in it."

In support of this, the letters dating from 1902 and concerning Nietzsche's contrast of Dionysian sadness with Apollonian self-sufficiency and joy. "We possess nothing but the will and we must never let the children of vague desires breathe upon it nor the waters of sentiment rust the terrible mirror of its blade." (P. 434.)

And also in this assertive masculine vein: "I once cared only for images about whose necks I could cast various 'chains of office' as it were. They were so many aldermen of the ideal, whom I wished to master the city of the soul. Now I do not want images at all, or chains of office, being content with the unruly soul." (P. 469.)

After 1906 there were scattered signs of mellowing. Yeats wrote to Florence Farr (p. 472), "I shall get you to teach me meditation." And to his father, after railing against "generalisation" (p. 534), he yet ventures it (p. 568), and finally in 1914 temporizes (p. 588): "What you say is true about abstract ideas. They are one's curse. . . . Yet, in some curious way, they are connected with poetry or rather with passion, one half its life and yet its enemy." The next year, reporting reading the whole seven volumes of Wordsworth in the Dowden edition, he complained about the "reflective power," yet seemed to like the work, and may have been influenced by its prevailingly classical mode (p. 590). At any rate, the partial acceptance of abstractions marks the beginning of a basic turn.

By 1917 Yeats was planning to publish together his new poems *The Wild Swans* and his new philosophy, *An Alphabet,* in which to "Anima Hominis" of his dramatic period he had added "Anima Mundi": "I find the setting it all in order has helped my verse, has given me a new framework and new patterns. One goes on year after year gradually getting the disorder of one's mind in order and this is the real impulse to create." (P. 626.)

And again to Lady Gregory: "A very profound, very exciting mystical philosophy—which seems the fulfilment of many dreams and prophecies—is coming in strange ways to George and myself. . . . I live with a strange sense of revelation and never know what the day will bring. You will be astonished at the change in my work, at its intricate passions." (Pp. 643–644.) The passion is intricate now, rather than simple, as he had earlier tried to make it, because it contains its anti-self, Apollo with Dionysus, in explicit theory as well as in poetic practice.

The theory, *An Alphabet,* appeared under the title *Per Amica Silentia Lunae,* carrying us back to the beloved moon of Yeats's earliest balanced verse, the poems before 1895. *Under the Moon* had been their projected title. Under the moon, both early and late, Yeats found the "secret well of quietness" of those who "in youth wander in wild places" (p. 110), the classical poem joining clear heart and wild soul. Even before *A Vision* (Macmillan, 1938, p. 24), its metaphors of moon and sun had "helped me to hold in a single thought reality and justice." We may see then that Yeats was acutely conscious of both main changes discernible in the analysis of mode: the change from, and then toward, the mode of balanced predication. And this consciousness is present not only after the fact in the reminiscences of the *Autobiography,* but even step by step in the sequences of the *Letters.* For no other poet have we looked so closely at the detailed biography of relation between critical consciousness and practice: for some, the evidence is not available; for some, great change is not perceptible. For Yeats, the mode is a clear part of the life, and suggests further possibilities for the tracing of mode and style in individual biography.

CHAPTER TWELVE

THE RESOURCES OF LANGUAGE

LET ME suggest some possible connections between the selective modes discerned in this study and the further implicative powers of language, from three main points of view.

For the past three centuries we have been stressing an associationist psychology of language, emphasizing the range from image to concept, from concrete to abstract reference, from denotation to connotation in the literary senses of these terms as label and symbol. Art in its distinction from science, and poetry in its distinction from prose, have been seen to use language as concrete characteristically, to work at the image and symbol end of the scale, since the eye is the avenue to the heart, and sensation develops through association into significance. Dryden was one of the first to treat the image as the heart of poetry; Wordsworth's triad was "thoughts, feelings, images"; and still today the term *poetry* calls up first the term *imagery,* for Imagists, Symbolists,

Metaphysicists alike. Critics and philosophers as different from each other as Richards, Dewey, Santayana, Charles Morris, Kenneth Burke stress the presentative, immediate, iconic, symbolic force of sense image as poetic.

On the other hand, the basic distinction made by classical rhetoric was between language as literal and language as figurative, with art on the side of figure. Literal language is usual, whether abstract or concrete; figurative is unusual: archaic, foreign, coined, transformed—in some way altered from the usual expectation, noting likeness in unlikeness, as the poet is peculiarly able to do. From Aristotle through such Elizabethan handbooks as Puttenham's, and sparely still in rhetorics today, figurative language, trope, rather than image, is treated as poetry's essential. Some present scholars like Spurgeon and Tuve and Wheelwright blur the two distinctions, treating of metaphor only when it is concrete, of image particularly when it is achieved by metaphor. But basically the two kinds of distinction rest upon different interests: the associational, in psychological truth of impression and conception; the rhetorical, in the truth of natural order as seen in classes and in definitional procedures.

A third kind of distinction is made today particularly by linguists with semantic interests, between descriptive and normative language, between neutral and evaluative, with poetry as especially normative and evaluative because of its strong emotional force. So as eighteenth-century associationism stressed the aesthetic of imaging power of poetic language, and as classical rhetoric stressed the cognitive or double-knowing power, so semantics stresses the emotive, singling out a force which the others had assumed in impression or type.

The point most needing clarification, I think, is that poetry is not bound to any one of these theories and ranges, but shares in all. The poem need not use a merely aesthetic or a merely emotive or a merely figurative material; it is shaped out of all the possible characteristics of language, and no single sort of language may be called poetic by definition. The scientist indeed may use his language as evaluatively or as figuratively as the poet does. The clear-cut Dewey-Richards debate whether it is science or poetry that "orders, controls, consolidates" makes a good example of the possibilities. In the first place we must recognize, and usually do, that every poem conditions its own language by its arrangement. In the second place, we must remember that the language which the poem selects as well as arranges is already conditioned in structure and emphasis by the beliefs of its general users. Language is not a raw and amorphous material, but individually and socially shaped, and contains within it, at least in the Indo-European forms that we know, all the working characteristics which have from time to time been attributed to poetry alone or prose alone. A word may be used concretely or abstractly, neutrally or normatively, literally or figuratively, as the need demands and as the context guides.

Consider for example the word *man* in the sentence "A man is walking down the street." There is always a general assumption of a neutral "dictionary" reference for this word. We feel we know in general what a man is, at the descriptive or denotative or literal points on the respective scales. A man, of generally visualizable shape, pointoutable, not a cat and not a hero, walks down the street in simplest reference. This is the sense in which I have used *reference* in this study, as relatively independent of context, as preserving certain agreed-upon and definable characteristics throughout. *Man* makes very good material for poetry just as neutral as this; no term is simply used more often.

But further, depending upon the frame of reality and the chosen emphasis, the reference may be extended to meaning in the various ways we have noted. A preceding sentence may read, "A penguin waddles ahead of me in his comical upright position." Then "A man is walking down the street" may become metaphoric, *man* and even *walking* being substitute terms from another class, able to suggest the significant parallels, however few, between the classes. Metaphor acts upon unlikeness not of things but of kinds; some sense of continua, if not of natural classes, is necessary to all such substitution, because a play upon definition is being made in the stress on likeness of accidental rather than essential properties, or of sufficient rather than necessary conditions. It is in their necessary, their defining characteristics that penguins are unlike man, and their unresolvable unlikeness provides the basis for the few sufficient striking likenesses of metaphor; the nucleus and periphery of meaning are held in tension.

If, on the other hand, the details of sensory image or of symbolic implication are important, then the penguin will not do, and becomes a matter of verbal wit as it would have in the eighteenth century, which would prefer, "A man is walking down the street; strong and sinewy, he reminds me of my youth, or of Youth." He works here along a line from sense impression to concept of significance. Prepared for, he could be treated as symbol, as Mallarmé treated *l'azur,* or as objective correlative—"for all the history of grief."

Thirdly, our sentence may read, "Out in the west where men are men, a man is walking down the street." Here the implications are normative—by *man* one means the best, the essence, and a lot of men walking around under the descriptive definition are not "really" men at all. "The times aren't as good as they used to be, and they never were," is a fine example of such usage recognized, as is Gertrude Stein's rose. Our grammar itself allows for the normative, in optative subjunctive verb constructions, and in the comparative-superlative forms of adjectives. While poets naturally exercise their sense of value in the very selection of terms to use, selecting *man* to mention thousands of times more often than *penguin,* they do not by that very selection make the use normative, for they may be wishing to shape a substance they treat as neutral; rather more often it is the critics who use a normative terminology, employing "this is a *poem"* for "this is a good poem." While poets may wish to use some normative materials and to shape some normative wholes, like cognitive, or like aesthetic, the only one they are bound to by definition, so far as I can see, is the aesthetic whole, toward which even a nonaesthetic material may undergo transformation.

These three resources of language, the normative, figurative, and symbolic, extend the relative neutralities of definition by greater or less degree of emphasis upon defining characteristics. The normative stresses and intensifies certain qualities considered essential by definition; it is a centripetal force. The symbolic may stress necessary traits also, but usually fewer, and in centrifugal association. The figurative stresses accidental, sufficient, traits, by substitution setting up a relation between two centers; it thus adds to or "ornaments" the natural, while the normative embodies the natural, and the symbolic suggests it. A neutral usage would require a synonym of necessary and sufficient qualities; a normative, one of intensified necessary qualities; a symbolic, one of selected and perhaps attenuated necessary or sufficient qualities; and a figurative, one of substitution on the basis of merely sufficient qualities, likeness within fundamental unlikeness. As a poem dominantly figurative consider Wyatt's "Lover Beseecheth His Mistress":

Forget not yet the tried intent
Of such a truth as I have meant;
My great travail so gladly spent,
    Forget not yet!

Forget not yet when first began
The weary life ye know, since whan
The suit, can service none tell can;
    Forget not yet!

Forget not yet the great assays,
The cruel wrong, the scornful ways,

The painful patience in delays,
    Forget not yet!

Forget not! oh! forget not this,
How long ago hath been, and is
The mind that never meant amiss,
    Forget not yet!

Forget not then thine own approv'd,
The which so long hath thee so lov'd,
Whose steadfast faith yet never mov'd:
    Forget not this!

The terms of this poem are almost wholly abstractions; that is, references to concept. The piling up of and design of abstractions is so strong, in fact, that the slight deviation at the end becomes climactic, when in the line "Whose steadfast faith yet never mov'd," *steadfast,* at first taken abstractly, is seen to imply a direct action, a concrete translation into *never mov'd*. The simple abstract reference is so little extended in any direction that the slightest extension becomes effective. So the metaphoric hyperbole of "none tell can" and "never . . . never" casts an implication of superlative upon all the merely positive terms. As a whole, the words are not much "loaded," not much extended from a literal center. It is the sound pattern and the sentence pattern which provide the strong reinforcement of the hyperbole and help achieve a wholly figurative poem, a piece of fiction wrought out of the literal relationship by trope. In such an effort, concreteness may be useful but nearly irrelevant; the poets who are working carefully and precisely along one range of linguistic powers are apt, that is, to use other powers slightly and with relative nonchalance. What we assume provides the nonexploited background to what our interest focuses upon. So Wyatt uses abstract and normative language toward metaphoric ends.

We may note that commonly in the mode of metaphysical poetry in the seventeenth or nineteenth centuries, the bias is put on conceptual language by metaphoric construction. In the eighteenth and twentieth centuries sublime, the bias is symbolic, on fairly concrete and often figurative materials. In classical eras, the bias is normative, upon literal materials. The figurative would seem to be the most verbal construction, and the symbolic associative the least.

Keats's "Bright Star" provides a useful example of the symbolic, because it is briefer than most of its forebears of Milton, Thomson, or Collins and less intricate than its successors of Pound and Thomas, yet like these it emphasizes the embodiment of concept in image and the adjectival qualities of image.

> Bright star! would I were steadfast as thou art—
> Not in lone splendour hung aloft the night,
> And watching, with eternal lids apart,
> Like Nature's patient, sleepless Eremite,
> The moving waters at their priestlike task
> Of pure ablution round earth's human shores,
> Or gazing on the new soft-fallen mask
> Of snow upon the mountains and the moors—
> No—yet still steadfast, still unchangeable,
> Pillow'd upon my fair love's ripening breast,
> To feel forever its soft fall and swell,
> Awake for ever in a sweet unrest,
> Still, still to hear her tender-taken breath,
> And so live ever—or else swoon to death.

We may recognize the *bright star,* the *night,* the *waters,* the *mountains,* the terms of *eternal, pure,* and *forever,* the motion of *rise* and *fall,* all as characteristics of the sublime mode, and we may see then also how the function of these terms is primarily imagistic with symbolic overtones. The star is seen as image; its overtones are of steadfastness, an associated rather than a definitional quality. The moving waters are seen to wash, but felt also to wash sacredly. The fair love's breast is an image of softness, a symbol of eternal breath. The very centering of interest in sense impression, as in much modern symbolist poetry, leads to the implication of concept behind the sense, and often thus to associated sense, to personal connotation, to adjectival harmonics of related qualities and synaesthetics.

The balanced mode within classical style moderates between these extremes of predicative metaphor and of adjectival image-symbol, giving us rather a close to literal statement, working within a frame of normative acceptance of optatives and superlatives. Yeats's "Her Praise" is an example:

> She is foremost of those that I would hear praised.
> I have gone about the house, gone up and down
> As a man does who has published a new book,
> Or a young girl dressed out in her new gown,
> And though I have turned the talk by hook or crook
> Until her praise should be the uppermost theme,
> A woman spoke of some new tale she had read,
> A man confusedly in a half dream
> As though some other name ran in his head.
> She is foremost of those that I would hear praised.
> I will talk no more of books or the long war
> But walk by the dry thorn until I have found
> Some beggar sheltering from the wind, and there
> Manage the talk until her name come round.
> If there be rags enough he will know her name
> And be well pleased remembering it, for in the old days,

Though she had young men's praise and old men's blame,
Among the poor both old and young gave her praise.

The first and refrain lines are fully and explicitly normative. Then the casual neutrality of "I have gone about the house" is given heavy norm by the familiar and loving types, the proud author and the young girl. We respond in that we accept the sense of norm for type. Then the poem grows in its concentration toward praise, by the abandoning of other topics, and by the eventual focus on the most specific term *rags,* not as image or figure but as most minute representative of the norm of the poor, who most literally, yet also characteristically, gave her praise. In this poem, predications and modifications are balanced, because neither subordination of concept nor qualification of concept is the function of the sentence structure primarily, but rather an effort at essentialization of concept, in the classical belief that such essentialization is possible: the belief in "embodiment" rather than knowledge of the truth, expressed in Yeats's very last letter.

Reference, even in its barest selection, rests in belief; so that before we even look at patterning, at the complications of theme and tone in the full arrangements of style, we may see in the simplest presences of terms themselves, in their proportioning and their various possibilities of intensification, some of the bases of their use in some of our assumptions about value and reality. Our native active and thoughtful mode is visible at once in lively verbs and in metaphorical extensions, that is, in both clausal and figurative subordinations which rest in the belief of metaphysically subordinate and microcosmic man. Our sublime and rare extremes of the eternal, as distinct from the temporal, are visible at once in our epithets of cosmos and seer, in our images which are symbols of the ineffable, and rest in the belief of a receptive and prophetic man. Our classical essentializing of human situations is visible at once in the balances of human terms and norms, the structure between clausal and phrasal, the location between microcosm and macrocosm in the level world, and rests in our belief in man as able to achieve his own balances.

The range from a word to a belief is a vast range, but a word itself may span the distance, as an adjective suggests, a verb conveys, a noun essentializes, in symbol, figure, or norm, the fullest possible resources of understanding.

If it is possible for us to conceive of continuities of usage, from parts of speech to sentence structures, to extensions by figure, norm, and symbol, to modes, styles, eras, and beliefs, in certain recurrent configurations of language in poetry, then we may be persuaded to ask certain questions about poetry as history. Perhaps poetry gives us history in an intensive form—the shape of values selected and stressed by artistic forces. Perhaps the terms and structures which a poet most cares about tend to be those which a group, even an era, most cares about, as they represent the basic choices of the time. The language we speak, and even more the language we versify, may be seen to be a loaded language, carrying the weight of chosen values.

We may be able to see, then, in close detail the process of progression and change from one frame of values to another, as we have seen the diminution of metaphysical values in the poetry of the eighteenth century, and the gradual return of these same values in the nineteenth, or as we have seen the steady slow emergence of sublime thought and expression into English poetry of the eighteenth-century revolutionary period, and the persistence of mediating forces of moderation from time to time. We surmise, if artistic choice provides a valid clue, that there are various kinds of change from generation to generation, or even within one life. The change by pull, driving toward a new force, as toward eighteenth-century sublimity by Milton; the change by push, intensification of an old force, as of sublimity by Blake; the change by reaction or opposition, as against sublimity by Coleridge; the change by moderation, as toward or away from sublimity by Dryden or Wordsworth. In the early twentieth century, the push by Frost and Auden; the reaction and possibly the pull toward new forces by Pound, Sitwell, Thomas; the moderation by Yeats, Eliot, and Stevens.

René Wellek says in his *History of Modern Criticism* (p. 8): "We must first recognize that there is an inner logic in the history of ideas; a dialectic of concepts. An idea is easily pushed to its extreme or converted into its opposite. Reaction against the preceding or prevailing critical system is the most common driving force of the history of ideas, though we cannot predict what direction a reaction will take or tell why it should come at a certain time. One has to leave something to the initiative of the individual, the luck of the gifted man devoting his thought to a particular matter at a given time."

Pierre Guiraud says in *Les Caractères statistiques du Vocabulaire* (Paris, 1954, p. 74): "Je crois que toute œuvre comporte un cohésion et une économie internes que se reflètent dans le style; et que certains traits du langue, convenablement choisis, sont révélateurs, selon l'expression de M. L. Spitzer, de cet 'etymon spirituel' vers lequel ils doivent nous conduire."

Combining these ideas, allowing for forces perhaps more complex than dialectic, yet of simple substance as well as mysterious spirit, we may learn the relationships of the luck of the gifted man to the luck of his language and his generation. While some historians suggest an autonomy for poetry, or for art, one may learn that through language poetry is bound to its society and shares in the terms and choices of that society; but the possible ways of correlation are still to be learned. We may study the relation of poetic language to prose language, and to musical and graphic forms. We may study poetic mode as a part of biography. At very least, because of the stability of certain configurations, we may learn to recognize certain terms and structures as representative of certain whole forms and attitudes. As a word, like an atom, is itself a complex universe of meanings, with certain centers and extensions, so language has its molecular stabilities and persistences, its organizations and variations; so we may learn from it not as a miscellany of usage but as a pattern of value.

At least we may consider the pattern set forth by this study of language forms and structures in the poetry of individuals and their eras: first, a clear agreement in English usage, an active moral and metaphysical predication giving way to an appreciative balanced mode and later to a celebrative phrasal one, to recur again in the strength of the nineteenth-century ballad and the twentieth-century metaphysical poem; second, the mode which has had no literary name but "pre-romantic," but which we have called the "sublime" phrasal and adjectival kind of its own, predominating through a century and beyond, into ours; third, the classical mode of balance, not merely a combining of two extremes, but a characteristic complex of vocabulary, sound, and structure, occurring between extremes. Then also the whole motion through these, toward the present, of the increasing force of a concrete and specific language. And finally the singularity of every poet, who, while he shares something with many, and much with a few, has always his own distinguishing qualities of combination, his habits of word and measure, of phrase and sentence.

CHAPTER THIRTEEN

STYLE AND CHANGE

As we discuss motives of change, other than destiny and evolution, the starting and leaving off of styles in art may come clearer for us. We see that it is not necessarily a man's fate to paint a picture in a certain way any more than that it is his arbitrary and individual decision. Artists—as men—participate in their times, the motives, purposes, rebellions, reactions of their times, so that the combination of individuality and generality in any work is one of its wonders, yet one of its most natural traits.

The "convention and revolt" in poetry, of which John Livingston Lowes wrote early in the century, is more and more being understood and delineated by art historians, today, with especial skill by James Ackerman in the *Journal of Aesthetics:* Traditions, materials, techniques, all are part of the chosen solutions to problems which the artist undertakes for himself, the product of a tension between the stability of human schemes and the capacity for human inventions and individualization. A style successively develops an original solution, moving away from it, not toward an inevitable ideal further solution, but toward individual modifications of the original or of its modifications, until some sense of satisfaction and then of lessened interest may be reached. So the growth of a style is seen by many as a motion away, rather than a motion toward. Of the artist, Mr. Ackerman says, "He accepts and rejects aspects of what he finds in things about him and he adds something of his own. By his choice and by his contribution he moves a step—sometimes a leap—away from the past. . . . In his terms the future is a void—how can he move toward it?" (*Journal of Aesthetics,* Spring, 1962, p. 231.)

I would propose that we do not have to abandon one of these in favor of the other; that, indeed, we may discern not one or two but three basic pushes and pulls made by the work of art in its temporal context. I would offer evidence from linguistic and sociological studies like those of Mentré and Agnes Young. The first premise is that there is some working unity to a generation; the second, that generations differ in their relation to each other, sometimes progressive, sometimes reënforcing, sometimes reactionary, and that these require looks not only backward, not only forward, but all around.

A. Duraffour's study of pronunciation in a French community, "Trois phénomènes de nivellement phonétique en Franco-Provençal" (*Bulletin de la société de linguistique de Paris* XXVII, 1927), shows unity of pronunciation not in community or in family, but in the three generations: over sixty, under thirty, and between. R. Menéndez Pidal's *Origines del Español* (Madrid, 1926), shows that in certain groups of early years the uses of older forms are decreased, uses of newer forms increased, with much vacillation in the middle years.

"It seems therefore, that the 'generation' is a real unit of measurement of linguistic change . . . life seems to create groups of those who are fully employed, and those who are coming forward to their responsibilities . . . At some date around thirty years the young man or woman acquires the responsibilities which continue till about sixty, and which make all between thirty and sixty in a special sense contemporaries." (William J. Entwhistle, *Aspects of Language,* London, 1953, p. 36.)

Let us look at the way the major language of poetry moves with its users, the adjectives, nouns, verbs most used by a poet, at least ten times or more in a representative thousand lines. A summary list is appended. Consider the poetry of England in its first great era, the Elizabethan. The basic vocabulary was established by this time. Poets agreed largely on the emphasized terms for their religious, courtly, and pastoral worlds. Then Spenser, Sidney, Sylvester, Campion contributed an abundance of rich emotions and values in newly stressed words like *muse, virtue, joy, new, sad, happy,* so that those who wrote in the first years of the new century, Ben Jonson, John Donne, George Sandys, Fletcher, Wither, Herrick, Quarles, Herbert, Carew, Shirley, were able to look about them and to discard and add frugally as they wished. They added a few verbs, *meet, appear, praise, write;* and discarded some courtly trappings from the past: *gold, fortune, hell, knight, lady, cruel, desire.* Their successors in turn dropped the formal feelings of the pastoral: *gentle, shepherd, faith, grief, woe,* and so on, to add a more classical vocabulary of *care, fate, soft, sense, shine.* Two early conventions were thus dropped, as Ackerman suggests, by a sort of wearying and rejection, and more general action and sensation were added, with a sense of freer choice. An equilibrium was established by mid-century.

Then the poets born in mid-century and publishing toward its end, after the Restoration, set a new tone. They dropped little, but added much, a whole new set of meanings: Roscommon's *wild,* Oldham's *vain,* Blackmore's *human, various, land, sky,* Pomfret's *charm, mighty, delight.* Here, perhaps prepared for by the classic sensory terms, we have the beginnings of men's, of poets', sense of and response to the natural world in its scope and variety. The new tendency moves quickly. Within a generation, *sky,* for example, will become a term of major importance for half a dozen poets or more. Yet Blackmore, the innovator, was berated by the men of his age as a bad poet with foolish ideas. Is there not here a sense of the future, felt, derided, yet accepted and moving forward?

The next generation, turning into the eighteenth century, confirms this feeling by dropping more than it adds, as if clearing the way, ex post facto, for materials already initiated—very concisely and critically now abandoning the terms of intellect, representing an outmoded faith, which Blackmore has supplanted. In the face of the rich new natural vocabulary, the old terms of human concept and action go: *common, true, sin, town, sight, word, wit, begin, write,* these and others are lost to poetry—not so many to be lost again for a hundred years. It is a milestone of change, this abrupt abandoning of a conceptual vocabulary in favor of a sensory descriptive one. There is room in poetry now, through the eighteenth century, for new words of two main kinds: more of the words of nature which we have already seen begun, like *deep, wide, green, golden, dark, silent, mountain, field, shade, song, breathe, pass,* many of which will persist into the present, and words of an artifice in nature which will last no more than a century: *fool, maid, nymph, scene, behold.*

Now again in the late eighteenth century, in the generation born in the 1730's to 1760's, we have the phenomenon, as in the two preceding late centuries, of addition before subtraction; of a minimum of discarding of major terms, preceding and accompanying a maximum of additions. First Sidney and Spenser, then Blackmore and Pomfret, now Crabbe, Bowles, Blake, make the step forward—this time into a new inner world: *cold, pale, black, white, grey, own, home, child, mother, morning, memory, foot, ear, pleasure, sorrow, wave, wood, feel, hold, sleep, turn, weep.* It is in this world, with its more recently added outward counterparts like *moon, star, water, body, bird, wing, shadow, house,* and especially with the innovations of mid-nineteenth century *dead, red, rain, stone,* that we still reside. For again, since this great period of innovation, the process has been one of a relieving loss of words—all through the nineteenth century the abandoning of the formalism and enthusiasm of the eighteenth: the *noble, sacred, divine, gentle, proud, wise, woe, pleasure, fame, virtue, sense, scene, mighty, appear, behold,* which we have not so long ago seen introduced. In like manner, American poets abandoned their eighteenth-century *shore, stream, strong, beautiful, holy,* in favor of *snow* and *leaf* and *stone* and the English *nothing*. If the pattern continues, it will be the poets now growing up who will initiate a new central subject matter in primary vocabulary.

In recapitulation we may see the most new words added by minor poets like Sidney, Sylvester, Blackmore, Bowles, Swinburne, born in mid-century and writing toward its end. We may see adding before diminishing, as if, in the next generation, the first of the new century, the new words finally pushed out the old. And finally the publishing middle generation provides the least activity and the fewest extremes, seeming to capitalize on, to make use of, the balance provided them. So the first generation seeks out the new, from some new source like the classical; the second discards, criticizes, dislikes, clears out. The third profits from both, tends to confirm.

By what justification do I speak of "first" generation and imply an order? Historically, the first considerable number of poets writing in modern English was the group born in the middle of the sixteenth century, writing at the end, in the famed Elizabethan golden era. Spenser, Sidney, Chapman, Daniel, Drayton, Sylvester, Marlowe, Shakespeare, Campion, these are all great names, and close together in age. Before them, modern English vocabulary in poetry has had about a century to establish itself—from the Ballads on through the pastoralists like Googe and Breton. So, first of all, it is not necessary that the Elizabethans add a new vocabulary, but they do: it is our first soundly characterizing addition. The next such major addition comes in each of the following end-centuries, with the "neo-classicists" like Blackmore and Pomfret, the romantics like Crabbe, Blake, and Bowles, and the Victorians like Swinburne. In these generations, in each of four centuries, new material is major—about half of all additions throughout—and loss of material gradually develops. In the generations following, that is, those born at the turn of each century and publishing at the beginning of the next, added and abandoned material are both moderate. And thirdly, for those born early and publishing midway, additions are minimal; losses strong at first, then weak.

Content, too, supports the pattern, even if historically one had chosen to start elsewhere, as indeed I first tried to. That is, the innovations of the Elizabethan are of a new sort, looking to classical materials in a way that had not been done before, whereas the next two generations first slightly modified this large step, as much by what they gave up as by what they added, and so for each century.

It is not so much necessity or loss, then, which seems the mother of invention, as a turn to new material, a refreshment, it may be, from classical literature, or from natural world, or from inner self, or from an objective correlative. Only after the new world has been named and recognized, is the old explicitly repulsed, and most strongly in the third, the old, generation when omission is for a while almost as strong as innovation, until both subside to a minimum of activity before the new youthful period of search. We cannot draw here a parallel to the seasons: we do not find a tentative spring, then a full summer, then a slow decline; but rather we see repeated in four centuries the pattern of sudden burst of new energy—summer at once—then stages of lessening and consolidation, more as we think of the human analogy.

But we should not merely think in groups and tendencies. What about the individual artist, whom Mr. Ackerman wisely keeps his eye upon? Of one hundred and twenty poets, about three fourths make some contribution to change by addition or elimination. And of these ninety, a third are both first and last to use terms, while many more initiate only, and only a few merely cling to the past—most notably the nineteenth-century Tupper who was the last to use a whole slate of terms! Campion was a fine turner-over of the language; so also were Herbert, Pomfret, Crabbe, Bowles, Wordsworth, Moore, Keats. How did they work?

Wordsworth worked, as Crabbe, Blake, Bowles, Burns, Coleridge, Moore did, first to bring in the natural world to poetry, but second not to lose the more formal processes by which the eighteenth century had already made this attempt. So his additions were of the words *young, tree,* and *pray,* his retention of *mountain* for the last time. Note how he hovers, his poetry stepping into the new simplicity without losing the old ceremony. Keats followed in the use of *tree,* participated also in the new use of *moon, dream, star,* and added his own *wing.* But also, like Wordsworth, he was the last to retain a number of formal eighteenth-century terms of scope and feeling: *divine, pleasure, wide, woe.* In the poetry of both we can hear this very richness of tone which comes from exploring the new without letting go of the old—an abundance and an ambiguity.

> There is a blessing in the air,
> Which seems a sense of joy to yield
> To the bare trees, and mountains bare,
> And grass in the green field.

This is the simple direction and simplicity so new and strange in Wordsworth's time. And into this bare world, Wordsworth draws the old poetic mountains, in the eighteenth century more grand, more awesome, more sublime, domesticating them here in a powerful way which may indeed lose for them their place of awe.

Keats on the other hand gives to the new words, *star, tree, wing,* the old awe.

> Tall oaks, branch charmèd by the earnest stars,
> Dream, and so dream all night without a stir,

Save from one gradual solitary gust
Which comes upon the silence and dies off,
As if the ebbing air had but one wave.

So his *woe* is too huge for *mortal tongue,* his *wide* is a *wide wilderness,* a *wide quietness,* his *rest divine, upon exalted couch,* his *wings, silver, argent, angelic.* So the push of the past can be tangible in new sensibility, the pull of the future strong in old forms and references.

When we describe a style, we need to know what combination it makes of these forces—the power of the past, poise of the present, potentiality of the future. The individual artist, with some influence from the state of art in his generation, decides whether to try to reach out for something new, or to help establish the new just reached for, or to value the old and familiar before it is ignored and rejected. One generation, one individual, moves away from the hardened strictures of another; one strives to strengthen the tentative efforts of another. How do we know our future? Like our past, it is all around us.

MAIN USES ADDED AND DROPPED BY POETS IN SUCCESSIVE GENERATIONS

1470	1500	1530	1570	1600	1630	1670	1700	1730	1770	1800	1830
	Add:	19	6	8	12	9	10	25	12	3	6
Basic ANV (Initial major uses)	96 + 26	new	meet	care	cloud	nymph	green	foot	strange	shadow	dead
		proud	appear	fate	hour	fool	sing	home	bird	last	bed
		sad	pride	wind	age	seem	breathe	hold	body	house	watch
		happy	voice	wake	wild	pass	leave	own	moon		red
		long	praise (v)	soft	vain	maid	golden	child	water		rain
		muse	write	sense	human	deep	silent	pleasure	dream		stone
		sight		shine	various	wild	truth	feel	star		
		virtue		poet	land	behold	dark	black	woman		
		bright			sky	mountain	field	pale	blue		
		sacred			charm		shade	morning	dim		
		grow			mighty			sleep	the dead		
		divine			delight			turn	wing		
		air						weep			
		earth						mother			
		sea						cold			
		joy						white			
		part						ear			
		fly						snow			
		move						wave			
								word			
								gray			
								memory			
								young			
								tree			
								pray			

1470	1500	1530	1570	1600	1630	1670	1700	1730	1770	1800	1830
	Drop:	5	7	6	6	12	2	7	11	10	11
		law	knight	gentle	look	word	work	fame	noble	woe	wise
		people	gold	shepherd	grace	wit	flame	foe	muse	proud	teach
		ground	lady	faith	face	fall		please	sacred	divine	virtue
		father	fortune	woe	show	true		move	meet	fly	sense
		fame	cruel	seek	place	common		bold	pride	appear	mighty
			desire	grief	part	begin		praise (v)	care	wake	nymph
			hell			town		various	fate	scene	fool
						sin			age	wide	maid
						prince			vain	shade	behold
						kind			charm	pleasure	ear
						sight			mountain		pray
						write					

CHAPTER FOURTEEN

THE POETRY OF PRAISE: AN AMERICAN MODE

OFTEN WE think of the main tradition in American poetry as that of the intense and cryptic metaphors of Emerson, Dickinson, Frost, and Eberhart, and we think of the very opposite style of Whitman as almost alien, unexplainable. Under the scrutiny of the metaphysical new critics for whom irony and paradox are major criteria of value, the loose clusterings of *Leaves of Grass* seem to become an historical anomaly.

What I should like to try briefly is to describe the historical nature of the high style which we see not only in Whitman but also in Anne Bradstreet, in Whittier, in Pound and Hart Crane, to suggest its essential differences in structure and vocabulary from other basic American styles, and to suggest what are its powers for our future.

The classical rhetoricians distinguished three sorts of style- the low or colloquial, the middle observational and meditational, the high, ceremonial. Critics today have not taken these distinctions as useful, because they have wanted to treat all poetry as a function of the first or second, low or natural, styles. For example, T. S. Eliot, though he has made allowances for Milton, and though he defines three different *voices* in poetry, makes these voices all non-Miltonic, all versions of dramatic colloquial poetry. The high style has been ignored, or at best, since Pope's *Peri Bathous,* has had an unfavorable press. Yet if we think of the high style also as *deep,* not only as empyrean but as subterranean and submarine, we may recognize its serious function for the present day. To clear and polished surfaces, it adds depths, however murky; to the objectivities of thought, action, and the thing in itself, it adds the subjectivity of inward feeling tumultuously expressed. Like the word *altus* in Latin, which means both high and deep, it relates the gods of the solar system to the gods of the solar plexus. Indeed it is one of the three great modes of poetry through time, and we may look to see how, historically, it has come so strongly into practice in America in its special complex of sound-structure, sentence-structure, and sense.

When American poetry began with the American revolutions of the seventeenth and eighteenth centuries, it was a poetry not of revolt but of enthusiasm, not analysis of America's situation but panegyric for the American land. In a century and a half it has not materially changed; despite the fashions of irony, drama, and complex involvement, in the present day, still a prevailing tone is praise; and still a prevailing substance, the country's bounty and beauty. "My country 'tis of thee, Sweet land of liberty, I love thy rocks and rills, Thy woods and templed hills . . ." These words have prospered and endured longer and stronger than the militant political ones for "Columbia, the Gem of the Ocean," of "Oh, say, can you see by the dawn's early light What so proudly we hailed at the twilight's last gleaming." Our popular care has been not so much for the America of conflict, trouble, and doubt, as for the America of triumphant abundance. "From the mountains, to the prairies, to the oceans white with foam."

Thinking of the satiric models of the late eighteenth century, of

Pope, for example, whom American gentlemen idolized; thinking of America's own native skepticism in the later generation of Emerson and Holmes; and thinking of the jazz of the twentieth century, we may well call into doubt any generalization about our poetic tradition until we look at its sources.

In the first place, consider the nature or natures of English poetry from which America stemmed, the poetry, that is, of the Renaissance of the sixteenth and seventeenth centuries: we can think what it is like if we think of Chaucer and the Chaucerian tradition: a lively, active, humorous, and intensely human poetry, with people in it, and the sense of their relationships, their stations, high and low, with lords, knights, ladies, kings, fathers and sons living, loving, seeking, giving, taking, telling, in a world of interaction. This world of Skelton, Sackville, the pastoralists and the satirists came to a narrower lyrical focus in two ways: in the specific relation of a courtier to his lady, the poetry of courtly love and Donne's mockery of it; and in the specific relation of the poet to his God, as in the metaphysical verse of Herbert, Herrick, and Vaughan. Speaking either to lady or to God, the poet was colloquial, argumentative, dramatic; the lyric could be the scene from a play; and it was usually more figurative than literal in expression, using irony, exaggeration, and transformation of accepted categories to make its intellectual point. As a whole, this has been called the poetry of wit; there have been many admirers of it but few inheritors in America: none, except perhaps Frost, so close as Hardy or Auden in England.

Concurrent with this verse in the sixteenth and seventeenth centuries ran a kind which was consciously more classical, more objective and observational. It tended to use a long smooth line rather than intricate stanzas, and to describe rather than to argue, in the tradition of Virgil's *Georgics* or of Horace's *Satires*. For a while in England, its function was mainly satiric or deliberative: to mark the fall of a prince in history and cause, to analyze and mock something so specific as political factions or something so general as the foolishness and corruption of mankind; this was social poetry, and its greatest successful exponents were Dryden and Pope, whom the American colonists read avidly in order to keep track of what was wrong in London and the world, as they would read Arnold in the nineteenth century and T. S. Eliot in the twentieth. The more positive and cheerful descriptions of the land and its products, in the Virgilian tradition, grew up more slowly in England and for some reason less richly, but as they grew, served to support and strengthen a third kind of poetry which was just beginning to emerge, and which did not reach full force until the revolutionary and democratic eighteenth century, the poetry of rhapsody, the ode, hymn, dithyramb of praise. Familiar in the Homeric Hymns and in the Odes of Pindar, and powerfully joined by the Hebraic tradition of the Psalms, this was the form which grew in force from Spenser and Sylvester to More and Milton and which provided the whole basis of the vast odes of the eighteenth century, Thomson's pioneering book of *The Seasons,* the work of the Wartons, and Blake's *Prophetic Books.*

This third kind of English poetry, along with its more classical Virgilian counterpart, was what America brought across the ocean in full force. Not the earlier humanistic verse prevailed here, nor the satiric, nor even the religious and metaphysical work of the seventeenth century, traces of which we see in such early poets as Edward Taylor; but rather the newest, most revolutionary verse which England had to offer, the work of the Whig democrats, of the Protestants, and of the philosophers of benevolence like Shaftesbury and Locke, the work of men not more than a generation older than the first solid poetic group in America; the writers of the new nation, John Trumbull, Timothy Dwight, Philip Freneau, Joel Barlow, and their successors Sigourney, Percival, Drake, and Halleck. These took on wholeheartedly the new vocabulary of English rhapsody, and carried it into the present, while

England herself in the nineteenth century nearly abandoned this tradition, returning to it in the twentieth under the leadership of American augmentation and innovation.

This is not the pattern of relationship and development we are usually given by scholars, yet it is a believable one, if we remember some clear distinctions. First, both the religious verse and the social verse of the seventeenth century, which the Puritans might have brought with them directly, with their love of moral criticism and their sense of a personal god, was after all not *their* sort of verse, but indeed the verse they were fleeing, as it was aristocratic and intellectual rather than democratic and enthusiastic. The good Puritan book was the Bible itself, and works most reliant on Biblical language and concept, like Sylvester's translation of Du Bartas's *Divine Week,* for example, meant most to the first tentative and isolated poets of America like Anne Bradstreet. This "tenth muse lately sprung up in America" was more Hebraic than the other nine muses; and sought sometimes the high style of ceremony, not always the low style of colloquy, because she held strongly to Biblical and Pindaric tradition.

Also, the high style seemed suited to the high adventure of America. Remembering that a translation of Ovid's *Metamorphoses* was the first English poetry written on this continent, by George Sandys in Virginia, as early as 1616, we may realize that men's minds were attuned to the idea of marvels and transformations here, of richness and abundance and of a suitably rich diction. Not Horace's mellow humor, not Catullus's sophisticated individuality, but something rarer, if we must be classical, like Ovid or like Virgil, would do better; and nothing was too good.

Thirdly, the political mentor of the constitution makers was John Locke, and it is not unnatural that our poetical mentors should have been his friends and followers, successors to the revolution of 1688, not old-regime roundheads but new parliamentarians, libertarians, latitudinarians, believers in progress and the pursuit of happiness. Here was the psychology of sense and common sense, of the marvels of wonder and imagination; here was the philosophy of men born equal and much alike; here was the cosmic science which followed Newton and Boyle, seeing the universe in wider and wider terms; here was the belief in physical laws and universal truths.

These all fitted together, the alliance of Protestant with Whig in political enthusiasm, the sense of the high style, the philosophy of universals, in encouraging a general ceremonious American style, stressing not what was peculiar or individual, or singular in America, but what it shared with the universe at large, namely, nature itself, in its abundance and splendor. Eighteenth-century philosophers and critics had noted that the materials of satire were particularities, the oddities of men, the specific details which stood for trivia; by an inversion of logic, then, the poets in America felt that when they wrote about their country's own singularities they were in a sense mocking her—thus the many satiric poems, half-hearted in their specific characterizations which seemed to lead away from praise, yet eager to record the qualities and characteristics of the American scene.

Here was a dilemma for the poets: how to write a great and noble poem about a special place and situation, America, when universality not specialness was great and noble. The answer came gradually, in the stressing of those traits in which the country was not singular but was, rather, superlative, the traits of natural divine endowment. Once this pattern of emphasis was established, it was not broken even by those later nineteenth-century poets who cried for the romantic richness of distinguishing detail: they got no further complexity of human American character nor even more complexity of nature. There was a lot of talk about more bobolinks and grasshoppers for the realism of the scene, but poetry persisted in lofty generality, in the sublime and universal mode which crossed the Atlantic from England and established itself strongly on these shores in philosophic democracy, and protestant theology of praise of the works of God. We are often confused when we look back upon this transit, because we expect a low, modest, and sober plain style from puritans and democrats. But the eighteenth-century democracy of man was based in the universality of sense impressions, the common accessibility of beauty, and the development from sense to soul; the eighteenth-century religion of protestant dissent, while it opposed the artifice of stained-glass windows in churches, hailed with joy the art of nature as the most direct revelation of God's handiwork. So the high style of beauty and praise was considered natural.

Just how did this high style sound? We have heard it in the lofty passages of the Bible, possibly in Homer, Pindar, and Lucretius, and in English in Spenser, Sylvester, and Milton. But most precisely we may hear it in that work of their own day, which eighteenth-century American poets admired so profoundly and perpetuated so vigorously, James Thomson's poem *The Seasons*. Here are the introductory lines to his "Hymn on the Seasons." Notice the long rolling blank-verse invocation, the progressive round of scene and time, the sense of illimitable and almost inexpressible power, all characteristics of the sublime style.

> These, as they change, Almighty Father! these
> Are but the varied God. The rolling year
> Is full of thee. Forth in the pleasing Spring
> Thy beauty walks, thy tenderness and love.
> Wide flush the fields; the softening air is balm;
> Echo the mountains round; the forest smiles;
> And every sense, and every heart, is joy.
> Then comes thy glory in the Summer-months,
> With light and heat refulgent. Then thy sun
> Shoots full perfection through the swelling year:

The poem continues through the other seasons, and through the farthest reaches of the universe, and ends with a restatement of ineffable power:

I cannot go
Where universal love smiles not around,
Sustaining all yon orbs and all their suns;
From seeming evil still educing good,
And better thence again, and better still,
In infinite progression. But I lose
Myself in him, in light ineffable!
Come then, expressive Silence, muse his praise.

In an early preface to his poem "Winter," 1726, Thomson wrote what he thought about the state of poetry in the early eighteenth century, and what should be done about it. After his own century, more American poets than English believed in him and followed his advice. He said:

". . . Let poetry once more be restored to her ancient truth and purity; let her be inspired from heaven, and in return her incense ascend thither; let her exchange her low, venal trifling subjects for such as are fair, useful, and magnificent . . . Nothing can have a better influence towards the revival of poetry than the choosing of great and serious subjects, such as at once amuse the fancy, enlighten the head, and warm the heart. [Then he in effect anticipates and rejects the poetry of the Waste Land.]: To be able to write on a dry, barren theme is looked upon by some as the sign of a happy, fruitful genius:—fruitful indeed! like one of the pendant gardens in Cheapside, watered every morning by the hand of the Alderman himself . . . A genius fired with the charms of truth and nature is tuned to a sublimer pitch, and scorns to associate with such subjects . . . I know no subject more elevating, more amusing; more ready to awake the poetical enthusiasm, the philosophical reflection, and the moral sentiment, than the works of Nature. Where can we meet with such variety, such beauty, such magnificence? All that enlarges and transports the soul! . . ."

This was the belief which, though often in milder language, would prevail in American poetry, even into the work of the reformed Alderman of Cheapside, in the sublime passages of his *Four Quartets*, and into more youthful symbolic splendors of Ezra Pound, Hart Crane, and Richard Wilbur. It was a doctrine which met with tough opposition from English skeptics or even classicists from Dr. Samuel Johnson to Coleridge, Arnold, and Hulme; but it was a doctrine which found no great opposition on the new continent, rather a soil fertile for rich growth, with growing transcendentalism and modern imagism not stays but aids.

One might almost call it a doctrine native to America, because even a century before its enunciation by Thomson, it was practiced with enthusiasm by America's first muse, Anne Bradstreet. In her poem, "Contemplations," she writes the stiffer and simpler language of the seventeenth century and of Sylvester, but with the sweeping panegyric spirit of the century to come.

Here are the first two stanzas:

Some time now past in the autumnal tide,
  When Phoebus wanted but one hour to bed,
The trees all richly clad, yet void of pride,
  Were gilded o'er by his rich golden head;
Their leaves and fruits seemed painted, but were true
Of green, of red, of yellow, mixèd hue.
Rapt were my senses at this delectable view.

I wist not what to wish, yet sure, thought I,
  If so much excellence abide below
How excellent is He that dwells on high,
  Whose power and beauty by his works we know!
Sure He is goodness, wisdom, glory, light,
That hath this under world so richly dight.
More heaven than earth was here, no winter and no night.

Later in the poem Bradstreet devotes more famous lines to "I heard the merry grasshopper then sing/ The black-clad cricket bear a second part"; but these are not so closely American as her general spirit of praise: "More heaven than earth was here, no winter and no night."

In time with the ringing of the Liberty Bell, the positives grew more superlative and competitive, as in Dwight's "Greenfield Hill" (I, 1–41).

As round me here I gaze, what prospects rise?
Etherial! matchless! such as Albion's sons,
Could Albion's isle an equal prospect boast,
In all the harmony of numerous song,
Had tun'd to rapture, and o'er Cooper's hill,
And Windsor's beauteous forest, high uprais'd,
And sent on fame's light wing to every clime.
Far inland, blended groves, and azure hills,
Skirting the broad horizon, lift their pride.
Beyond, a little chasm to view unfolds
Cerulean mountains, verging high on Heaven,
In misty grandeur.

Then there was, in early romanticism and late, free modulation of line-structure and implication—as in Lydia Sigourney's "Tomb of a Young Friend":

I do remember thee.
                There was a strain
Of thrilling music, a soft breath of flowers
Telling of summer to a festive throng,
That fill'd the lighted halls. And the sweet smile
That spoke their welcome, the high warbled lay
Swelling with rapture through a parent's heart,
Were thine.
          Time wav'd his noiseless wand awhile,
And in thy cherish'd home once more I stood,

Amid those twin'd and cluster'd sympathies
Where the rich blessing of thy heart sprang forth,
Like the moss rose. Where was the voice of song
Pouring out glad and glorious melody?—
But when I ask'd for thee, they took me where
A hallow'd mountain wrapt its verdant head
In changeful drapery of woods, and flowers,
And silver streams, and where thou erst didst love,
Musing to walk, and lend a serious ear
To the wild melody of birds that hung
Their unharm'd dwellings 'mid its woven bowers.
Yet here and there, involv'd in curtaining shades
Uprose those sculptur'd monuments that bear
The ponderous warnings of eternity.

Or Timrod's "The Cotton Boll":

Yonder bird,
Which floats, as if at rest,
In those blue tracts above the thunder, where
No vapors cloud the stainless air,
And never sound is heard,
Unless at such rare time
When, from the City of the Blest,
Rings down some golden chime,
Sees not from his high place
So vast a cirque of summer space
As widens round me in one mighty field,
Which, rimmed by seas and sands,
Doth hail its earliest daylight in the beams
Of gray Atlantic dawns;
And, broad as realms made up of many lands,
Is lost afar

Behind the crimson hills and purple lawns
Of sunset, among plains which roll their streams
Against the Evening Star!
And lo!
To the remotest point of sight,
Although I gaze upon no waste of snow,
The endless field is white;
And the whole landscape glows,
For many a shining league away,
With such accumulated light
As Polar lands would flash beneath a tropic day!

At the same time, a larger more social sweep: as in Thomas Holly Chivers' "The Rising of the Nations":

Millions of millions now are groaning, groaning
  Beneath the grinding weight of Despotism,
While bloody Anarchy, unmindful of their moaning,
  Plunges them deeper into Hell's unsunned Abyssum!
While Earth, now slimed beneath his vile pollution,
  Echoes the wailings of their desolation,
Until the remnant, ripe for revolution,
  Answers the music of their soul's salvation,
Uttered by Liberty upon th'immortal Mountains,
  From all the vallies, out of every habitation—
Coming, like many rills from new-born Fountains
  Fresh opened in the Earth from long-descending rains,
Which, gathering into one great onward rushing river,
  Distending, overflows its banks, till all the plains
Are inundated with its everspreading waters—
  Still gathering volume as it flows forever;—
So did they gather in one mighty multitude,
  As if the Nations from the four great quarters

Of all the earth had migrated in one great flood,
  With one great common sympathy, to overthrow
  This mighty Monarch of the world—this foe
To human greatness—this great Devil to the Free—
This damned Abaddon of the Sons of Anarchy!

The sublime poets were political poets; they were moved by vast social forces, and exercised a public rhetoric, as Pindar did, for public purposes. For all of them in America, from Barlow and Trumbull on, we may let John Greenleaf Whittier do the speaking, for he spoke from the troubled middle of the century, with a passion we are still feeling. Here are some stanzas from his "Lines, Suggested by a Visit to Washington in the 12th Month of 1845":

With a cold and wintry noon-light,
  On its roofs and steeples shed,
Shadows weaving with the sunlight
  From the gray sky overhead,
Broadly, vaguely, all around me, lies the half-built town outspread.

Through this broad street, restless ever,
  Ebbs and flows a human tide,
Wave on wave a living river;
  Wealth and fashion side by side;
Toiler, idler, slave and master, in the same quick current glide.

Underneath yon dome, whose coping
  Springs above them, vast and tall,
Grave men in the dust are groping
  For the largess, base and small,
Which the hand of Power is scattering, crumbs which from its table fall.

Base of heart, they vilely barter
  Honor's wealth for party's place:
Step by step on Freedom's charter
  Leaving footprints of disgrace;
For to-day's poor pittance turning from the great hope of their race.

Then, after a vision of the South's anguish, and the nation's highest purposes, the final exhortation:

Let us then, uniting, bury
  All our idle feuds in dust,
And to future conflicts carry
  Mutual faith and common trust;
Always he who most forgiveth in his brother is most just.

From the eternal shadow rounding
  All our sun and starlight here,
Voices of our lost ones sounding
  Bid us be of heart and cheer,
Through the silence, down the spaces, falling on the inward ear.

Manifold traits of the sublime style are here: the visionary spirit and invocative tone, the irregular line length and harmonic use of sound, the sense of mankind as one great body, with personifiable characteristics, the exclamations and superlatives, and even the figures, of the restless river, the eternal shadow, and the voice of silence falling on the inward ear. I know none more directly representative of this whole American tradition than Whittier.

While in Whittier we have its representation, in Whitman we have its extreme. More visionary, more invocative, more adjectival, more cumulative and harmonic than any other poet in English, even more than Blake, Whitman is the great, and American, culmination of the sublime tradition. Each of us can recall a dozen or a hundred passages from *Leaves of Grass* which embody these traits we have been thinking of. To begin to quote is not to know where to end. But here is an early passage, "On Journeys through the States," with its free-swinging line and its all-encompassing attitude:

On journeys through the States we start,
(Ay through the world, urged by these songs,
Sailing henceforth to every land, to every sea,)
We willing learners of all, teachers of all, and lovers of all.
We have watch'd the seasons dispensing themselves and passing on,
And have said, Why should not a man or woman do as much as the seasons, and effuse as much?
We dwell awhile in every city and town,
We pass through Kanada, the North-east, the vast valley of the Mississippi, and the Southern States,
We confer on equal terms with each of the States,
We make trial of ourselves and invite men and women to hear,
We say to ourselves, Remember, fear not, be candid, promulge the body and the soul,
Dwell awhile and pass on, be copious, temperate, chaste, magnetic,
And what you effuse may then return as the seasons return,
And may be just as much as the seasons.

Every particular has its place in the list, every list its place in the whole poem, and every whole poem its place in geography and universe. Smallness and greatness are equal in this cycle of meaning. Through Whitman, Emily Dickinson, Marianne Moore and others, America has fostered the sense of size not only in greatness, but in smallness also, in the most minute and loving detail. As Whitman said in "Song of Myself,"

I chant the chant of dilation or pride,
We have had ducking and deprecating about enough,
I show that size is only development.

And therefore the gamut, the interest in degree, of small to large and little to great, in the careful and fond details of the most sweeping verse.

In a particular way, Whitman naturalized the sublime: he located it in individual bodies and souls, not only by specifying the sublime, but by generalizing and expanding the human. Like his contemporaries in America, he fostered the Whig poetizing of earth, sea, and land—the expanses of nature—and then in his own way gave them a human presence, in woman, mother, child; in water, which could be both human and natural, and in the human, natural counterparts of hair and grass. This sharing of physical values, this passiveness of holding and beholding, sleeping and waiting, has been characteristic of much poetry since Whitman—of Pound, Eliot, Lawrence, Crane, Roethke. While for Blake, Keats, and others before Whitman, sublime figures were externalized, for Whitman and those after him they were internalized; earth felt through body, body through earth.

As the historian Bancroft wrote to Prescott in 1848, in terms like Whitman's, "Go forth, then, language of Milton and Hampden, language of my country, take possession of the North American Continent! Gladden the waste places with every tone that has been rightly struck on the English lyre, with every English word that has been spoken well for liberty and for man! . . . Utter boldly and spread widely through the world the thoughts of the coming apostles of liberty, till the sound that cheers the desert shall thrill through the heart of humanity . . ."

I have been making here a number of generalizations which run counter to some standard descriptions of American poetry. I have suggested first that the Protestant-democratic style is not the plain English but the high Greek and Biblical style; second, that of two major and almost opposite Romantic styles it was again not the dramatic one of Coleridge but the high one of Thomson and Blake that most affected American nineteenth-century romanticism; third, that the prevailing balanced style in America, often called classical, represents a steady and conscious effort at compromise between extremes: between the lowly and plain in poetry, for which the country has so much affinity, and, at the other extreme, the sublime, the worshipful Sunday poetry early adopted and enthusiastically maintained; and fourth, that when the two nations separated politically at the end of the eighteenth century, it was America, not England, that carried on the eighteenth-century poetic tradition, and it is now America which is taking the lead in returning this tradition to England, with an increasing consolidation of interests and powers.

Let me now substantiate these suggestions in a way more precise than I have used heretofore, that is, with a description of the *language* of the two poetries since about 1800. Looking at representative work of the fifty leading poets of each nation in the past century and a half, we discover that to an amazing degree they share a common vocabulary; yet in the degree in which they differ we may learn a great deal about their differences in ideas. Most poets, we find, have about fifty words which they use with great frequency and consistency; these are terms of content—nouns, adjectives, and verbs—in addition to the connective and auxiliary terms which are most frequent. The repeated terms of content tend to indicate the major interests and attitudes of the poet: what he most cares about repeating, as poetry as an art of repetition. If every one of our hundred English and American poets had his own special fifty terms for emphasis, we would of course be lost in a welter of individuality, with something like one hundred times fifty, or five thousand major terms to consider. But in actuality poets seem to draw from the agreed-on terms of value in their time, and to share a good deal of substance in their writing, so that we may find that there are not five thousand but just about two hundred and fifty terms of substance on which at least four poets in this period agree, and of this number, one hundred and fifty, or three fifths, are agreed upon by both British and Americans. We may see then that we can very justly talk about modern English poetry, meaning both British and American since 1800, since in such large proportion its substance and its values are the same in both countries, and since common verse forms and sentence-structures support the likeness. (See Tables.)

The shared terms are words of basic human values, as one would expect: such adjectives as *good, great, old, sweet, high, true, happy, little, long, deep, wide,* and the colors *black, white, green,* and *red;* such subjects as *god, man, love, time, nature, day, night,* and *world;* such actions as *coming* and *going, giving* and *taking, making* and *seeing.* The main course of development of these terms in usage through five centuries from Chaucer to the present has been from the more abstract to the more concrete; that is, from words like *good, true,* and *wise* to the colors we have mentioned, or from nouns like *fortune* and *virtue* to nouns like *wood, water,* and *stone.* This is the field of agreement within the language, and it is a large one. Now how about the field of disagreement, that Atlantic which separates the language of the two bodies of poetry?

If we think about what English poetry was like at about 1800, the time of the new nation in America, we can almost guess the difference. On the one hand in England was the strong sublime tradition of the eighteenth century, of Milton, Thomson, Blake, Keats. On the other hand was the new metaphysical revolution against this old sublimity, led by Coleridge and Wordsworth in the *Lyrical Ballads,* by Byron and by Thomas Moore in their lyrics, and later by the Pre-Raphaelites: this was active psychological romanticism of the ballad tradition. It was this second kind which, despite the efforts of Longfellow, did not stand the sea-change to the new continent and never fully prospered here. It was the first kind, the sublime tradition, which came early and stayed late. Exactly what we may call a Coleridgean vocabulary, of sensitive psychological discriminations, is what characterizes the nineteenth-century British poetry as distinct from American; that is, such metaphysical nouns as *spirit, sorrow,* and *memory,* and such delicate objects as *bird, moon, wing, shadow,* and *rain,* modified by *golden* and *grey.* There is a quality of dramatic and atmospheric vignette in the poetry of nineteenth-century England which we find much less in America.

On the other hand, America both continued the more strong and enthusiastic terms of eighteenth-century sublimity and added new ones of its own, which are now moving back into British poetic usage. *Fair, new, bright,* and *dark* were major eighteenth-century terms which died out in British poetry but crossed over to America; *pure, strong, warm, clear,* and *beautiful* were the epithets which America added. Words of physical beauty and warmth like *breast, face, flame, fire, sun, sky, sea, home* and *land, mountain* and *morning,* were dropped by the British romantics, for their too great obviousness and solidity, but then fostered by America for their very richness of substance, and added to by *shore, stream, river, music, rose, wall, snow,* and *leaf.* Verbs of thought and action like *think, rise, seek, meet,* were increased by *get* and *walk,* to an effect of greater active involvement. Even the single most distinguishing trait of the eighteenth-century sublime style, its concern with sound and silence, with hearing and music, is strongly perpetuated in present American emphasis on *music, voice,* and *silence.* And the most recent British abstract term, the *nothing* of Auden, is balanced on the positive by the *being* of Wallace Stevens.

So in 1800 and again in 1900 we have an American poetry with a language clearly its own: verbs of bodily motion, nouns of natural motion and power, adjectives of positive intensity. James Gates Percival then, like Hart Crane now, walked to observe shore, hill, brook, roses, in order to participate in their miracle:

—or the walk
On the rude shore, to hear the rushing waves,
Or view the wide sea sleeping—on the hill
To catch the living landscape, and combine
The miracles of nature in one full

And deep enchantment—or to trace the brook
Up to its highest fountain in the shade
Of a thick tuft of alders, and go down
By all its leaps and windings, gathering there
The forest roses, and the nameless flowers,
That open in the wilderness, and live
Awhile in sweetest loveliness, and die
Without an eye to watch them, or a heart
To gladden in their beauty—
("The Wreck," ll. 81–102)

So in the twentieth century we have the American sublime of Hart Crane, of Pound, of Marianne Moore, of younger poets in great number. Central in this present-day tradition is Hart Crane's "Voyage," with its suns and waves, seas and bodies, hands and waters, stars and meadows, and the long measures of the lines reaching out toward the cycles of the seasons, the praises of space and the embodiment of eternity.

And yet this great wink of eternity,
Of rimless floods, unfettered leewardings,
Samite sheeted and processioned where
Her undinal vast belly moonward bends,
Laughing the wrapt inflections of our love;

Take this Sea, whose diapason knells
On scrolls of silver snowy sentences,
The sceptred terror of whose sessions rends
As her demeanors motion well or ill,
All but the pieties of lovers' hands.

And onward, as bells off San Salvador
Salute the crocus lustres of the stars,
In these poinsettia meadows of her tides,—

Adagios of islands, O my Prodigal,
Complete the dark confessions her veins spell.

Mark how her turning shoulders wind the hours,
And hasten while her penniless rich palms
Pass superscription of bent foam and wave,—
Hasten, while they are true,—sleep, death, desire,
Close round one instant in one floating flower.

Bind us in time, O Seasons clear, and awe.
O minstrel galleons of Carib fire,
Bequeath us to no earthly shore until
Is answered in the vortex of our grave
The seal's wide spindrift gaze toward paradise.

Far as the state of mind of this poetry is from Trumbull's, Barlow's, and Percival's a century before, it is in their tradition, their spirit and vocabulary, America's far more than England's in the intervening years, in its combination of massive physical presence and paradisal vision, and in its renewed effort toward making a private speech properly public.

Hear how the phrases of the vocabulary echo and reverberate in such a skillful younger poet as Richard Wilbur, in *Things of This World:* such phrases of the American tradition as "wholly at home," "massed voices," "a wild shining of the pure unknown," the sun's "warm look," "mind in its purest play," "a wall of stone," the "confident morning sound," "leaves were all its voice," "as clear as mountain water," "as the sea receives a stream," "birds in the burning trees," "A blazing girl with skin like polished stone," "a far-out breast of green," "her hair . . . a moving shade," the "stilled land," the "self-established tree," "tides of leaves," "heavy streams," "unbridled waters," "the summer's final mass," "complete music," "the man of snow," "the purest rain," this is the intense bodily and visionary language of both the past and the present. Wilbur keeps constantly pulling toward reality, by much specific reference, by neat verse forms, by an ironic or humorous disclaimer at the end of a poem, and thus again is like Trumbull, Barlow, Dwight, and Halleck, Holmes and Whittier, never quite as willing as Whitman or Crane to get lost and stay lost in the empyrean. Because some kind of Yankee temper in the American poet leads him to keep making remarks about his vast enterprises and moderates his praise of his land, the sentence structure of American poetry is closer to balance in more poets than one would surmise from their vocabulary and free verse forms. The hard sense of the week's business moderates Sunday's worship. Aside from the most extremely panegyric poets, Trumbull, Dwight, Barlow, Whittier, Chivers, Whitman, Lowell, Louise Guiney, Pound, Moore, Crane, Bishop, Rukeyser, Wilbur, and Hecht, most use a moderated balanced structure; some even represent the active verbal structure more dominant in England; of these we see that Emily Dickinson and Robert Frost are our strongest New England extremes, our skeptical consciences against sublimity.

"You know who the Titans were, don't you," said Robert Frost to a vast audience in a university gymnasium. "You remember those great sublime mythical figures? You remember the Titantic?" It is that undercutting and ironic spirit that has held much American sublimity in check.

Then, too, I think, American criticism has held sublimity in check. Especially recently, but throughout our history, our critics have been ironists, or have spoken from a cooler English point of view. Most of the new critics are anti-sublime poets and theorists; and of so-called pure poetry we have had little critical defense, unless we have seen it in the work of the French, of Baudelaire's and Mallarmé's pure sublime. Nevertheless, there have always been some to champion such flights: not only the myriad eighteenth-century gentlemen who took their pens in hand to praise Milton and Thomson, but serious critics like John Neal who complained of his contemporary Bryant that "He wants fire

—he wants the very rashness of a poet—the prodigality and fervour of those, who are overflowing with inspiration." (*American Writers,* ed. F. L. Pattee, 1957.) Or like Longfellow, who spoke for "the height, and depth, and purity of . . . moral nature, . . . the bold irregularities of human genius." (*Essays from the North American Review,* ed. Rice, 1879.) Or like Noah Webster, who got aid from the poet Trumbull in the writing of his "Dissertations on the English Language," and made use of the poet's major terms as he wrote of the *purity* and *strength* of that language in America (Boston, 1787). Or like John Pickering who made in 1816 a *Collection of Words and Phrases Peculiar to the United States,* in which he noted a number of terms, among them *freshet* for a stream, and *evoke* as a verb, which were not current in England but could be traced to the poetry of Milton and Thomson; and the noun *temper* which in England implied coolness; in America, warmth; and the adjective *aweful,* from the noun of wonder, *awe,* which for most of the country meant wonderful, but for New England meant something unpleasant, as in an "awful time." For New Englanders, wrote Pickering, "Every thing that creates surprise is awful."

Perhaps none recognizes more clearly the pull and tug between Yankee skepticism and the sweep of Sublimity than some of the Yankee realists themselves; not so much the humorists who deflate, as the sheer reporters and describers, who feel that the sublime is part of the everyday real in America. Such a one was Hamlin Garland, who at the beginning of our century was famed as one of the first great realists, following in the footsteps of William Dean Howells. Garland had one grandfather who was Yankee—"his speech neat and nipping," and one grandfather who was Scotch-Irish—"He was like Ezekiel, a dreamer of dreams. He loved the Old Testament, particularly those books which consisted of thunderous prophecies and passionate lamentations . . . The songs he loved best were those which described chariots of flaming clouds, the sound of the resurrection trump,—or the fields of amaranth blooming on the other side of Jordan." Garland understood, therefore, the special American combination of the harsh labor of the everyday world with the sometimes splendor of its surroundings and the hopes of its future. By his use of both the word "epic" and the word "romantic" he makes us realize that these are in our country still eighteenth-century terms, with Miltonic meanings: "epic" means "large-gestured and splendid," "romantic" meant to be bounded by "chaos and black night." Most of all poems, Whitman's *Leaves of Grass* filled Garland with the sense of poetry: "a keen sense of the mystery of the near at hand." Therefore into the realism of the near at hand, even the stark bitterness of such books as his *Son of the Middle Border,* from which these quotations have been taken, comes the mystery of the sublime in many such passages as this: "Deep as the breast of man, wide as the sea, heavy-handed, supple-stocked, many-voiced, full of multitudinous, secret, whispered colloquies,—a meeting place of winds and of sunlight—our fields ran to the world's end."

The drama of O'Neill and the fiction of Faulkner each in its own way gives us again this vision of the mystery in the near at hand, and confirms in the sublime style of the prose of America the sublimity of its poetry. The importance of this sublimity will, I think, increase with time. Of all the modes it has been least consciously explored and defined, least critically championed. Yet Dylan Thomas in England and Hart Crane in America have spoken with this voice what Whitman spoke, what the prophets spoke, to the young poets: "Come then, expressive silence, muse his praise."

This American poetry of praise has a long free cadenced line, full of silences, symbols, and implications. It has a cumulative structure, building up to a height of force and feeling, whether in imprecation or in rhapsody. It has a phraseology of resounding sound and of warm responsive sense, suggestive of heights and depths beyond the reach of form or reason. As at its worst it can be dangerously loose, semiconscious, and irresponsible; at its best it can be powerfully aware of moving forces and meanings. Strong as it was in England in the work of

Keats, Tennyson, and Dylan Thomas, it has been more widespread and more central to tradition in America, with added impetus from poets of the Orient as well as of Europe. What can it mean to our future?

It can portend for our poetry a strong sense of ceremony and of public concern, strong personal and passionate comments on public issues, a highly vocal and expressive function of evaluation for the poet —comparable to the role played by Pindar, for example, in his celebration of the Olympic Games—a calling up and praising of great figures of our life, or perhaps a denouncing them, but at any rate a perceiving and portraying them, larger than life, in a great frame of human values and human concerns. It can be not only personal and ambiguous, but social and magnanimous, in the magnanimity of a poetry which transfigures what it values.

TABLES

I have tried to bring together all the information I have gathered for two hundred poets, one hundred and fifty British and fifty American, from Chaucer to the present, in such a way as to suggest the basic patterns of relation between poet and poet in the use of language, and at the same time to provide the most straightforward chronological arrangement of materials for those who may have other questions to ask, about single poets, single eras, single types, or single terms.

Some believe that only for the individual poet can the facts be significant. But rather, it seems to me, the individual is most singular in the way he makes use of the materials available to him; in his peculiar combination of traits rather than in the traits themselves. Therefore, the way to see the individual whole is in the pattern of his work, and in his relation with other poets, other writers, other artists, other people, in time and in type.

These tables suggest some of the relationships evident in the use of language, the medium to which the poet gives form by the forces of repetition. Tables 1 and 2 together show the major uses of measure, proportions of reference, and repeated terms, of two hundred poets in order of birth date. Tables 3 and 4 show some of the patterns to be seen in this basic material—the types of interrelated content, structure, and sound which recur for the poet as he composes, and which seem to be related most strongly to the time in which he lives. I hope that the reader, looking at these materials (especially the simplest ones, in Tables 1 and 2) with his own interests in mind, will see new questions to be asked and forms of answers other than those which have occurred to me.

There is also the warning that no complete reliance should be put on any single item listed, inasmuch as the whole collection has been made by a number of different people, including me, for a number of different purposes, so that all sorts of misreadings must have come into existence despite efforts to avoid them. At least, within the suggested scope of pattern of usage, the reader can locate his own interest and establish his own greater accuracies, granting if he will my premise that an important part of the history of English poetry is the history of its language.

The assistants who through the generosity of the Faculty Committee on Research have aided in this study are: Michael Cooke, Phillip Damon, Mary Emma Elliott, George P. Elliott, Elizabeth Kaupp, Jean Lynch, Harriet Polt, John and Muriel Ridland, Jack Thornburgh, Robert Smutny, W. L. Stover, Beverly Wilson, and Jean Wirth. I also owe special thanks for advice to Professors Edgar Anderson, F. W. Bateson, James R. Caldwell, Alfred Kroeber, Benbow Ritchie, and Hanan Selvin.

Six terms in this study I use with special limitations of meaning: _poet_, _era_, _mode_, _proportion_, _major word_ or _use_, and _innovation_. _Poet_, I use to stand for the major text studied. Sometimes it is indeed almost all the poet's work, being about a thousand lines; sometimes it is only a small part of his work, but, so far as I know, characteristic. Generalizations are pertinent only to the text here named. For Wordsworth and Yeats, as distinguished from Donne, Dryden, and Eliot, for example, the change from one mode to another is a characterizing fact of biography, and for such poets particular care should be taken to note which text is referred to.

About poets to be included there is not much possible disagreement, although every reader will miss among the two hundred some he believes to be more important than those included: Fulke Greville, perhaps, or Henry King, or Christopher Smart, or John Clare, or Kipling, with more coming to mind for the recent years. But because I have been concerned with all eras, not just those now in favor, I have tried to include ten poets for every thirty or forty years, that is, thirty poets for every century, with the consequent inclusion of more so-called minor writers in early eras. Ghosh's chronological handbook, _The Annals of English Literature_, has provided a reasonably objective basis for inclusion; indeed, only about fifty poets listed by Ghosh are not included here, and they are mostly recent—Dobson, Dowson, Lang, for example.

Era is a concept for which theorists have had little clear basis of distinction. We take century lines as marks of convenience. With the suggestion in mind that about thirty years represents a generation, I found the first clear and ample generation of poets after Chaucer's time to be those born about 1470 and beginning publication in 1500, the "early sixteenth-century" poets. So Dunbar, Hawes, Skelton, with the Ballads, begin the birth-span of 1470-1500; Wyatt and Surrey begin that of 1500-1530 (with a little extension into the 1540's because of the poetic sparseness of the period); and Spenser and Sidney begin the mid-century, that is, the poets who published at the century's end. These thirty then represent the whole sixteenth century in its sequence. So too, the centuries 1670-1770, 1770-1870, and the incomplete two-thirds 1870-1930. In addition, I have listed ten early poets, around the time of Chaucer, and fifty American poets for the nineteenth century (1770-1870) and the twentieth (1870-1930) paralleling the British: a total of one hundred and fifty British and fifty American. Note that birth dates have been used throughout as being more simple and stable than publication dates; and that publication dates are assumed to be, as they usually are, about thirty years later. Note that Tables 3 and 4 as finally worked out on this hypothesis of generations now suggest a somewhat different pattern: that of innovation by poets born in mid and late century, following a certain stasis in poets born at the beginning; thus perhaps a grouping of those born in the '50's-'80's, and publishing at the turn of the century. In Tables 3 and 4 we also see a larger meaning of era, not by one generation but by groups of three, amounting in effect to the conventions of the three central centuries, seventeenth, eighteenth, and nineteenth.

Mode is the term I have used to suggest certain relatively stable complexes or conventions of usage, in reference, sound, and structure, as these are established by agreements in poetic practice and survive and recur through time. The predicative mode, for example, combines a high proportion of verbs and clausal structures with a vocabulary of concept and a stanzaic verse form. It was the mode of poets in the Renaissance, most particularly of those called metaphysical, and survives today in the colloquial meditations of Frost and of Auden. As a style is a persisting complex of interrelated habits founded on values, I take mode to be part of style, a complex of habits specifically in the use of language. In both the selection and the arrangement of the materials of art, the quantity of materials as well as the quality is important: not only what is chosen but how often, not only how strongly emphasized but how recurrently. One may speak of Picasso's blue period, for example, not only because he used a little blue with much emphasis but because he used much blue with little emphasis. Habitual choices underlie the vivid traits of mode as of style.

Proportion is one part of poetic mode. As Tables 1, 2, and 4 indicate, there is a close relation between the proportions of referential parts of speech and the context of such reference. We see that English poetry began by being highly predicative, that is, with a strong dominance of verbs and of clausal structures, in connection with a strongly conceptual vocabulary of reference and a formal stanzaic sound pattern, and that this metaphysical mode, subsiding in the eighteenth century, recurred again with some force in the nineteenth. We see, on the other hand, from Spenser to Thomson, the increase of the adjectival phrasal mode along with allusive reference and internalizing of sound pattern. And we see, between these extremes in each century—most strongly in the twentieth—the classical mode of balance, combining equal phrasal and clausal structures with literal reference and descriptive statement in formal sound pattern. These three main complexes of practice underlie more individual and temporal traits of style and provide certain significant continuities of agreement.

Related to proportion is the choice of major or most frequent referential terms. As we learn from such technical studies as G. Udny Yule's _Statistical Study of Literary Vocabulary_, Pierre Guiraud's _Les Charactères Statistiques du Vocabulaire_, Godfrey Dewey's _Relativ Frequency of English Speech Sounds_, Helen Eaton's _Semantic Frequency_, Einar Haugen's _Norwegian Word Studies_, Vernon Lee's _The Handling of Words_, R. A. Sayce's _Style in French Prose_, Charles Osgood's _Measurement of Meaning_, concordances by Bandy, Hanley, and others, and the Thorndike-Lange word-lists, the referential vocabulary of adjectives, nouns, and verbs is about half the total in a text, the other half including connectives, most adverbs, and other sorts of particles. Of this referential vocabulary, the few most-used words make up about fifty or sixty per cent. In a verse text, for example, as I discovered independently of these other studies, the total of nouns, adjectives, and verbs that occur about ten times (seven to twelve times) in a thousand lines (approximately seven thousand words) comprises some fifty separate words, and these constitute about half the nouns, adjectives, and verbs—or a fourth to a sixth of the whole text.

Major word or _major use_, then, means the words used about ten times or more in a thousand lines. These are given in Table 2, with numbers in parentheses indicating more than ten uses. One may assume the strong frequencies of the auxiliaries _to be_, _to have_, _to do_, as well as the verb _to say_; these are counted in the total proportions of Table 1, but not separately listed in Table 2. Among adjectives, the frequent numerical adjectives like _all_ and _some_ have been counted but not listed; so, too, the proper nouns. Adjectives include compared forms; verbs, all forms but the participles, which, in disagreement with some modern linguists, I take to be most significant in their adjectival, phrasal functions. Indeed, it is the substitution of such forms as _the blowing wind_ for _the wind which blows_ that makes one of the main differences between phrasal and clausal modes. Adjective totals including at least thirty per cent participial adjectives are marked with asterisks in Table 1; they are among the highest in proportion.

Noteworthy in the list given in Table 2 is the basic agreement in usage among poets: to a strong degree in any one time, and even, though to a lesser degree, through time. If every one of the two hundred poets had used his own individual group of fifty or so major words, the total number of words would have been 200 x 50, or 10,000. Instead, the list contains only the 260 words that were used by at least four poets within the defined time, plus the 600-700 individual dominant words. Yet no two poets choose just the same words to emphasize; agreements appear within diversities. For what I have called Innovation, or first major appearance, see Ch. 13.

TABLE I

Of the two hundred poets listed in Table 1, the first ten were born in the century or so before 1470. From birth date 1470 on, there are ten poets in each thirty or forty years; that is, thirty in each century. The order is chronological, with the fifty American poets of 1770-1930 following the fifty British of 1770-1930. Texts are the first thousand consecutive lines of a major poem or sequence of poems, with exceptions noted, and with editions chosen, when possible, for availability. Measures are indicated by line length and line grouping. The fairly stable four-accent or five-accent lines provide 7,000 or 8,000 words in a thousand lines. Of these total words, the total terms of reference—that is adjectives, nouns, and verbs—as distinguished from articles, pronouns, connectives, and most adverbs, amount to about half. Within these terms of reference, the proportions vary, from Minot's five adjectives, fourteen nouns, and ten verbs in ten lines, a dominance of verbs over adjectives of two to one, or Langland's three to one, to Lydgate, James, and Henryson, for whom verbs still dominate, but only by a small proportion. We find as we turn the pages to the sixteenth and seventeenth centuries, that the weight of verbs lessens, that Chaucer's 7A-15N-11V establishes a fair norm, but that not until Fletcher in 1582 do we get any strong adjectival emphasis. Such proportions as 10A-10V, or 9A-8V may be called balanced, and, we shall find, tend to be accompanied by a special sort of vocabulary. The adjectival emphasis of Fletcher is to be noted again in Milton and More and then very strongly in the eighteenth century; the predicative recurs in the early nineteenth century; and the balanced, in the late nineteenth and twentieth in both England and America.

A summary of this pattern of change is shown in Chapter 1, and is one I have discussed more fully there: the basic agreement among the poets of the Renaissance in the use of a language complexly clausal and highly predicated; the slow beginnings in the "aureate" poets like Hawes and Dunbar, and then Spenser, then the swift rise through Milton to the eighteenth century, of an opposite stress, the use of modification instead of predication, of participles instead of clauses. And meanwhile the persistent, in our day dominant, emphasis of some poets on a balance of these two extremes—in Shakespeare's sonnets, for example, and in Fairfax's epic translation—of the classical norm of Horace, Ovid, Virgil, the 10-20-10 of the balanced style: two nouns, one adjective, one verb in the line.

Nouns, we may note, do not seem to provide the basis for an emphasis of their own, but seem to equal the total of verbs plus adjectives, with a few early exceptions in lesser nouns, as for Hoccleve, Heywood, Wyatt, Donne, and some of the particularly strong Miltonic users of adjectives, and with certain modern exceptions in strong nouns, as for Halleck, Whitman, Whittier, Sterling, Pound, Lowell in America, and Sitwell, Raine, Nicholson, Thomas in England. In these few exceptions, indeed, we may see an eventually significant shift toward a more heavily substantive verse in the twentieth century.

But these suggestions which have interested me are only a small part of what may be seen even in Table 1. The reader interested in any individual poet--in Langland, for example, on the first page of the table, —may learn much about him just from these simple figures. Reading from right to left, one may note his large number of total words, reflective of his long and full lines, and then secondly his unusually large number of repeated adjectives, nouns, and verbs in relation to total words. Repetition is poetry's basic device of form, but few use it so strongly for simple, basic terms as Langland does. Few also use so many verbs in proportion to adjectives: 18 to 6, or 3 to 1. And few until later use a measure of lines without any repetitive pattern of rhyme. From these brief figures, then, we may draw a sense of the difference between Langland's language and that beginning to flourish in his day, as in Chaucer for example. Langland's long line was controlled by accent and by repetitions within rather than at the end of lines—by repetitions of major references, especially of actions rather than of qualities.

TABLE 1

TEXTS, MEASURES, AND PROPORTIONS FOR 200 POETS

Birth date	Poet	Work and edition (first 1,000 lines)	Measure	Adj.	Nouns	Verbs	Total ANV	Total words
		Pre-1470 poets						
ca. 1310	Laurence Minot	Poems, 980 lines. (Poems, ed. Hall, 1887.)	4' (5'-3') lines	530 (5)	1,410 (14)	1,000 (10)[a]	2,940	6,850
ca. 1325	John Gower	Confessio Amantis, Prologue, 500 lines, I, 500 lines. (Works, ed. Macaulay, EETS, 1900.)	4' couplets	410 (4)	1,190 (12)	1,010 (10)	2,610	6,210
ca. 1330	William Langland	Piers, through III. (Ed. Skeat, 1886.)	4' lines	550 (6)	2,100 (21)	1,770 (18)	4,420	8,790
ca. 1340	Geoffrey Chaucer	Prologue, 860 lines, Knight's Tale, 140 lines. (Works, ed. Robinson, Cambridge, 1933.)	5' couplets	650 (7)	1,530 (15)	1,060 (11)	3,240	7,680
ca. 1350	Author of Pearl	Pearl. (Pearl, ed. Gordon, Clarendon Press, 1953.)	4' stanzas	720 (7)	1,440 (14)	1,070 (11)	3,230	7,050
ca. 1350	Author of Gawain	Gawain. (Gawain, ed. Gollancz, Oxford, 1940.)	5' stanzas	930 (9)	1,740 (17)	1,130 (11)	3,800	8,820
ca. 1368	Thomas Occleve	Complaint, Dialogue. (Works, ed. Furnivall, EETS, 1892.)	5' stanzas	580 (6)	1,300 (13)	1,350 (14)	3,230	8,000
ca. 1370	John Lydgate	Fall of Princes, Temple of Glass, 500 lines each. (Ed. resp. Bergen, 1923-27, Schick, 1891.)	5' couplets, stanzas	630 (6)	1,600 (16)	880 (9)	3,110	6,900
ca. 1394	James I	Kingis Quair. (Poems, ed. Skeat, 1911.)	5' stanzas	650 (7)	1,610 (16)	1,030 (10)	3,290	7,300
ca. 1430	Robert Henryson	Cresseid, plus six poems ff. (Poems, ed. G. G. Smith, 1908.)	5' stanzas	810 (8)	1,630 (16)	980 (10)	3,420	6,900
		Sixteenth-century poets						
1470	Ballads	Ballads, first 18. (Ed. W. M. Hart, 1916.)	4' stanzas	570 (6)	1,340 (13)	1,090 (11)	3,000	7,800
1470	William Dunbar	Thistle, Targe, Synnes, Makaris, 700 lines. (Scottish Text Soc., 1919.)	5'-4' stanzas	550 (8)	1,130 (16)	500 (7)	2,180	4,850
1470	Stephen Hawes	Pastime of Pleasure, through X, 900 lines. (EETS, 1928.)	5' stanzas	770 (9)	1,200 (13)	710 (8)	2,680	6,480
1470	John Skelton	Colin Cloute. (Ed. Hughes, 1924.)	2' couplets	400 (4)	980 (10)	710 (7)	2,090	4,720
1474	Gawin Douglas	Palice of Honour, Eneados, 500 lines each. (Works, 1874.)	5' stanzas	820 (8)	1,750 (18)	890 (9)	3,460	7,600
1475	Alexander Barclay	Eclogue V. (EETS, 1928.)	5' couplets	780 (8)	2,160 (22)	1,170 (12)	4,110	8,200
1480	Thomas Sternhold	Psalms of David, first 25. (Huntington Lib., 1631.)	4' stanzas	410 (4)	1,100 (11)	840 (8)	2,350	4,800
1488	Miles Coverdale	Ghostly Psalms, through XLVI, "Psalm of David." (Ed. Pearson, 1846.)	4' stanzas	480 (5)	1,230 (12)	940 (9)	2,650	6,100
1490	David Lindsay	Squire Meldrum. (Works, ed. Laing, 1879.)	4' couplets	620 (6)	1,340 (13)	920 (9)	2,880	5,960
1497	John Heywood	Proverbs, and Epigrams, 500 lines each. (Ed. resp. Sharman, 1874, and Spenser Soc., 1864.)	5' stanzas	700 (7)	1,200 (12)	1,060 (11)	3,960	7,430

[a]Parentheses show proportions in ten lines; so, 5S-14N-10V in ten lines, for 500A-1400N-1000V in 1000 lines.

TABLE 1 (continued)

Birth date	Poet	Work and edition (first 1,000 lines)	Measure	Adj.	Nouns	Verbs	Total ANV	Total words
1503	Thomas Wyatt	Songs, Rondeaus, Odes. (Works, Boston, 1854.)	5' stanzas	700 (7)	1,200 (12)	1,060 (11)	2,960	7,430
1517	Henry Howard, Surrey	Sonnets, etc. (Poems, ed. Padelford, 1920.)	5' stanzas	740 (7)	1,750 (18)	1,320 (13)	3,810	7,840
1520	Thomas Churchyard	Chippes. (Ed. Collier, Early English Poetry, Despises, Siege, Farewell, less 50 lines. 1866-70.)	5'-3' stanzas	540 (5)	1,670 (17)	1,510 (15)	3,720	8,350
1520	Robert Crowley	Epigrams, thr. XVI. (Works, ed. Cowper, EETS, 1922.)	2'-4' stanzas	440 (4)	1,090 (11)	980 (10)	2,510	5,900
1529	William Baldwin	Mirror for Magistrates, first 400 lines, and Cambridge, Clarence, York, 1,120 lines. (Mirror, ed. Campbell, 1938.)	5' stanzas	790 (7)	2,190 (20)	1,380 (12)	4,360	9,160
1536	Thomas Sackville	Induc. and Buckingham in Mirror for Magistrates, 1,050 lines. (Ed. Campbell, 1819.)	5' stanzas	900 (9)	1,880 (18)	1,040 (10)	3,820	8,300
1540	Barnabe Googe	Eglogs, Epitaphes, Sonnets. (Ed. Arber, 1871.)	4' stanzas	520 (5)	1,240 (12)	900 (9)	2,660	5,600
1540	George Turberville	Epitaphes, Epigrams, etc. (Ed. J. P. Collier, 1866.)	4' stanzas	480 (5)	1,340 (13)	960 (10)	2,780	5,860
1542	George Gascoigne	The Steele Glas. (Works, ed. Cunliffe, 1912.)	5' bl. verse	850 (9)	1,800 (18)	1,210 (12)	3,860	8,110
1545	Nicholas Breton	School and Fort of Fancie. (Works, ed. Grosart, 1879.)	3' stanzas	510 (5)	1,120 (11)	820 (8)	2,450	5,300
1552	Edmund Spenser	Faerie Queene, Amoretti, 500 lines each. (Oxford, 1910.)	5' stanzas	1,150 (12)	1,590 (16)	1,100 (11)	3,840	8,100
1554	Philip Sidney	Eclogs, and Astrophel, 500 lines each. (Cambridge ed., 1912-26.)	5' stanzas	1,030 (10)	2,090 (21)	1,290 (13)	4,410	8,950
1559	George Chapman	5th Juvenal, 300 lines, Hymn to Apollo, 834 lines. (Works, ed. Swinburne, 1875.)	5' lines	*970 (8)	2,030 (18)	1,170 (10)	4,170	9,270
1562	Samuel Daniel	Delia, 700 lines, and Rosamund. (Ed. Sprague, 1930.)	5' stanzas	750 (8)	1,730 (17)	1,270 (13)	3,750	8,170
1563	Michael Drayton	Idea, and Pastorals, 500 lines each. (Oxford ed., 1932, ed. Hebel.)	5' stanzas	940 (9)	1,770 (18)	1,190 (12)	3,900	7,670
1563	Joshua Sylvester	Divine Weekes. (Ed. Grosart, 1880.)	5' couplets	1,060 (11)	1,900 (19)	850 (9)	3,810	7,160
1564	Christopher Marlowe	Hero and Leander, 800 lines, Ovid, Eleg., 200 lines. (Ed. Tucker Brooke, 1910.)	5' couplets	*940 (9)	1,640 (16)	1,320 (13)	3,900	7,860
1564	William Shakespeare	Sonnets, 1,050 lines. (Cambridge ed.)	5' stanzas	1,000 (10)	1,780 (17)	1,130 (10)	3,910	8,520
1567	Thomas Campion	A Booke of Ayres, and Two Bookes, thr. 17. (Works, ed. Vivian, 1909.)	4' stanzas	710 (7)	1,560 (16)	1,070 (11)	3,340	7,500
1570	Edward Fairfax	Translation of Tasso's Recovery of Jerusalem. (New York, Putnam's, 1845.)	5' stanzas	950 (10)	2,010 (20)	1,020 (10)	3,980	7,720

*An asterisk indicates that 30 to 40 per cent of the adjectives used are participial, in contrast to 10 to 25 per cent of those without an asterisk.

TABLE 1 (continued)

Birth date	Poet	Work and edition (first 1,000 lines)	Measure	Adj	Nouns	Verbs	Total ANV	Total words
		Seventeenth-century poets						
1573	Ben Jonson	Underwoods, through XV, 1,070 lines. (Oxford edition.)	5'-4' stanzas	630 (6)	1,470 (14)	1,230 (12)	3,330	7,580
1576	John Donne	Songs and Sonets, 1,010 lines. (Random House.)	5'-4' stanzas	660 (7)	1,300 (13)	1,230 (12)	3,190	7,100
1578	George Sandys	Song of Solomon, Jeremiah, 1,200 lines. (Works, ed. Hooper.)	5'-4' couplets	*930 (8)	2,040 (17)	1,050 (9)	4,020	6,310
1582	Phineas Fletcher	Purple Island. (Poems, ed. Grosart, London, 1869.)	5' stanzas	*1,350 (14)	1,830 (18)	990 (10)	4,170	8,200
1588	George Wither	Vox Pacifica. (Misc. Works, Spenser Soc., 1872-1878.)	5' stanzas	660 (7)	1,460 (14)	1,100 (11)	3,220	7,940
1591	Robert Herrick	Hesperides, 1,090 lines. (Poems, ed. Grosart, 1876.)	5'-4'stanzas	770 (7)	1,410 (13)	1,180 (11)	3,360	6,750
1592	Francis Quarles	Shepherds Oracles. (Works, ed. Grosart, 1880-1881.)	5' couplets	960 (10)	1,730 (17)	1,280 (13)	3,970	8,150
1593	George Herbert	The Church, through "Mattens." (Oxford ed., 1941.)	5'-3' stanzas	600 (6)	1,450 (15)	1,060 (11)	3,110	7,260
1595	Thomas Carew	Poems, 1640. (Roxburghe Library.)	5'-4' couplets	750 (8)	1,480 (15)	1,100 (11)	3,330	6,700
1596	James Shirley	Poems. (Ed. R. L. Armstrong, 1941.)	4' couplets, stanzas	720 (7)	1,440 (14)	1,070 (11)	3,230	6,900
1606	Edmund Waller	Poems, 1,050 lines. (Works, ed. C. Clarke, 1862.)	5' couplets	1,180 (11)	1,940 (19)	1,030 (10)	4,150	7,700
1608	John Milton	Nativity, L'Al., Il P., Lyc. Comus. (Minor Poems, ed. M. Y. Hughes, 1939.)	5'-4' lines	*1,200 (12)	1,550 (16)	770 (8)	3,520	6,720
1609	John Suckling	Fragmenta Aurea. (Ed. A. H. Thompson, 1910.)	5'-3' couplets stanzas	560 (6)	1,260 (13)	1,170 (12)	2,990	6,500
1613	Richard Crashaw	Steps to the Temple, 1,080 lines. (Poems, ed. A. R. Waller, 1904.)	5'-4' stanzas	1,060 (10)	1,900 (18)	1,140 (11)	4,100	8,000
1613	John Cleveland	Poems, 1,050 lines. (Poems, ed. J. M. Berdan, 1903.)	5'-4' stanzas	*770 (7)	1,740 (17)	1,020 (10)	3,530	6,670
1614	Henry More	Psychozoia Platonica. (Poems, ed. Grosart, 1818.)	5' stanzas	1,160 (12)	1,760 (18)	1,030 (10)	3,950	7,720
1615	John Denham	Cooper's Hill, ff., 1668 text, 1,090 lines. (Works, ed. Banks.)	5' couplets	750 (7)	1,550 (15)	980 (9)	3,280	6,820
1618	Abraham Cowley	Mistress, 1,030 lines. (Works, 8th ed., London, 1693.)	5'-4' stanzas	730 (7)	1,330 (13)	1,170 (11)	3,230	7,350
1618	Richard Lovelace	Lucasta, 1,040 lines. (Poems, ed. C. Wilkinson, 1925.)	5'-4' stanzas	860 (8)	1,380 (13)	1,000 (10)	3,240	5,870
1621	Andrew Marvell	Poems, 500 lines through Coy Mistress, 500 lines, Appleton House. (Poems, ed. MacDonald, 1952.)	5' couplets	*660 (7)	1,360 (14)	900 (9)	2,920	7,700
1622	Henry Vaughan	Silex Scintillans, and Poems, 1,050 lines. (Ed. Grosart, 1871.)	5'-2' stanzas	750 (7)	1,300 (13)	950 (9)	3,000	7,120

TABLE 1 (continued)

Birth date	Poet	Work and edition (first 1,000 lines)	Measure	Adj.	Nouns	Verbs	Total ANV	Total words
1631	John Dryden	Absalom and Achitophel, 1,030 lines. (Ed. Noyes, 1950.)	5' couplets	*1,020 (10)	1,950 (19)	1,060 (10)	4,030	7,800
1633	Earl of Roscommon	Poems, through Prospect, 480 lines, Horace's Art of Poetry, 480 lines, 1717.	5' couplets	940 (9)	1,680 (17)	1,120 (11)	3,740	10,250
1653	John Oldham	Trans. Horace and Juvenal, 1,300 lines. (Works, 1854.)	5' couplets	1,130 (7)	2,330 (17)	1,510 (11)	4,970	10,400
1655	Richard Blackmore	Wit, 350 lines, Nature, 500 lines. (Collected Poems, 1718), "Vanity," "Happiness," "Morning Thought," 150 lines.	5' couplets	1,185 (12)	1,990 (20)	1,010 (10)	4,190	6,970
1659	Thomas Creech	Odes, etc., of Horace, 1,030 lines. (Tonson, 1737.)	5' couplets, stanzas	830 (8)	1,800 (18)	1,360 (13)	3,990	5,890
1661	Samuel Garth	Dispensary. (London, 1726.)	5' couplets	880 (9)	1,960 (20)	1,180 (12)	4,020	7,600
1663	William Walsh	Poems, 1,060 lines. (British Poets, 1810, ed. Chalmers.)	5'-4' stanzas	820 (8)	1,550 (15)	1,310 (13)	3,680	7,390
1664	Matthew Prior	Poems on Several Occasions, 200 lines, Solomon, 800 lines. (Cambridge ed., 1905.)	5' couplets	*1,160 (12)	1,910 (19)	870 (9)	3,940	7,300
1667	John Pomfret	Poems on Several Occasions, Choice, 100 lines, Death, 220 lines, Love Triumphant, 500 lines. (Chalmers, 1810.)	5' couplets	*1,070 (11)	1,440 (15)	1,170 (12)	3,680	5,140
		Eighteenth-century poets						
1672	Joseph Addison	4th Georgic, Ovid Met., Horace Ode III, 1,070 lines. (Works, London, 1811.)	5' couplets	*1,120 (10)	2,000 (19)	1,160 (11)	4,280	7,566
1675	William Somerville	Hobbinol. (London, 1740.)	5' bl. verse	*1,650 (17)	1,910 (19)	840 (8)	4,400	7,200
1676	John Philips	Cyder. (Poems, ed. Thomas, 1927.)	5' bl. verse	1,275 (13)	1,795 (18)	748 (7)	3,818	7,190
1679	Thomas Parnell	Nightpiece and poems ff., Hymn, Hermit, Anne, Piety, Swift, 970 lines. (Works, 1722.)	5'-4' couplets	*990 (10)	1,830 (19)	990 (10)	3,810	6,815
1683	Edward Young	The Complaint. (New York, 1868.)	5' bl. verse	*1,010 (10)	1,990 (20)	1,040 (10)	4,040	7,400
1685	John Gay	Fables, First Series. (Works, ed. Arbur, 1926.)	4' couplets	658 (7)	1,654 (17)	987 (10)	3,299	6,460
1688	Alexander Pope	Rape of the Lock, and Eloisa, 200 lines. (Vol. II, Poems, ed. Tillotson, 1939.)	5' couplets	*1,090 (11)	2,020 (20)	1,110 (11)	4,220	8,200
1699	Robert Blair	The Grave, 800 lines. (Engl. Poets, ed. Chalmers, XV, 1810.)	5' bl. verse	*890 (11)	1,330 (17)	710 (9)	2,930	5,900
1700	John Dyer	Grongar Hill, Walk, 720 lines, Fleece, 1,030 lines. (Works, ed. Maurie.)	5' couplets	1,310 (13)	1,960 (19)	810 (8)	4,080	7,509
1700	James Thomson	The Seasons, Winter, rev., 1749, 1,070 lines (Works, Oxford ed.)	5' bl. verse	*1,660 (16)	1,880 (18)	800 (7)	4,340	7,704
1709	John Armstrong	Art of Preserving Health. (Lit. Misc., 1804.)	5' couplets	1,450 (15)	1,820 (18)	870 (9)	4,140	7,300
1709	George Lyttelton	Progress of Love, Soliloquy, Blenheim, Ayscough, Monody, 1,130 lines. (Works, 1774.)	5' couplets, stanzas	1,170 (10)	1,880 (17)	970 (9)	4,020	8,360

TABLE 1 (continued)

Birth date	Poet	Work and edition (first 1,000 lines)	Measure	Adj.	Nouns	Verbs	Total ANV	Total words
1709	Samuel Johnson	London, Vanity, Prologues, plus 7 poems ff., 1,020 lines. (Poems, ed. Smith and McAdam, 1941.)	5' couplets	*960 (9)	2,110 (21)	1,060 (10)	4,130	7,380
1714	William Shenstone	The Schoolmistress, Hercules, Taste, 175 lines. (Works, 1764.)	5' stanzas	*1,190 (12)	1,910 (19)	1,110 (11)	4,210	7,800
1716	Thomas Gray	Poems, 1742 ff. 1,090 lines. (Oxford, 1937.)	5' stanzas	*1,090 (10)	1,870 (17)	890 (8)	3,850	7,818
1721	Mark Akenside	Odes. (Works, 1808.)	5' bl. verse lines	990 (10)	1,730 (17)	750 (8)	3,470	5,600
1721	William Collins	Poems, 1742 ff., 1,060 lines. (Oxford ed.)	5' stanzas	*1,260 (12)	1,800 (17)	920 (9)	3,980	7,703
1722	Joseph Warton	Enthusiast, Odes. (Engl. Poets, ed. Chalmers, XVIII, 1810.)	5' lines	*1,290 (13)	1,850 (19)	820 (8)	3,960	6,450
1725	William Mason	Musaeus. (Poems, London, 1764.)	5' stanzas	1,170 (12)	1,760 (18)	960 (10)	3,890	7,450
1728	Thomas Warton	Odes, Isis. (Engl. Poets, ed. Chalmers, 1810.)	5' couplets, stanzas	*1,450 (15)	1,890 (19)	810 (8)	4,150	6,260
1730	Oliver Goldsmith	Village, Traveller, Hermit. (Poems, New York, 1890.)	5' couplets	*1,120 (11)	1,910 (19)	1,050 (11)	4,080	7,400
1731	William Cowper	The Task. (Poems, London, 1931.)	5' bl. verse	*1,130 (11)	1,730 (17)	840 (8)	3,700	8,000
1731	Charles Churchill	The Ghost, 500 lines, plus Famine, 500 lines. (Works, Oxford, 1956.)	5' couplets	920 (9)	1,780 (18)	920 (9)	3,620	8,000
1752	Thomas Chatterton	Clifton, Bristowe, Hastings, Eclogues, 900 lines. (Works, ed. Skeat, 1891 ff.)	5'-3' couplets, stanzas	*810 (9)	1,680 (19)	890 (10)	3,380	5,782
1754	George Crabbe	Village, 500 lines, Eustace Gray, 200 lines, Parish Register, 200 lines. (Poems, ed. Carlyle, 1908.)	5' couplets	*1,010 (11)	1,750 (19)	1,030 (11)	3,790	6,800
1757	William Blake	America, etc. (Poetry and Prose, 1939.)	5' lines	*1,200 (12)	2,400 (24)	1,030 (10)	4,630	7,700
1759	Robert Burns	Poems, 1786-1794, "Cotter" through "Epistle." (Edinburgh, 1793.)	5' lines	950 (10)	1,580 (16)	950 (10)	3,480	7,000
1762	William Bowles	Sonnets and Other Poems. (8th ed., London, 1802.)	5' stanzas	*1,310 (13)	1,860 (19)	1,000 (10)	4,170	7,600
1763	Samuel Rogers	Pleasures of Memory. (Works, Philadelphia, 1854.)	5' couplets	*1,110 (11)	2,040 (20)	1,080 (11)	4,230	7,900
1770	William Wordsworth	Lyrical Ballads, omitting groups between "Anecdote" and "Old Man." (Complete Poetical Works, Cambridge ed., 1904.)	5'-4' stanzas	*940 (9)	1,560 (16)	940 (9)	3,440	6,596
		Nineteenth-century British poets						
1772	Samuel Taylor Coleridge	Ancient Mariner, and Christabel, 1,300 lines. (Rinehart ed.)	4' stanzas	790 (6)	1,750 (13)	1,200 (9)	3,740	8,170
1774	Robert Southey	Poems, through Sonnet 15. (Bath, 1795.)	5' stanzas	1,000 (10)	1,720 (17)	920 (9)	3,640	7,860
1775	Walter Savage Landor	Hellenics, first 9. (Oxford ed., 1937.)	5' bl. verse	750 (8)	1,560 (16)	1,230 (12)	3,540	8,460

TABLE 1 (continued)

Birth date	Poet	Work and edition (first 1,000 lines)	Measure	Adj.	Nouns	Verbs	Total ANV	Total words
1777	Thomas Campbell	*Theodoric*, and *Pilgrim*. (Oxford ed., 1907.)	5' couplets	*1,020 (10)	2,140 (21)	1,220 (12)	4,380	8,640
1779	Thomas Moore	*Irish Melodies*, 600 lines, and *Lalla Rookh*, 300 lines. (Oxford ed., 1915.)	4' stanzas	650 (7)	1,520 (17)	840 (9)	3,010	6,700
1784	Leigh Hunt	*Rimini*, and *The Feast*, 1,050 lines. (Oxford ed., 1923.)	5' couplets	*1,100 (10)	1,950 (19)	1,100 (10)	4,150	8,730
1788	George Gordon Byron	*Hebrew Melodies*, 500 lines ff. plus 200 lines each, *Manfred*, *Childe Harold*, *Don Juan*. (Oxford ed., 1921.)	4' stanzas	700 (6)	1,620 (15)	1,020 (9)	3,340	8,000
1792	Percy Bysshe Shelley	*Poems*, 1820, through "Arethusa." (Random House.)	5' stanzas	960 (10)	1,970 (18)	870 (9)	3,800	7,980
1793	Felicia Dorothea Hemans	*Works*, "Restoration," 518 lines, through 106 lines of "Edith." (Boston, 1864.)	5'-4' stanzas	*1,280 (13)	2,040 (20)	850 (9)	4,170	7,860
1795	John Keats	*St. Agnes*, *Odes*, etc., and *Hyperion I*, 1,210 lines. (Random House, 1951.)	5' stanzas, bl. verse	*1,470 (12)	2,200 (18)	940 (8)	4,610	9,040
1799	Thomas Hood	*Elm Tree*, *Haunted House*, *Bridge*, *Song of the Shirt*, 1,040 lines. (*Works*, ed. Jerrold, 1920.)	4'-3' stanzas	1,000 (10)	1,460 (14)	670 (6)	3,130	5,840
1803	Richard Horne	*Orion*, through Book II, line 190. (London, 1928.)	5' lines, bl. verse	*1,200 (12)	1,280 (13)	900 (9)	3,380	7,580
1806	Elizabeth Barrett Browning	*Romance of Page*, 26 sonnets, *Rosary*, III, 8. (*Works*, Macmillan, 1903.)	4' stanzas	760 (8)	1,610 (16)	1,020 (10)	3,390	7,900
1809	Alfred Lord Tennyson	*Poems*, 1842; Vol. I, first 21 poems, "Claribel" and ff. (Oxford ed.)	4' stanzas	*1,000 (10)	1,380 (14)	640 (6)	3,020	6,080
1810	Martin Tupper	*Proverbial Philosophy*, first 12. (1st and 2nd series, Philadelphia, 1845.)	6' lines	*1,300 (13)	2,980 (30)	1,510 (15)	5,790	9,170
1812	Robert Browning	*Pippa*, 500 lines, *Dramatic Lyrics*, "Cavalier" through "Laboratory," 500 lines. (*Works*, 1887.)	5' stanzas	760 (8)	1,580 (16)	1,210 (12)	3,550	6,980
1819	Arthur Hugh Clough	*Ambarvalia*, first 64. (*Poems*, ed. Lowry, 1951.)	5'-4' stanzas	*930 (9)	1,660 (17)	800 (8)	3,390	6,950
1822	Matthew Arnold	*Strayed Reveller and Other Poems*. (Oxford ed., 1922.)	5' stanzas	*920 (9)	1,470 (15)	860 (9)	3,250	5,580
1828	George Meredith	"Jerry" and 25 sonnets from *Modern Love*, 500 lines, plus *Westermain*, 300 lines. (Scribner, 1912.)	5'-3' stanzas	730 (9)	1,420 (18)	930 (12)	3,080	6,390
1828	Dante Gabriel Rossetti	*Poems*, 1850 ff., "Damozel" through "Ave," 900 lines. (Dutton.)	4'-3' stanzas	450 (5)	1,460 (16)	690 (8)	2,600	5,210
1837	Algernon Charles Swinburne	*Poems and Ballads*, II, through "Ave," 1,230 lines. (McKay ed., 1910.)	5' stanzas	1,320 (11)	2,380 (19)	1,100 (9)	4,800	10,490
1840	Thomas Hardy	*Poems of Past and Present*. (Macmillan, 1925.)	5' stanzas	550 (6)	1,150 (12)	810 (8)	2,510	6,240

TABLE 1 (continued)

Birth date	Poet	Work and edition (first 1,000 lines)	Measure	Adj.	Nouns	Verbs	Total ANV	Total words
1844	Robert Bridges	Growth of Love, 500 lines, Poems, 1890 200 lines, Classical Metres, 200 lines. (Oxford, 1929.)	5' stanzas, lines	870 (10)	1,740 (19)	800 (9)	3,410	7,230
1844	Gerard Manley Hopkins	Poems, "Pool" through "R. B." (Oxford, 1948.)	5' stanzas	990 (10)	1,960 (20)	1,030 (10)	3,980	8,430
1849	William Ernest Henley	In Hospital 460 lines, London Voluntaries, 360 lines. (Poems, Macmillan, 1921.)	5'-4' lines	1,050 (13)	1,370 (17)	580 (7)	3,000	5,650
1856	Oscar Wilde	Poems, 1882, "Eleutheria," "Garden of Eros," "Impressions du Theatre," 870 lines. (Boston, 1882.)	5' stanzas	880 (10)	1,510 (17)	600 (7)	2,990	4,530
1859	Alfred Edward Housman	Shropshire Lad, and Last Poems, 500 lines each. (Collected Poems, Holt, 1950.)	4' stanzas	470 (5)	1,480 (15)	1,040 (10)	2,990	6,000
1859	Francis Thompson	Misc. Poems, 720 lines, "Tryst" to "Dead Cardinal"; plus "Hound." (Poems, Oxford, 1937.)	5' stanzas	*770 (8)	1,470 (15)	740 (7)	2,980	6,100
1864	Stephen Phillips	Marpessa, Wife, Christ, 800 lines. (Dodd Mead, 1922.)	5' lines, bl. verse	*890 (11)	1,390 (17)	780 (10)	3,060	6,480
1865	William Butler Yeats	The Tower, 1,100 lines. (Collected Poems, Macmillan, 1952.)	5' stanzas	960 (9)	1,760 (16)	980 (9)	3,700	7,350
		Twentieth-century British poets						
1873	Walter de la Mare	The Listeners, through "Exile," 500 lines. (The Listeners, Holt, 1916), and The Veil, through "Monologue," 536 lines. (Poems, 1935.)	4' stanzas	*950 (9)	1,450 (14)	770 (7)	3,170	6,070
1878	John Masefield	Salt Water Ballads and Misc. Poems, through "Holy Peter," 1,030 lines. (Poems, Macmillan, 1953.)	5' stanzas	*1,130 (11)	2,210 (22)	1,170 (12)	4,510	9,500
1878	Edward Thomas	Collected Poems, through "Gone Again," 1,020 lines. (New York, 1921.)	4' stanzas	700 (7)	1,700 (17)	950 (9)	3,350	7,200
1885	D. H. Lawrence	Pansies, through "Touch," 1,030 lines. (Complete Poems, London, 1957.)	5'-3' lines, stanzas	*1,000 (10)	1,560 (15)	1,120 (11)	3,680	7,200
1887	Edwin Muir	First Poems, and Labyrinth, through "Good Town," 1,070 lines. (Collected Poems, Faber, 1952.)	4' stanzas	800 (7)	1,570 (15)	980 (9)	3,350	7,290
1887	Edith Sitwell	Green Song and Other Poems, 750 lines (New York, 1946), and Street Songs, 350 lines (New York, 1942.)	5' stanzas	*1,060 (10)	2,510 (23)	960 (9)	4,530	9,060
1892	Richard Aldington	Complete Poems, "Images" through "Sunset." (London, 1948.)	3' lines	880 (9)	1,290 (13)	610 (6)	2,780	5,030
1893	Wilfred Owen	Poems, through "Inspection." (New Directions, 1949.)	5'-4' stanzas	880 (9)	1,750 (18)	1,030 (10)	3,660	6,900
1895	Robert Graves	Poems, 1938-1945, 750 lines (London, 1948), and Collected Poems (1938), last 11 poems.	4' stanzas	*900 (9)	1,500 (15)	780 (8)	3,180	6,460
1896	Edmund Blunden	Poems, 1914-1930, Experience and Soliloquy, through "Reliques," 1,100 lines.	5' stanzas	*1,290 (12)	1,920 (17)	980 (9)	4,190	7,690

TABLE 1 (continued)

Birth date	Poet	Work and edition (first 1,000 lines)	Measure	Adj.	Nouns	Verbs	Total ANV	Total words
1907	W. H. Auden	Poems, through "Trouble," 630 lines (Collected Poetry), and In Time of War, 380 lines (Random House, 1945.)	5' stanzas	750 (8)	1,590 (16)	1,030 (10)	3,370	7,220
1907	Louis MacNeice	Springboard, Poems, 1941-1944, 1,060 lines.	5' stanzas	*970 (9)	1,960 (18)	1,080 (10)	4,010	8,360
1908	Kathleen Raine	The Year One, through "7th Day." (Collected Poems, London, 1956.)	5' stanzas	*590 (6)	1,690 (17)	730 (7)	3,010	6,000
1909	Stephen Spender	The Still Centre, through "Two Kisses." (Faber, 1939.)	5' stanzas	*900 (9)	1,890 (19)	740 (7)	3,530	7,640
1912	Anne Ridler	The Golden Bird. (Faber, 1951.)	4'-5' stanzas	*800 (8)	1,770 (18)	910 (9)	3,480	7,030
1913	George Barker	Selected Poems, through "Holy Poems," 1,020 lines. (Macmillan, 1941.)	5' lines	*950 (9)	1,900 (19)	820 (8)	3,670	7,320
1914	Norman Nicholson	The Pot Geranium, through "Turn for the Better." (Faber, 1954.)	5' stanzas	*770 (8)	2,140 (21)	680 (7)	3,590	7,010
1914	Dylan Thomas	Selected Writings, first 29 poems. (New Directions, 1946.)	5' stanzas	*1,020 (10)	2,300 (23)	790 (8)	4,110	7,960
1921	Elizabeth Jennings	A Way of Looking, plus Poems, through "Adopted Child." (London, 1955.)	5' stanzas	*610 (6)	1,450 (15)	1,130 (11)	3,190	7,050
1922	Thomas Gunn	Fighting Terms, 1954, plus Sense of Movement, through "Motorcyclist's Vision," 1,020 lines.	5' stanzas	*860 (8)	1,630 (16)	1,100 (11)	3,590	7,540
		Nineteenth-century American poets						
1750	John Trumbull	Minor Poems, 1,028 lines. (New York, 1922.)	5'-4' stanzas	1,130 (11)	2,050 (20)	1,010 (10)	4,190	7,340
1752	Timothy Dwight	Greenfield Hill, 1794, through II, 430 lines. (Conn. Wits, ed. Parrington.)	5'-4' stanzas	1,190 (12)	2,190 (22)	1,050 (11)	4,430	7,830
1752	Philip Freneau	Poems, 1797-1815, through "Suitors," 1,030 lines. (New York, 1815.)	5'-4' stanzas	*880 (9)	1,690 (16)	1,030 (10)	3,600	6,670
1754	Joel Barlow	Hasty Pudding, 1796.	5' lines	1,380 (14)	2,110 (21)	1,100 (11)	4,590	7,800
1790	Fitz-Greene Halleck	Poetical Writings, 1,010 lines. (Ed. Wilson, 1869.)	4' (3'-5') stanzas	630 (6)	2,150 (21)	670 (7)	3,450	7,020
1791	Lydia H. Sigourney	Poems, through "Huguenot Pastor." (New York, 1841.)	5'-4' stanzas	*810 (8)	1,710 (17)	780 (8)	3,300	6,700
1794	William Cullen Bryant	Later Poems, 1,045 lines. (Poems, Philadelphia, 1851.)	5'-4' stanzas	*920 (9)	1,790 (17)	900 (9)	3,610	7,760
1795	Joseph Rodman Drake	The Culprit Fay, 638 lines, through "To a Friend," 100 lines. (Life and Work, Boston, 1935.)	4' stanzas	760 (8)	1,900 (19)	870 (8)	3,530	7,590
1795	James Percival	The Wreck, 1,044 lines. (New York, 1823.)	5' stanzas	840 (8)	1,640 (16)	1,040 (10)	3,520	8,240
1802	Edward Coote Pinkney	Poems, 1825, through "Rodolph, II." (Works, Macmillan, 1926.)	4' stanzas	730 (7)	1,540 (15)	750 (8)	3,020	6,450

TABLE 1 (continued)

Birth date	Poet	Work and edition (first 1,000 lines)	Measure	Adj.	Nouns	Verbs	Total ANV	Total words
1803	Ralph Waldo Emerson	Poems, 1,005 lines. (Boston, 1899.)	4' stanzas	660 (7)	1,530 (15)	820 (8)	3,010	6,140
1807	Henry Wadsworth Longfellow	Ballads and Other Poems, 1842. (Cambridge, 4th ed.)	4' stanzas	*860 (9)	1,930 (19)	1,040 (10)	3,830	6,810
1807	John Greenleaf Whittier	Poems, 1837-1865, Early Verses, "Exile" through "Isabel." (Cambridge, 1894.)	4' stanzas	*1,060 (11)	1,960 (20)	740 (7)	3,760	7,050
1809	Thomas Chivers	Virginalia. (Brooklyn, 1942.)	6'-5' stanzas	*1,130 (11)	1,900 (19)	730 (7)	3,760	7,850
1809	Oliver Wendell Holmes	Poems, 1836, "Ironsides" through 150 lines of "Poetry." (Boston, 1850.)	4' stanzas	*740 (7)	1,430 (14)	890 (9)	3,060	6,310
1809	Edgar Allan Poe	Poems, 1845, "Raven" through "Israfel." (Crowell, 1892.)	5' stanzas	*930 (9)	1,660 (17)	790 (8)	3,380	7,360
1813	Jones Very	Poems, 1839, first 71 sonnets. (Boston, 1883.)	5' stanzas	*870 (9)	1,750 (18)	1,250 (13)	3,870	8,460
1819	James Russell Lowell	"Launcal," "Brittany," and first 100 lines of "Prometheus." (Poems, Cambridge ed., 1897.)	5'-4' lines, stanzas	1,150 (12)	1,860 (19)	1,070 (11)	4,080	8,650
1819	Walt Whitman	"Song of Myself," 500 lines, "Exposition," 250 lines, "India," 250 lines. (Poems, Everyman, 1947.)	6' lines	*1,330 (13)	2,790 (28)	1,040 (10)	5,160	11,050
1829	Henry Timrod	Poems, 1860, 1873, through "An Exotic." (Houghton Mifflin, 1899.)	5'-4' lines, stanzas	710 (7)	1,540 (15)	740 (7)	2,990	6,100
1830	Emily Dickinson	Poems, 1863, Nos. 700-780, 1,020 lines. (Harvard, 1955.)	4'-3' stanzas	440 (4)	1,130 (11)	720 (7)	2,290	4,880
1839	Joaquin Miller	Songs of the Sierras, 1871. (Boston, 1871.)	5' stanzas	930 (9)	1,610 (16)	960 (10)	3,500	7,410
1841	Edward Rowland Sill	The Heritage, 1868, through "Dead Bird." (Houghton Mifflin, 1889.)	5'-3' lines	1,010 (10)	1,690 (17)	1,090 (11)	3,790	7,260
1842	Sidney Lanier	Poems, 1877, "Hymns" through "Stirrup Cup." (Scribner, 1912.)	5' stanzas	960 (10)	2,150 (22)	950 (10)	4,060	8,230
1850	Eugene Field	Western Verse, 1889.	4' stanzas	490 (5)	1,390 (14)	790 (8)	2,670	5,980
1850	Ella Wheeler Wilcox	Poems of Passion, 1883. (Chicago, 1892.)	4' stanzas	850 (9)	1,610 (16)	1,110 (11)	3,570	8,100
1861	Louise Guiney	Roadside Harp, 1893, through "Footnote."	5' stanzas	900 (9)	1,520 (15)	740 (7)	3,160	6,600
1869	William Vaughan Moody	Poems, "Gloucester Moors" through "Jetsam." (Houghton Mifflin, 1901.)	5' lines	1,070 (11)	1,730 (17)	1,140 (11)	3,940	8,630
1869	Edward Arlington Robinson	Children of the Night, 950 lines. (Collected Poems, Macmillan, 1948.)	5'-4' stanzas	660 (7)	1,380 (15)	850 (9)	2,890	7,600
1869	George Sterling	The Testament of the Sun, 1903, through "Testament of the Sun." (Wood, 1903.)	5' stanzas	740 (7)	1,740 (17)	710 (7)	3,190	6,650

TABLE 1 (continued)

Birth date	Poet	Work and edition (first 1,000 lines)	Measure	Adj.	Nouns	Verbs	Total ANV	Total words
		Twentieth-century American poets						
1875	Robert Frost	A Further Range, through "10 Mills." (Collected Poems, 1939.)	5'-4' stanzas	770 (8)	1,490 (15)	1,110 (11)	3,370	7,380
1879	Wallace Stevens	Transport to Summer, first 20 poems. (Knopf, 1947.)	5' lines, stanzas	860 (9)	1,850 (19)	950 (10)	3,660	7,550
1883	William Carlos Williams	Early Martyr, 465 lines, Adam and Eve, 585 lines. (Collected Poems, 1938.)	3' lines	*540 (5)	850 (8)	420 (4)	1,810	3,100
1885	Ezra Pound	1st Cantos. (New Directions, 1948.)	5'-3' lines	*740 (7)	1,960 (20)	610 (6)	3,310	7,220
1887	Marianne Moore	8 poems from Selected Poems (1935), plus Nevertheless (1944.)		*930 (9)	1,830 (18)	680 (9)	3,440	5,700
1888	T. S. Eliot	The Waste Land, and ff., through "Marina," 900 lines. (Macmillan, 1944.)	5'-3' lines	*640 (7)	1,490 (17)	730 (8)	2,860	6,620
1892	Edna St. V. Millay	Collected Lyrics, through "Journey." (Harper, 1943.)	4' stanzas	760 (8)	1,260 (13)	1,110 (11)	3,130	7,150
1894	E. E. Cummings	IXI. (Holt, 1944.)	3' lines, stanzas	580 (6)	1,130 (11)	710 (7)	2,420	4,980
1897	Robinson Jeffers	Counsels and New Poems, last 540 lines. Be Angry, first 480 lines. (Selected Poems, Random House, 1941.)	6' lines	1,560 (16)	2,810 (28)	1,590 (16)	5,960	15,300
1899	Hart Crane	The Bridge. (Collected Poems, ed. Frank, 1946.)	5'-3' stanzas	*1,030 (10)	2,030 (20)	800 (8)	3,860	6,890
1904	Richard Eberhart	Poems New and Selected, plus Burr Oaks, 250 lines. (1947.)	5' stanzas	820 (8)	1,500 (15)	930 (9)	3,250	6,410
1905	Robert Penn Warren	Selected Poems, 1923-1943, "Pots" ff., through "Question and Answer." (New York, 1944.)	5' lines, stanzas	820 (8)	1,790 (18)	1,060 (11)	3,670	7,700
1908	Theodore Roethke	The Waking, 1933-1953, 1,060 lines. (New York, 1953.)	4' lines, stanzas	*800 (8)	1,580 (16)	800 (8)	3,180	6,680
1910	W. T. Scott	To Marry Strangers. (New York, 1945.)	5' stanzas	*940 (9)	1,540 (15)	1,040 (10)	3,520	7,930
1911	Elizabeth Bishop	Poems, 1955, through "Fish," 1,030 lines. (Boston, 1955.)	4' lines, stanzas	*870 (8)	1,480 (14)	760 (7)	3,110	6,660
1913	Muriel Rukeyser	Beast in View, 1944, 1,040 lines. (New York, 1944.)	5' lines, stanzas	*970 (9)	1,800 (17)	820 (8)	3,590	6,550
1913	Karl Shapiro	Person, Place, and Thing, and V-Letter, 19 poems each, 1,039 lines. (Reynal, 1942, 1944.)	5' stanzas	1,000 (10)	2,160 (21)	970 (9)	4,130	8,350
1917	Robert Lowell	Lord Weary's Castle. (New York, 1946.)	5' lines	*740 (7)	2,130 (21)	1,010 (10)	3,850	7,460
1921	Richard Wilbur	Things of This World, 130 lines (New York, 1956), plus Ceremony, 1,030 lines (New York, 1950.)	5' stanzas	*960 (9)	1,750 (17)	880 (9)	3,590	6,570
1923	Anthony Hecht	A Summoning of Stones (1954), 1,030 lines. (New York, 1954.)	5' stanzas	*1,010 (10)	1,850 (18)	840 (8)	3,700	6,420

TABLE 2

Table 2 gives the list of major terms supplementing the list of major measures and proportions for the texts of Table 1. To use the same examples as in Table 1, we may see further how Langland's mode is consistent in its extreme. The adjectives he repeats most—false, fond, good, great, kind, poor, red, wise—which appear at least ten times apiece in the thousand lines, are, in the main, terms of human judgment and relation, as they are for his contemporaries, Gower and Chaucer. His nouns, like Gower's if not Chaucer's, are words of a religious society, with certain homely details of reference. Three of his nouns, like three of Gower's, are repeated more than ten times apiece, as indicated by the numbers in parentheses: king (40), mede (60), truth (30). His main verbs, differing from both Gower's and Chaucer's, stress in ask, bring, find, like, maintain, show, and teach, the theme of inquiry, of learning, which is central to the poem. Repetition of other verbs of this sort, in action after earnest action in the poem, accounts for the high proportion of verbs in the text.

Every poet presents a unique combination of choices: Chaucer's early interest in old and young, for example, his urbanity in gold and town and name; his consciousness of speech in tale, word, speak, and tell. Turning the pages, we may note how some poets more than others rely on a basic stock of repeated terms: note, for example, the difference between Douglas' paucity and Coverdale's abundance. Sometimes such repetition may represent a fully used device of form; sometimes it may seem an inadequacy of invention. As a whole, the nineteenth-century poets seem the ones most interested in the thematic powers of word repetition.

We may note also the general likeness of one major vocabulary to another in any one time, present as well as past, and even certain major likenesses as well as differences between past and present. Indeed, about a fourth of all the major terms are used throughout the five centuries.

Place too seems to support agreement, though not so strongly as time. The American poets of 1770-1930 agree mainly with their British contemporaries, but in some main terms, especially those for natural forces, agree more strongly among themselves, and follow their eighteenth-century predecessors rather than their contemporaries in England. Note how the major terms of Barlow, Dwight, Trumbull, Whittier, Whitman, and even moderns like Pound and Crane, sound more like the terms of Thomson and the Wartons than like those of Shelley or Arnold or Browning.

At the end of Table 2 are lists of the major words and proportions of twenty poetic texts in other languages and of twenty prose texts in English, in order to suggest, however briefly, some of the possible relationships needing study. We may see again how strong a force time is, in the likeness to our own of our contemporaries' vocabulary in other tongues. We may see the likeness of actual classical major terms to the major terms in our own self-termed classical poetry. In the prose texts of the seventeenth and twentieth centuries we may note proportions and vocabularies closely similar to those of poetry, with two major exceptions: topic seems a more controlling force in the choice of nouns, and the phrasal mode seems less frequent, at least in the prose here observed.

My hope is that each reader of Tables 1 and 2, interested in a particular poet, will find some illumination of character in these lists of the proportions and terms which his poet relies upon.

TABLE 2

MAJOR ADJECTIVES, NOUNS, VERBS FOR 200 POETS

Major words occurring approximately ten times or more in a thousand lines; twenty times or more indicated in parentheses. Specific omissions, here, though counted in totals, are: numerical adjectives, proper names, auxiliaries and <u>to be</u>, <u>to have</u>, <u>to do</u>, <u>to say</u>.

Poet	Adjectives	Nouns	Verbs
		England	
Minot, 1310	bare fair false good (20) great keen stout worth	bale battle boast bow care deed day dance folk god* (30) guile heart king (20) knight land lord man (80) mede might night pride prince right shame side sin steed town time while will word	abide bear begin bring (20) come (30) dare dight dwell fall fare find fight flee give go girt help hear hide save send see take tell think wene win
Gower, 1325	good (20) great holy wise	book cause Christ church clerk day ensample ear eye god hand heart law life love (30) man (70) point priest schrift son thing time truth vice wisdom wit word world (40) wyse	befall begin cast fall go hear know keep see schrieve set speke stand take tell think understand wot write
Langland, 1330	false fond good great kind poor red wise	cat cheek Christ conscience friar god heaven king (40) law life love mede (60) mercy people rat simony soul tongue truth (30) wit word work	ask bring find can (know) hear leve like maintain quoth show teach
Chaucer, 1340	fair good great high old poor worthy young	day gold hand heart horse knight lady lord man (40) tale thing time town way wine word	begin come give go keep know love make ride see speak take tell win
Gawain Poet, 1350	clean comely dear gay good great green (30) hende high new rich (20) stiff (strong)	athel arm burne (man) court day dais frehe (man) gold gome (man) god hall hand head king (20) knight (30) lady life lord man (30) meat mirth secg (man) table wonder world year	ask come find go hear hold know laugh let like look make quoth ride see seem serve sit (20) stand tell think win wone (dwell)
Pearl Poet, 1350	clean dear fair great (20) gentle high mascelless precious rich	adubbement apocalypse apostle bank bliss (20) Christ courtesy day date god (20) gem ground grace heaven jewel jeweler lamb (20) life lord (20) man (20) mote pearl (40) queen right speech spot stone vine water world	bear call come deem find gan give know leve quod rise see sit stand take think wone (dwell) work
Hoccleve, 1368	good (20) great (20) wise	book cause conceit day (20) death friend (30) friendship god (40) gold grace harm head heart labour life lord (20) man (80) manner matter might people reason sickness sooth spirit study thing time wight (20) wise wit (20) woe word world	come (20) deem fall give go hold keep know (20) lay let list pass rede see (30) speak stand take (20) tell thank think (20) wist
Lydgate, 1370	good great fair fresh high new old	auctor beauty book fortune god heart joy king lady life love man manner story thing woe	find love make see (30) take
James I, 1394	bright fair (20) fresh full good little sweet (20) white	adventure bird book cause comfort cure day (20) eye flower folk fortune god grace ground hand heart heaven joy law life (20) love (30) man matter mercy mind nature pain service song thing thought time vertue way wight	come (20) find give go list live make (20) see (30) set sing stand take think turn
Henryson, 1430	fair (30) false gay golden good great (20) green true worthy	care day end eye face flower (20) father god (20) hair hand heart heaven joy king knight lady (20) lip love (30) man (20) night pain thing time wind word	come (20) give go hear know look lie quoth pass

Ballads, c. 1460 ff.	bonny dear fair golden good green handsome old red silver young (20)	bed child church day father (20) hand heart home king lady life lord (30) love man (30) mother (40) sister son steed time word	come (70) die go leave lie (30) look make (30) play see (30) sing speak take (30)
Skelton, 1460	good great holy noble	bishop church friar god gold lord man people	come go make know speak take
Dunbar, 1470	awful bright clear fair full fresh green lusty noble red sharp shene sweet tender white	beam beast beauty bird dame dance day death field fowl flower (20) god lady leaf light love May morrow nature queen rose sky	affray come go hail make rise see (20) sing take think
Hawes, 1470	busy clear common fair (30) famous good (30) great (40) high holden labell noble (20) old perfyt pucell royal true whole	color cunning dame fame flower grace head king lady man matter mind name poet reason science thing time tower (20) truth way (20) word world	appear begin behold call go know make see set shine show take
Douglas, 1474	gentill good great fresh lustie sweet	book day eloquence god gold lady man nature poet tree thyng tyme water werk (20) wit word world	follow know make show wot
Barclay, 1475	good great (20) poor rural	citie (50) dayes fortune god (20) ground herd honour (20) labour (20) lady life lord (20) man (60) payne people pleasure plowman shepherd thing (20) time town winter	come dwell give live make see tell (20) think
Sternhold, 1480 1480	great holy just poor wicked worldly	foe god (50) hand heart (30) heaven king life lord (100) man (50) mercy mind power soul thing world	give hear keep know make (20) see stand take
Coverdale, 1488 1488	dear eternal free good great (30) holy (20) strong sweet worthy	Christ day (20) death (20) enemy evil faith father (20) flesh god (80) the good grace heart (20) heaven hell hour law life lord (50) love man (30) mercy (20) might mind name need night pain power right saviour sin (20) son (20) spirit tentation thing (20) verity will (20) word (20) world	bear believe break bring call come (20) deliver die fall forgive fulfill give (20) go help keep live love make (20) pray put rejoice rise see sin show stand take trust
Lindsay, 1490	English fair good great (30) noble young	arms day deed field gear god hand (20) horse (20) king lady (20) land life lord love man (60) shield ship spear (20) squire (60) steed (20) time war (20)	come fight get give go know lie love make (20) pass play put quod run see (30) take (30) think
Heywood, 1497	good (60) ill merry (20) old (20) poor rich sweet wise young	day eye friend god (20) hand heart love maid man (60) mind thing (30) time wedding (20) widow wife (20) year	begin bring come (30) find go (20) know look make (20) quoth (30) speak see (20) show (20) take (20) tell think (20)
Wyatt, 1503	blind cruel dead dear fair good great true	cause death desire faith fire fortune grace heart (50) life love (20) man mind pain (30) place reason sigh tear thing time woe	find go hear know love make please see seek take think (20)
Surrey, 1517	good great green pleasant secret sweet true woful	beauty breast (20) day death desire eye face fire flame heart (40) heat lady lord love (40) man (20) mind (20) nature night pain place sun thing thought (20) time winter woe year	bring come find (30) give go know (30) lose make (20) methinks see (40) seek serve show take teach think (20)

*god includes God and the gods.

TABLE 2 (continued)

Poet	Adjectives	Nouns	Verbs
Churchyard, 1520	gcod (20) great (20) small (20) sweet	band camp charge day (20) end enemy fame fear fight foe fortune friend god hap harm life man (70) mount name queen pen shot soldier (20) thing (20) time (20) town trench war (20) way wit world	bear begin bring (20) come (30) fall find (20) get give go (20) hear know (30) lay leave look (20) make (50) put run see (30) seek seem serve set shoot show sit slay speak stand take tell think use win
Crowley, 1521	great poor sore true wicked (20)	blood Christ day duty end father fault flock god (30) the good ground hand (20) heart hell house king land lord (20) man (50) pain people place the poor rede rent sort thing (20) time way word world	buy call come crave dwell feed find get give (20) go hear keep know lay live (20) make (20) see (20) seek send take (30) tell think work
Baldwin, 1529	cruel false good old true	brother day death father fortune god (20) heart king (30) land law life love man (30) mind right prince son thing (20) time	come (20) die give make see seek take (20) think
Sackville, 1536	chief cruel woeful	blood eye day death fear fortune god hand heart (20) king life (20) love man murder night prince state tear thing tyrant woe	bear begin come (30) die fall find give go know make (20) see (40) seek take tell think
Googe, 1540	cruel good great high old pleasant	fame fancie gryef heart hell love (20) man name payne shepherd thing time (20)	die give let lie live see tell
Turberville, 1540	friendly good	beauty fame flame god hand heart (20) hope love (20) man pain pleasure	fall give know make (20) see (20) seem tell think yield
Gasgoigne, 1542	common (20) filthie foul good (20) great high pleasant strange trusty worthy	cause day deed (20) delight eye glasse (40) god (20) gold heart king (20) knight life lord (30) love lust man (40) mind (20) priest (30) prince steele thing time soldier world youth	behold come (20) find give go keep live make (30) pray (20) see (60) seem serve show sing speak tell think
Breton, 1545	fine foolish good great little old strange	art asse delight eye fancie (30) flower friend god hand head heart kind love man mind scholar school sir thing time toy way (20) youth	bring come find gin give go learn lie make (20) see take teach tell think
Spenser, 1552	black blind dear fair (20) foul full gentle good great (20) little naught new proud sad sweet (20)	day eye (30) heart (20) heaven lady life (20) love (30) man (20) night thought word world	come find give hear know lie look make (20) see (20) take tell think
Sidney, 1554	fair gold good (20) great (20) happy high inward long old own poor rich sweet (20) true wise	beauty being breast day desire eye (30) fool fortune friend hand heart (30) heaven hell life love (60) man mind muse nature praise sight shepherd soul sun thing thought virtue wit word	behold come find give go know learn love make (40) run see (20) seek seem show speak take think yield
Chapman, 1559	bright fair glorious golden good great high poor rich sacred	ear eye god gold heaven king life man (30) praise son	bear come fall give (20) grow know make (30) see (30) serve take (20)
Daniel, 1562	chaste cruel fair (30) good great happy (20) high poor own sweet (20) unkind	art beauty (30) breath day death desire (30) disdain eye (40) faith flower grief hand heart (40) honour (20) hope (30) life love (40) man muse night pity power soul sun tear thought time (30) world (20) youth (30)	come find (20) give go know let lie live (20) look love (20) make (20) read see (30) show take think yield

Drayton, 1563	fair good great heavenly high sweet true	beauty day eye (20) god hand heart (20) heaven hope light love (30) man (20) night power prayer queen shepherd (30) sun thing thought virtue world	come give (20) go hear lie love make (20) play please see (30) sing sit take tell think
Sylvester, 1563	bright divine eternal fair glorious good great high immortal sweet mighty proud pure sacred (20)	air (20) art beauty day earth eye fire god (30) heaven light lord nature night nothing power sea soul spirit sun time water work world (30)	give make see seem
Marlowe, 1564	fair (20) gentle gold great poor rich sweet	arm beauty breast day eye god (20) hand (20) head heart heaven love (70) maid man (20) mind muse night thought time woman word world	come gin give go (20) kiss know lie love (20) make (30) see seek sing sit take (20) think win
Shakespeare, 1564	bright dear fair good great happy old sweet (30) true	beauty (30) day (20) eye (50) love (80) time (30) world heart (20) life man nature night (20) thing thought (20) youth	bring die find give (20) go (20) know lie live (20) look love (20) make (30) see (20) take
Campion, 1567	fair good great happy heavenly kind sweet (20) true	beauty (20) comfort day (20) death deed delight desire earth eye (20) fire fortune god grace grief hand heart (30) heaven (20) hell hope joy (20) kiss life light (20) lord love (70) man mind music night (20) pain part pity pleasure power sight song sorrow soul (20) spirit sprite stream sun thought (20) time way	come die (20) fear find fly follow give hear hold lie live (20) love (20) move prove see sing sleep speak view
Fairfax, 1570	bold Christian fair fierce full glorious good great (20) noble (20) old strong sweet	arm Christian conquest courage day death duke eye field fire foe glory god heaven hour image knight king lord (20) love (20) man might prince sea side sight soldier thought (20) time town troop tyrant war	begin bring come (20) fear find hear lay lie make (20) move quoth send take win
Jonson, 1573	good great poor proud sweet true	day eye face fire friend god grace hand heart life love (30) man (40) name nature son thing world	call come find fly give go grow hear know look love make (40) meet see take tell think
Donne, 1576	bad false good new poor true	day death eye face fear heart love (110) man name soul sun tear thing world year	come die fall find give go keep know love make see show take (20) tell think
Sandys, 1578	fair great high sweet	beauty breast daughter day death earth eye foe (30) god (30) heart heaven joy lord love man night power sin soul virgin woe wrath	appear come fall find give hear know make see show take tell
P. Fletcher, 1582	fair gentle good great (20) happy high little old new strong	art breast death earth grief heart (20) isle (30) life light love (20) man mind muse nature shepherd song soul time world	gan give know lie live make (20) rise see sing sit take
Wither, 1588	good great true	day eye fear folly foe god heart hope king man power pride sin thing time voice world	appear believe bring come fear find give hear (20) know make see seem take tell think
Herrick, 1591	dead good poor rich small sweet (20) true white	bed day eye flower heart lip love (40) man night part rose	bring call come (30) die fall find fly give go grow hear keep kiss know lie live look love make see show sing stand tell think

TABLE 2 (continued)

Poet	Adjectives	Nouns	Verbs
Quarles, 1592	common fair full gentle good great new poor sweet true	blood day ear (20) earth eye flock (40) god hand heart heaven lamb life love man power sheep (30) shepherd (70) soul swain thing time water word	come fear feed (20) find give go grow hear keep know lie look love make see speak stand take teach tell think
Herbert, 1593	good great (20)	art blood day (20) death dust earth eye faith fear glory god grace grief (80) heart heaven (20) joy king life (20) light lord love (20) man (20) name part place praise sin (30) sorrow soul (20) stone sun way (20) world (20)	bear bring come die drop feel fly give go know let make rise see seek show sing take write
Carew, 1595	cold fair pure sweet	beauty (20) blood day earth eye face fire flame god hand heart (30) lip love (60) man nature soul sun thing time year	die find fly give lie live love know make rise see show
Shirley, 1596	fair good great new sad	blood day eye face fire flame heart heaven king love (30) man name soul time	bring come find give hear know love make (30) see (30) sing tell
Waller, 1606	bold bright fair (30) good great high just new noble old proud sweet	care eye fate fire god heart heaven (30) love (40) man part power sea thing world	bring come find give grow hear know make (30) see seem sing stand tell
Milton, 1608	dark fair good great high holy old sad sweet	air day ear eye god heaven light night star sun wind	bring come (20) give go hear (20) keep know lie live make see sing sit
Suckling, 1609	dear fair good great kind little new wise	day eye face fire grace heart hope love man mind place sun thing time way wit	appear awake bring call come die find give go hold keep know lie look love make move see take tell think
Cleveland, 1613	good old strange sweet	eye lip love man nature soul tongue world	find give go know make see speak swear take think
Crashaw, 1613	black bright dark fair (30) full good great high new old poor proud rich sad soft sweet true	day death earth eye (50) fire god heart heaven (40) love man night part sin soul tear (20) world	bring come find give go keep know lie make (40) see show speak stand think weep
More, 1614	bright fair foul good (30) great happy high holy old sweet	earth eye fire god heart life (20) love man nature night sense son soul thing word	begin (20) call give go hight look make see shine speak stand take tell
Denham, 1615	dark good great noble old pious	eye fire god king love man name poet son thing world	bring come find fly give know make (30) see stand teach tell think
Cowley, 1618	fair great happy wise	art beauty body day earth eye fear fire god heart heaven light love (60) man (30) name nature part soul thing time woman world year	appear bring call come die find fly give go grow keep know live love make (30) move prove see seem shine show take think
Lovelace, 1618	black bright fair good happy new poor rich true	breast day death earth eye fire god heart heaven joy light love man night soul tear time thought world	bring find fly (20) give hasten hear know lie live love make see shine show weep

Marvell, 1621	fair great holy sweet (20)	day eye (20) flower (20) foot garden grass hand head heaven (20) lily love man (20) rose soul sun tear time world	die find go grow know lie live make (20) meet see (20) seem show take
Vaughan, 1622	dark fair full quick	blood cloud day (30) death earth eye god heaven hour life light (20) lord man night sin soul star sun tear thing thought time wing year	bring come fall find give go know make see shine sleep take think weep
Dryden, 1631	bad good high long old public true wise	arm day eye fate father friend god hand heart heaven (40) king (40) law (20) life love man (20) name time nature people (20) power (20) prince soul (30) youth	bring find give (20) know love make (30) please rise see think
Roscommon, 1633	good great new sacred wild	age art day death eye friend god (30) heaven hope joy love man (30) muse nature night pain poet power praise sense style	bring call come cry die find fly give know love make (20) please praise see (20) seize sing (20) teach think write
Oldham, 1653	common dear good great (20) new next old poor sure true vain wild	age art author day design end fire friend god language law man nature nothing play poet poetry rest rules sense (20) sir subject thing town verse way wit (20) word work	bring choose come give (20) grow know make (30) please take think write
Blackmore, 1655	bright divine fine good great happy high human pure superior vain various wild	brain day god head heaven land law learning life man mind (20) muse nature (20) nation power pride race reason sense (30) sky soul spirit sun thought (20) town virtue wit (50)	fill find give grow know make (20) raise see take
Creech, 1659	bad free good great high mean new noble old poor	art bayes fame friend god life man (20) muse poet sir son time way wit word (20)	fear fly give go live keep know make (20) take tell write (20)
Garth, 1661	great (20) new old	arm art day eye (20) fate god hour life power sky world	call fall find fly give know (20) lay make meet raise reign rise tell try
Walsh, 1663	bright charming fair false free great happy kind just new soft true vain (20)	arms beauty breast charm death eye (20) fame fate fear fire god heart joy life love (60) lover man muse pain (20) passion pity power soul tear thing time torment verse youth	begin find give grow hate know live love (20) make see (40) take think
Prior, 1664	great (20) various	care earth heaven man nature power reason sea thought throne	find know rise see
Pomfret, 1667	bright eternal fair gay great happy kind mighty sad secret soft true vain vast	arms blood care charms day death delight eye fate fear friend god (20) heaven joy life love (40) man night pain passion power reason (30) sight soul (20) thing youth (20)	bring come cry die (20) go know (20) live (20) make (20) see take
Addison, 1672	bright great high mighty vain	air arm art bee cell earth eye fire god (20) heart heaven (20) hive king light man night pain sky tree wind work	die find fly grow lie make raise rise run see (20) work
Somerville, 1675	bold fair great old proud rich soft vain	air arm (20) breast crowd (20) day eye (30) foe friend hand (30) head (20) heart (20) hope joy (20) king love man nymph rage soul voice youth	bear fall (20) fly hang hear see stand view

TABLE 2 (continued)

Poet	Adjectives	Nouns	Verbs
Philips, 1676	fair large little	apple art force fruit ground hand love nature soil	fall give know
Parnell, 1679	bright fair great long sacred soft sweet	air angel care day eye fame fear flame glory god heart heaven joy life light love man (20) mind music name nation night peace praise prayer sky (20) soul state sun time view war way world	appear come die fall go know make rise see seem sing
Young, 1683	eternal fair good great human immortal poor soft strong sweet wise	day death (30) earth (20) eternity eye fate (20) fool friend god heart heaven hour joy (20) life (40) man (60) nature (20) night scene soul thought (30) time (50) virtue world (20)	call die fall find fly give know make (20) see seem take think
Gay, 1685	wise	air art blood breast care eye gold hand heart heaven life man mind nature power praise virtue	cry fly give grow hear know pass see stand wake
Pope, 1688	bright fair new sad silver soft various	air (20) beauty (20) breast day eye (40) fate god hair hand (20) head (20) heart (20) heaven (20) king lock lord love (30) maid man (20) name night nymph (20) power prayer queen sky soul spirit star sun sylph thing	fall find fly give know lie make rise see (20) speak take think
Blair, 1699	great long	day death (20) eye grave hand heart life man (30) night soul thing time	come give go hear know make see tell think
Dyer, 1700	deep fair little proud soft sweet various wide	air day just eye flower fleece (20) god hand head hill life man nature ruin sheep (20) shepherd	behold hear lie rise see (20)
Thomson, 1700	deep fair fierce gay great happy long mighty pure sad wide wild	air cloud country day death eye flood friend hand heart heaven hill land life (30) man (20) mind mountain nature night (20) power scene sky (20) snow soul (20) storm sun thought wind winter world year	come fall hear know rise see stand swell
Armstrong, 1709	generous green human new soft tender various	air (30) art blood day food god heart heaven life (30) man nature (30) power (30) sky song soul world youth	bear breathe come give grow know live rise see yield
Johnson, 1709	gay general great new vain	age air art (20) day eye fate foe friend gold heart heaven king land life (20) love (20) man nature (20) power (20) pride scene virtue voice wealth woe world youth	behold come die find fly give know leave make please rise see
Lyttleton, 1709	dear fair gentle happy soft sweet (20) tender	breast day eye flower friend god hand heart (20) joy (20) life love (30) maid name pain power (20) soul thought world youth	come find give hear know love move please see (20) shine stand teach tell
Shenstone, 1714	fair (20) gay little lovely soft (20) sweet	air art beauty breast dame day eye (20) flower fool friend (20) god hand life love maid mind nature power scene sweets toil thought virtue youth	find fly give know please rise see (20) seem
Gray, 1716	golden human little solemn sweet wild	air day eye (20) fate flower friend god hand head heart heaven joy king love man muse night soul sun time way	come fly give go hear know leave rise see (20)

Akenside, 1721	divine fair lonely	air art breast care day earth eye friend god hand heaven hope hour joy life light love lyre man mind muse name nature nymph power (20) scene sky song soul sun tongue	bear behold fly give know move rise see
Collins, 1721	divine fair gentle golden green happy royal sad silent soft sweet (20) tender wide wild (20)	air day (20) eye (20) flower hand (20) heart heaven hour love (30) maid (30) man mind nature power scene shepherd son song soul thought truth virtue way youth (20)	bless call come find (20) hear (20) know lead leave love make rise see (20) sing teach
J. Warton, 1722	dark fair golden great high rich soft sweet wild	air beauty breast eye field friend god hand head (20) heart heaven joy love maid man mead nature night nymph soul virtue world muse (20) shade (20)	give hear lead love rise sit
Mason, 1725	bright fair free high light proud sacred soft sweet vain	beauty charm day eye fancy fate friend hand head heart heaven lay love man muse name nature poet power praise pride scene shade shepherd song soul strain time truth youth	bid come die flow give hear know lead meet rise see teach
T. Warton, 1728	ancient bold bright conscious divine fair golden gothic holy mild new old pensive proud rude sacred	art day eye fame freedom glory hand king mind muse nature power state truth youth	call mark rise see (20) shine sing stand strike
Goldsmith, 1730	dear good sweet	art breast charm (20) heart heaven joy land life love man (20) pride sky son time train way wealth woe world youth	fly give go know see (20)
Cowper, 1731	distant good soft sweet	air art beauty country day earth eye foot god heart life man (20) nature (20) scene sofa wind world	fall feel find love make see seem stand
Churchill, 1738	great happy mighty new simple vile	age art eye fate fear fool fortune friend head heart home honour hour knowledge land law love man (20) muse nation nature (20) place power pride rule sage skill son state swain thing time trade want way world	bring come fall find give hear hold keep know make rise see take think
Chatterton, 1752	bloody brave dead good great high mickle noble sweet	air arrow blood day earl eye father fight friend god ground head (20) heart (20) king knight life man (20) might mind plain saint son spear sun war way woe wound	come (20) die draw fall (20) fly give go live make rise see (20) seek sing stand take tell
Crabbe, 1754	fair great happy humble own poor proud rude sad	age care child day eye (20) fate fear field friend grief hand heart hope hour joy labour (20) life man (20) mind muse nymph pain peasant pleasure power pride scene song sun swain thought time view way woe year youth	ask behold come die feel find give go hear know lie live look make reign see (20) stand think
Blake, 1757	beautiful black bright dark divine eternal (20) gentle golden great happy human little (20) old pale red silent soft starry sweet terrible wild	air bosom child cloud (30) daughter day (30) death (30) earth eye fire flower foot furnace god hand head heaven (20) joy (20) lamb land life love (20) man (20) morning mountain night (20) son sun time valley (20) voice wheel worm	awake bring come fall find give go know hear hide live look love make pass rise see sing sit sleep smile stand take turn walk weep

TABLE 2 (continued)

Poet	Adjectives	Nouns	Verbs
Burns, 1759	auld dear great guid honest long noble poor (30) weary youthful	care eye father friend (30) god heart (30) heaven hope life (30) love man (30) mother pleasure power pride sea sir tear time year	bless come give go hear make (20) mourn see (20) take think
Bowles, 1762	beauteous bright cold (30) dark distant fair high mournful pale poor sad (30) silent soft sweet vain weary white wild	charm cliff day (30) delight ear earth eye fancy fate friend (30) heart (30) hill hope (20) hour (30) life (20) man morn (20) mountain pain pity scene (20) sense shade shore sight song sorrow sound spirit sun tear (20) thought tide time vale view virtue wave wind woe woods world year youth	bear behold bid come feel fly go (20) hear (20) love mark meet pass see seem think turn wait weep
Rogers, 1763	bright busy fond grey little old pensive rude sacred silent soft sweet (20)	age air breast charm clime cloud day evening eye (20) form friend hand heart (20) heaven hope hour joy life (20) light love maid memory mind nature night power rapture scene shade shore sky soul (20) spirit (20) stone thought time truth virtue voice world youth	breathe call charm die draw dwell feel flow fly gaze give hail hear know live love rise see smile soothe view wake weep
Wordsworth, 1770	cold dear deep green little old poor sweet warm wild young	day heart joy love mountain nature pain spirit sun thing thought tree wood year	love pray stand weep
Coleridge, 1772	black bright holy little poor sad strange sweet white	air bird body cloud day eye love mist moon (20) night rock sail sea ship sky sun water wind wood	blow fly love pray sing
Southey, 1774	calm deep good high sad soft sullen	bosom breast day (20) eye fear friend hand head heaven hour joy life love man memory morn scene sorrow soul tear time year	fly give hear know (20) love recall see (20)
Landor, 1775	long old soft sweet	arm breast daughter day (20) eye (20) father (20) god (30) hand head heart love (20) maid man (20) mother night sea song word	bring come (20) fall find give go (20) hear (30) know leave lie look love (20) rise see (20) sing speak take think
Campbell, 1777	bright fair long old (20) poor sweet true wild wise	day (20) eye father friend hand heart heaven life (20) light love man (20) mind (20) nature power son soul (20) spirit time word	bring come (20) give go (20) hear know look love make (20) see (20) tell think
Moore, 1779	bright (20) cold dark dear (20) light silent soft sweet young	chains day dream eye (20) freedom friend glory heart (30) heaven home hope hour joy life light (20) love man moon night pleasure shade smile (20) sorrow soul spirit star sun tear thought time valley woman world youth	bless come fall feel give go hang keep lie live look love make remember (20) see shine sleep smile tell think turn wake weep
Hunt, 1784	bright good great lovely old own proud sweet true	air bride day eye (20) friend god (20) hand head heart horse knight lady lord light poet princess spirit sun thing time	come (40) fall find give go (30) grow hear know look make pray rise see seem sit show take tell think
Byron, 1788	blue bright cold deep good own	blood bosom day (20) earth eye (20) father god hall hand heart (20) hour king land love man mother soul spirit tear thought voice wind year	appear behold come die feel give go know lie look love make pass see stand tell weep

Shelley, 1792	blue bright deep dim fair golden sensitive sweet (20) white	air breast child cloud day earth (20) eye flower garden grace heart heaven (30) life light love man night plant power sky soul spirit star sun wind world	arise bear come die hear lie make see
Hemans, 1793	bright (20) dark deep dim fair full high own proud rich sad strong wild	art day (20) earth (20) eye (20) hand head heart (20) heaven hour joy life (20) light (20) love (20) might mind power (20) scene (20) song soul (20) thought (20) time world (20)	breathe fall give hear live make rise seem tell
Keats, 1795	bright deep divine fair (20) full golden happy little old (20) pale sad silent silver soft (20) sweet (20) wide wing'd	air beauty cloud day (20) door dream ear earth eve eye (20) face fancy flower foot forest god (20) hand head heart heaven honour hour joy light love man moon night (20) pain pleasure sorrow soul star thing thought time tree voice wind wing woe world	bear come (20) die fall find give go know lie look make rise see (20) seem stand tell
Hood, 1799	dark daunted gloomy haunted hollow human lofty old plain sad solemn	bough death ear elm (20) eye hand love man sense spirit time tree (20)	come fall feel hang (20) lie make stand stitch take work (30)
Horne, 1803	bright clear deep gold great high (20) new own	air dream earth eye friend giant god (30) hand head heart king length life light love man mind night nymph power sense shadow soul stag thing thought time wood	become come feel find give hold know look make rise see take teach
E. B. Browning, 1806	brown fair good great high holy last little own sweet true young	angel bride day death dream earth eye (20) father (20) god (30) hand (20) heart (20) heaven knight lady (20) life love (20) maid man mother (20) nature night page (20) prayer rosary soul spirit sun thought woman word world	come (20) fall feel forbear go hear (20) know lie look (20) make pray ride see (20) sing speak stand take think
Tennyson, 1809	aweary clear dead deep dreary golden (20) good (20) great silver sweet white wild	day death earth eye (20) flower heart (20) hour life (20) light (20) love mind moon night (20) prime star sun time	come (20) fall go hear kiss lie look see sing
Tupper, 1810	dark deep good (20) happy mighty own precious secret silent strong sweet wise	beauty character dream ear earth evil eye flower fool friend god (30) the good hand heart (20) heaven humility joy king life (20) lord love man (100) memory mind (40) name power (20) right sin soul spirit sun thing (20) thought time truth (20) virtue wisdom (30) word (20) world (20)	behold come fear find give go hope know (30) learn lie live look love make rise see seem stand take teach think yield
R. Browning, 1812	black good great little white	blood crime day (20) eye friend god (20) hand heart heaven horse house king life love (20) man morning mother night song sun thing time wine word world	bring come (20) fall feel gallop give (20) go know laugh lie live look love make ride (30) see (20) speak take think
Clough, 1819	earthly gold good high human long old sweet true	day (30) duty eye god (20) heart (30) hope joy lady life light love (20) man (20) music soul (20) spirit thing thought time truth word	come (20) feel find give (20) go hear (20) know listen look make see seem speak take think
Arnold, 1822	dark great long old strong sweet white	day (20) earth eye god (40) hand heart joy king (30) law life (20) love man (50) memory nature night power soul tablets thing time world youth	bring come (20) give go (20) hear know make (20) see (30)

TABLE 2 (continued)

Poet	Adjectives	Nouns	Verbs
Meredith, 1828	fair great low new old strange sweet true	day earth eye (20) god heart heaven life light love (20) man mind name nature soul spirit star sun thing woman woods world	come feel find give go know hear look see seem
Rossetti, 1828	golden sweet	bower (50) day (20) death desire dream eye face flower (20) god (30) hand head heaven hour (20) light love (20) man night prayer shadow sleep song soul sun wind year	come fall give go hear know lie look make see sing speak stand
Swinburne, 1837	bitter bright dark dead (30) fiery full great green high last long old (20) pale sad soft strange sweet (20) white whole wild	air bed brother darkness day (50) death (30) dream dust earth eye (30) face father field fire (20) flower (20) foot (20) god (30) hand head heart (30) heaven (20) hope hour king leaf life light lip love man (40) moon night (40) place rose sea (30) shadow sky sleep song soul (50) speech spirit star summer sun (40) sun-flower sunrise sunset tear thing thought time wave way (30) wind wing word world year	come die fall find give go grow hear know leave lie look make (30) rise see (20) sleep stand take touch watch (20) weep
Hardy, 1840	dear fair good old sweet	creature day dream earth heart hope joy life lord love (20) man (30) shape soul thing (20) time woman word world	bear call come (20) find go hear know (30) look love make see show sing stand think
Bridges, 1844	dear fair gentle good happy long old sweet true	art beauty (20) bird day delight earth eye face god grace heart (20) joy love man (40) mind nature (20) night song spring summer sun thing time truth world	come give go hear hold know lie live look love make see sit stand take win
Hopkins, 1844	black blue bright dear fresh grey lovely sweet (20) wild	air (20) beauty (20) child Christ comfort day death earth eye fire flesh foot glory god grace hand heart heaven home life light lord love man mind mother nature night patience peace pool self spirit sun thing thought time way world year	come (20) fall find go hear keep know lie live look make see tread
Henley, 1849	bright cheerful dim gray green golden little old poor still strange	air bed day dream eye face heart life light man night shadow spring street voice woman	come go hear look make pass see seem tell
Wilde, 1856	black dead fair grey little old red (20) silent sweet white wild young	child day eye field food god gold hand head heart king land life lips love lover man moon night pain sea sky son soul star sun tree wall water wave wind world	come die fall find go grow hear kiss know lie love make see sing stand
Housman, 1859	happy high little still true young	day (20) god hand heart home lad (30) land love lover man (40) morning night thing time world	call come (20) die go hear keep lie (30) look (20) make see sleep stand take
Thompson, 1859	golden great mortal sweet	angel day death earth eye fear foot (20) god hand heart (20) heaven (20) life (20) love man nature poet sky song soul spirit star sun tear thing wind wing world year	come find go grow know (20) see (20) seek seem take turn

Phillips, 1864	beautiful deep dim great human pale slow sweet young	air bloom child Christ the dead earth eye (20) face (20) god hand life man night rain sea sorrow soul spirit thing time wind woman word world	come fall feel grow hear know look make remember see seem speak stand
Yeats, 1865	ancient great long old (30) wild young	bird body child day dream eye heart (30) life love man (40) mind moon mother night song soul stone sun thing thought time tree wind woman year	break bring call come cry find give go grow know lie make run seem sing stand take tell think
de la Mare, 1873	clear cold dark fair green old pale small sweet	air beauty bird breast darkness day (20) dream end eye (30) face flower foot hand head heart hour house life light man memory mind night shadow sky sleep snow star sun thing water wind wing world	breathe come (20) go know lie lean make see seem sing sit stand
Masefield, 1878	blue (20) bold cold dead fine golden green (20) grey last learned little long merry old (50) pale quiet red (20) sweet tall west white windy	bell bird brother dawn day eye fo'c's'le god hand head heart hill home land life lord man (20) mate moon music night place port pull rain road rose sail (20) sailor sea (60) sky ship (20) song soul star thing time tree town tune watch way wind wine world yarn	come (20) blow die get give go (30) hear know (20) leave lie pass see sing take tell wish
E. Thomas, 1878	bright dark dead fine good great long old (20) sweet white	age beauty bird child day (20) earth eye flower forest grass heart hill man (20) morning name night rain road something spring sun thing time tree wind wood year	begin call come (30) fall find give go hear keep know leave lie love make pass see seem sing stand take tell think turn
Lawrence, 1885	black dark dead dear dirty gold good great (20) little (30) living long new (20) old superior white wild young (20)	beast bird body bourgeois child creature day the dead (20) death eye flame flesh foot god (20) hand heart house life (50) machine man (60) mill mind mist money moon night people (20) sea sex sin soul sun swan thing water woman (20) work world worm	come (20) die feel fight find get (20) give go (30) know (20) leave live look make (20) put rise see think turn want work
Muir, 1887	good great little long old small strange	air (30) body day (20) dream earth end eye face father field flower friend grass ground hand head heart (20) hill house land life (20) light man maze memory mound peace pity place (30) plain road (30) rock sand sea shadow silence sky stream thought time (20) tree wall war way world year	come (30) die end fall (20) find go (20) grow hurry know (20) lead lie look make pass run see (40) seem sit stand (20) take tell turn walk watch
E. Sitwell, 1887	bright (20) cold dark dead gold (30) great (20) green last long old (30) young (30)	air day death (20) earth (30) eye hand head heart (110) heaven life light love (40) man (60) night (30) rose sun (50) time water world (70)	come (40) fall feel give go grow (20) hear know (20) lie (20) love make see (20) seem
Aldington, 1892	beautiful black blue brown cold dark dead dingy dull green grey little old red white (40) yellow	beauty bird cloud eye face flower garden girl god (20) grass hand leaf lip love mist night rain sea sky song sun town tree water wind wing	come hear know love make pass see stand turn
Owen, 1893	cold dead great happy old (20) pale young	air arm beauty blood boy (20) dawn day death eye (20) face god (20) hand (20) heart life love (20) man (30) night soul sun time voice war wind wound year youth	come die fall feel go grow hear know laugh look make see seem sing take watch
Graves, 1895	little old own	air day dream death eye god hand head heart love man moon night snow sun time	come die fall give go know make see

TABLE 2 (continued)

Poet	Adjectives	Nouns	Verbs
Blunden, 1896	bright dead gold gone green grey lonely new old (20) rich sweet white wild young	air beauty bell bird cloud day (20) delight earth eye (20) field friend ghost grass head heaven hour joy light love (20) man mill night soul spirit stone stream sun tear time (20) tree voice water way wind wing wood word year (20)	bring come (20) cry find go (30) grow hear know (20) lie (20) leap look make pass rise run see (30) seem shine sing stand stare take think turn
Auden, 1907	good great last little new old	child (20) day death earth (20) eye father fate heart home life (20) love (20) man (20) mother nothing thing time truth word world	come fall feel find give go grow know (20) learn look make (20) see (20) seem speak take
MacNeice, 1907	grey new old own	child day death eye hand heart life (20) man (30) mind night sky stone thing time voice water word world	bear blow come (30) die find give go grow know (20) leave make (20) see speak talk think
Raine, 1909	dark deep great green living white wild	bird (30) child cloud darkness the dead death dream dust earth (20) eye (20) face fire flower form hand heart (30) hill home house joy leaf life light love lover mind moon mountain nature night (20) pain place rain root sea sky (20) song sorrow (20) soul space spirit star stone sun (20) thought time tree (20) water wave (20) way wind (20) wing word world (30)	bear come draw go grow hide know let (30) lie love make pass see (20) stand take
Spender, 1909	deep great little white young	child day (20) death dream eye (40) hand (20) head heart life (20) light (20) love man mind night sky sun thought time (20) word world (20)	fall lie look make seem stare
Ridler, 1912	green new solid true	all being body child day the dead death earth eye glory god heart (20) heaven life light (20) love (50) man (20) movement (?) moon night nothing pain (20) peace place power sea (20) season spirit stone stranger time tree water wave word world	bear break come die fall find give (20) hear know (20) live lie love make (20) move see seem take
Barker, 1913	dark great red turning	air blood body bone cloud death eye face (20) fear figure god glory grave hand (40) head kiss love man morning mountain night pain place rock sea sky spirit star tear time (20) tree water wave wind word world youth	bleed come fall find go (20) hear know leap leave lie lift make mourn see (30) turn
Nicholson, 1914	black dead dry free old yellow	air bed bird bone child cloud day earth (20) eye (20) finger fire foot grass the green head heart leaf light (20) love man (20) night rain rock (20) roof sand sea (20) shadow shape sky (20) slate smoke stone street sun tide time tree wall (20) water (20) wind (30) window world	come fall hear know look make see (20) seem take watch
D. Thomas, 1914	black dead golden green red white	bell bird blood (20) bone boy child day death (20) eye (20) face grave hand (20) head heart (20) heaven house land light love (30) man (40) moon mouth night sea (30) sky sleep stone summer sun (20) time (30) tongue tower tree voice water weather wind (20) word world	break drive drop fall hold lie make (20) turn

Jennings, 1921	deep new simple strange true	being child (30) city country death dream (20) eye foot (?) hand heart hill image (20) journey kind landscape legend life light love (30) man (30) meaning mind (50) nothing (20) passion place power (20) room self shadow something sun symbol thing time thought (40) vision water way word world	bring build feel (20) find go grow hold keep know look love make (30) move (20) play see seem show speak stand take think turn watch
Gunn, 1923	dead great	all bed bird body boy day death ground head man miracle nothing street thought time wind world	come (20) feel find (20) go hold keep know (40) leave lie make move see (20) take think turn want
		America	
Trumbull, 1750	bright deep ethereal fair gay immortal infernal new pale sad wide vain	air arm art beauty bliss charm cloud day death eye face fame fate field fire flame foe form genius glory god grave ground hand heart hill joy land life light love man muse name nature night power praise plain pride realm scene shade shore sky (20) son song soul strain stream sun sword vale war wave way world	arise bid come charm draw hear rise (30) roll see stretch
Dwight, 1752	bright dark fair happy little lovely mild pure rich sweet	earth eye (25) field god grove hand heart heaven hill joy (20) land law life (30) man (20) mankind manners mind (20) peace pride sky son soul stream sun swain toil truth virtue world (20) year	call fill hail look know rise see (30) smile turn
Freneau, 1752	ancient common dear fair great little old vast	age aid arm breast cause day eye flame friend heart heaven home king law life love man (50) mind nature (20) peace power race reason shore state strength sun thing trade tyrant view war way work world (20) year	bid bring come (30) find give go hold learn live make mean rise see (40) send take tell think
Barlow, 1754	bright broad distant future glad great long new old proud rich strong sweet vast wide yon	bank bowl care clime coast course day (20) earth eye fame feast field flood fire grain hand head heaven height hill (20) isle joy land main man mass morning mountain muse name nation ocean plain power praise pudding race realm sea shore (20) side sight sky (20) son song soul stream sun time toil wave (20) way	bend bring call feed fly gain give lead lie meet pour raise rise (20) roll see seek sing spread take teach trace unfold
Halleck, 1790	blue bright cold dark green happy high last proud pure warm wild young	air beauty breath cheek day death dream earth eye (20) flame glory grave hand hair heart (30) home hour (20) heaven joy land (20) life love man manhood mind music name pride sea sky smile song summer tear thought time wind wing world	breathe come (30) die gaze give go hear know see sing stand tell
Sigourney, 1791	bright dark fair holy strong sweet young	breast brow death dust earth eye faith flower friend god hand head heart heaven home hour joy life light love (20) man mother prayer side sky soul tear time voice	come give look make mourn rise see speak stand take turn
Bryant, 1794	bright dark fair (20) free gentle green little mighty old soft sweet white wild	air (20) breast child day death dust earth (20) eye father flower god hand heart heaven hour life light love man night sky star stream sun thought world	come die fall grow hear know lie (20) look love rise see seem take

TABLE 2 (continued)

Poet	Adjectives	Nouns	Verbs
Drake, 1795	blue bright cold dark elfin fairy high lovely pure sweet warm wild	air arm blade breast cloud eye (20) fairy fay ground hand heart heaven hour land light love mountain night river shade shore side sky soul spark star tree wave wind	come fall fly give hear lie make rise see
Percival, 1795	bright calm clear cold dark deep fond full happy high long new pure sweet tender white wide young	air beauty cloud day earth eye (30) feeling flower happiness heart (40) hill joy life light love (40) man mind nature ocean sail sea ship shore sky sorrow soul spirit stream sun thing thought time voice vine water wave wind youth	awaken come (30) fade fall find give go (30) grow hand know live love look lay make meet pass rise see seek set spread stand take tell throw turn
Pinkney, 1802	bright fair good old	air day earth eye face hand heart heaven life (20) light love man mind name nature night pain sea sky sun thought time woman	come die go know look make see (20) seem (20) show
Emerson, 1803	good old proud sweet wise	beauty day earth eye (20) god (20) heart (heaven ?) home love man (20) morning nature (20) rose sea sky sun thing thought time world	bring come fall find go hear know lie love make see seem
Longfellow, 1807	beautiful bright clear dark deep gold good holy old white wild	atonement breast child (20) Christ day (20) death earth (20) eye (20) faith father (20) friend god (30) hand (20) heart (20) heaven (40) life (20) light lord love (20) maid man (20) mother night prayer sea spirit sun teacher (?) world	come fall go hear know lie look love rise see speak stand tak. think
Whittier, 1807	beautiful cold dark (20) deep dim fair fearful gray mighty old red warm wild	air arm blood brother brow cloud day death ear earth eye (20) gloom god hall hand heart (20) heaven hill home land life light love man (30) mountain night power scene sea shadow shore sky smile son soul sound spirit storm stream sun tear tide voice wall wave	bow come fall give go hear know mourn rise see shake smile stand tell
Chivers, 1809	beautiful (30) blessed bright called dark dear deep divine dutiful fair fatal (40) golden great heavenly high immortal long mild new own pure soft standing stately sweet (40) white wild young	angel (40) bank bay beauty brow (Christ) day (30) death delight dew earth Eden evening eye flower fountain glory (20) god (40) grave (20) grief heart (30) heaven (50) lady land life light (20) lightning lily lip love (30) moon (20) morning (20) mother mountain music name night palace river rose sea sky snow song sorrow soul (60) star (20) sun way word	blow come (20) die dwell farewell flow give (30) go (40) hear know leave live make see seem sing soar take weep
Holmes, 1809	bright little sweet	air aunt child earth evening (20) grave hour leaf line love man (20) name poet stone thing time year	ask come fall feel give go hear know lie look love make read see (30) seem shake take tell think turn
Poe, 1809	dear dim fair gold human sad sweet	air angel beauty bell (60) bird day door (20) dream eye (20) flower god heart heaven (20) home hope hour man moon mother name nothing night (30) raven rose sea sky soul (30) star thought time word world year	come die dwell fall feel go hear know lie roll see seem sing tell

Very, 1813	bright dark dead deep new (20) silent sweet	bird birth child day (40) death earth (30) ear eye (20) father (20) field flower foot god hand (20) heart (20) heaven hill hour joy leaf life (20) light (20) love (20) man morning night peace place rest robe sea sin soul (20) sound spirit (30) spring stream sun (20) thing tree voice way wind word year	ask bid bless call come (20) fall feel fill find (30) flow give (30) go grow hear (30) hide keep know (20) lie live (20) love look make pass rejoice rise see (20) seek sing speak stand tell turn wait walk wear
Lowell, 1819	bright deep dim fair good happy high little old sweet true young	air beauty breast day dream eye god hand heart (50) heaven hope life light love man nature night power soul spirit sky star sun thing thought world	come fall feel give go grow hear know lie look make rise see seem sit
Whitman, 1819	good great long old white young	blood child day death earth (30) eye god grass hair hand house land life man (40) mother night passage place poet sea soul (30) sun time water woman wood word work world year	behold come fall go guess hold know make pass see (40) sleep stand wait
Timrod, 1829	deep English (30) happy holy noble old sweet white	air charm day death dream England eye fame foe god grace hand heart (20) land life love maid peace (20) sea soul thought truth woman year	come die fall feel give grow hear know lie look love make see tell
Dickinson, 1830	good small sweet	bird day death face heaven hill life man nature night sea soul sun world	come die go know pass see stop
Miller, 1839	black bright brown cold dark dead fair fierce full good lifted long old pure red rich strong sweet tall true warm white young	air beast blood care cloud clover day (20) death eye face finger fire gold (30) hand hair head heart land life lip love maiden man night river sea side soul sun sword thing tide time tree wind world year youth	come (40) die give go grow hide hold know (20) lie lift look love reach ride run see seem sing stand take think turn
Sill, 1841	blue faint fair great human little new old small still white wild	air bird brain brook child cloud day dream earth eye face fire flower foot god hand heart heaven hill hour life light love (20) man (30) mountain place rock sea shadow sky song soul spirit splendor star sun thought tree voice wall wave week work world (20)	break come (20) die fall feel find go hear know leave let lie make rise seem set sit stand take think touch watch
Lanier, 1842	bright dear fair free green large little mild red sweet	art artist beauty bee child cloud dark day death dream eye face god hall hand heart (20) heaven height hill (20) light lord love (20) lover man (30) marsh (20) morn night pain plain sea (30) shade silence sky sleep song soul space spirit sun time (20) tree valley way wind wood world	bring come fall forgive go hold lie look make (20) pass run see seem shine stand tell turn
Field, 1850	fair little (40) long old sweet	boy child day eye hand heart hoyden joy man mother (20) night opinion sea song summer time way year	come (30) give go hear know lay love make see sing smile
Wilcox, 1850	bright cold dead dear deep fair good great last new old sad strange sweet true vast warm	art breast day dream eye face fire friend god hand heart hour joy kiss life love man music night passion past river rose silence soul star sun thing time valley way word world year youth	break come fall find forget give go grow hear hold know leave live look love make meet see seem shine sing speak think wait
Guiney, 1861	clear dear (20) good inexorable little old sweet wild young	beauty cloud eye father god heart (20) home king life light (20) love man night place soul spirit star sun tear thing time wall way weather wind world year	bear come fall find go hush keep know make pass see

TABLE 2 (continued)

Poet	Adjectives	Nouns	Verbs
Moody, 1869	blue bright dark dear deep good great little low old own sick singing strange strong sweet white wild young	battle boy child dawn day earth eye (20) face (20) god (20) hand (20) heart (30) hope hour land life light love man moon mother night road sea shade soul sound spirit star street sun thing tree way wind word	come (30) fall feel find give go (20) grow hear know lay look make (30) meet see sing sit stand tell turn walk
Robinson, 1869	dead (20) desolate good human lonely lost old sad	day dream eye (20) faith flame friend gleam glory god hand hell life light love man music night place shame song star thing thought time touch truth wall way wind wisdom woman word world year	break call come (40) fall feel find give go grow hear know look make read see shine sing tell think
Sterling, 1869	dark (20) deep (20) divine dread eternal fair holy human mortal pure unheard	art beauty cloud? day (20) death doom dream dust eye fate fire flame flower foot gloom god gulf hand heart hope hour infinity law life (20) light (30) love man mist music mystery night pain peace power quest sea sight silence sky (20) sleep song star (20) strife sun (30) thing throne time vision voice war way word world year	deem dream find gleam hold know lie see stand
Frost, 1875	good little old white	day (20) earth eye flower fly god hand head leaf (20) life light man mind night (20) sky snow thing time tree	ask bring come (40) find give go (20) know (20) leave look make (20) see (20) seem take think
Stevens, 1879	blue great human large old own real	air being day earth eye head heart life man (30) mind (20) moon music night (20) nothing sky soldier spirit sun thing time (20) world (20)	breathe come fall find go grow hear know lie make rise see seem speak think
Williams, 1883	black good green old white	day dream eye face flower hand love man mind night sea water world	come find go live ring see take
Pound, 1885	black dark dry gray old (20) pale white	air day face foot god house land light man (20) sea ship stone thing time voice wall water wave (20) wind woman wood year	come (30) get give go know leave lie make move see set stand
Moore, 1887	fine great little small white	bird body ear elephant eye heart life man neck thing thought trunk wing	fight fly go know lie live look make (20) see
Eliot, 1888	blue broken brown dead dry empty good lost white	air birth city day death desert eye face foot garden hair heart hour kingdom land life light man (20) mountain night people place rock (20) sea shadow silence stair time voice water way wind winter word (20) world year	hope know look make pray sing speak think turn walk
Millay, 1892	blue good great little (20) old own sweet	day (20) death earth (20) eye faith father flower god (30) hand (20) head heart (20) heaven life love night nothing rain sky soul sun thing (30) word world	bring (20) come (30) fall feel go (20) hear know (40) lie look love make see (30) seem speak think
Cummings, 1894	green little true	bird death dream earth everything eye god heart joy leaf life love man (20) mind mountain nothing sky spring sun thing time tree world	begin blow come give go know make sing tell

Jeffers, 1897	beautiful (20) dark cold good (20) great (20) high little (20) long new old (40) white young	air day child death dream earth eye (20) god hand (20) head home life (20) love (20) man (80) mind music night (20) power (20) sky sun thing time (20) war world (20)	come (30) die find give go (30) hear (20) know (20) lie live look (30) love make (20) see (30) seem take tell think (20)
Crane, 1899	bright green long new white	arm day dream eye (30) fire god hand heart heaven hill light man night sea sky snow star time (20) water wind wing	come go hear keep know (20) see (30) take
Eberhart, 1904	dead full good old shallow	air being blood day death earth eye fire hand heart life light love man (40) mind night nothing place reason sense sky spirit sun thing time tree truth wind world (20) year	come (20) get go know let lose make (20) see seem think
Warren, 1905	big (20) black good great little (20) long (20) new old (30)	beginning the dark eye (20) face (30) flame friend hand head heart hill innocence land (20) leaf light lip love luck name (20) night place river (30) section stranger time (20) tree water wind word	call come (20) die get (20) give go (20) hear know (20) leave lose make ride see seek sit stand stop take think try
Roethke, 1908	cold dark dead great long old small soft	air bird bone cloud day dirt ear eye face fish foot grass ground hand hat head heart house leaf life light (20) moon mouth night nose place rain root rose stem stone sun time tree water (20) weed wind (20)	come (20) go (20) hear keep know (20) let look make move sleep see sing stand stay
W. T. Scott, 1910	cold dark dead deep long old young	air child day (20) death earth face fire flower girl hair hand (20) heart hope hour light love (30) man (20) memory night (20) poet sky snow spring stone sun (20) time (20) winter word world	come die go (20) hear hold know (40) leave lie look make (20) move remember see speak take think turn walk write
Bishop, 1910	black blue dead fine green little long old small white	balcony bird cloud coffee day eye head heart light line miracle monument moon night river sea (20) ship side sky sun water	catch come fall go hang lie look make move run see (20) stand (20) think turn
Rukeyser, 1913	black born dark free great living naked real white	air animal bell bird blood body breast cave child city cloud color darkness darling day death (30) door dream evening eye face (20) fear fire garden girl god grave grief hand head heart land leaf life (20) light love (30) lover man (20) moon myth name night nothing pain river sea shadow shoulder sky sound spirit star stone sun time tree voice wall water woman word world (30) year	arrive become come (20) enter fall find give go lead live love make move run see stand take turn walk
Shapiro, 1913	black green new old sweet white	air child day death (20) eye (30) hand head heart home kiss life light love man night sky soul time war world	bring come (20) die fall go hear lie look (20) make rise see speak take
Lowell, 1917	black blue dead great old red	blood body bone child Christ day death eye (20) face father (20) fire glass god hand head heart house ice king life light lord man night sea snow stone time tree water (20) wind world year	break come cry die fall go hear make see walk

TABLE 2 (continued)

Poet	Adjectives	Nouns	Verbs
Wilbur, 1921	blue clear great pure sweet	air beast bird darkness day dream eye (20) face god hand head land leaf light man (20) mind night nothing sea (20) sky soul sound stone sun (20) thing thought tree voice water (20) wave wind word world	come (20) cry dream fall find give go (20) hear know let make rise stand see (20) think turn
Hecht, 1923	being old white	air (20) blood body the cold eye finger fist flesh foot god hand heart lady life love man (20) name nature nothing pain place tree water (30) wind world	come drown fall go know lie make put rise see set stand think

APPENDIX TO TABLE 2

Poet, work and proportions of ANV	Adjectives	Nouns	Verbs
		Twenty poets in other languages (first 1,000 lines)	
Lucretius, 98 B.C. De Rerum Natura (ed. Bailey, 1907). 1,030A-1,800N-1,380V.	alternus certus clarus inans infinitus magnus mutatus solidus verus	aer aetas aevum animus aqua arbusta aura caelum cibus corpus (90) dictum finis genus homo ignis (30) imber inane (30) lignum locus lumen mare matena materies modus mars motus natura (50) nihil (50) oculus ora ordo os, ossis pactum pars (30) primordium (20) principium ratio (40) res (170) sanguis semen sensus sol spatium summa tempus (20) terra (30) umor ventus verbum versus verum vis	alo cerno consisto constituo consto (30) creo (20) cresco debeo dico dissolvo do facio fio (20) for gero gigno habeo mitto muto necesse est (20) nequeo ostendo pereo possum (100) puto queo refero relinquo teneo video (50) voco
Virgil, 70 B.C. Georgics, 500 lls. (Loeb, ed. Fairclough), 630A-1,180N-530V. [Aeneid, 200 lls. 210A-570N-220V]	altus densus ingens laetus levis magnus medius novus pinguis tenuis varius	ager agricola aequor caelum campus cura dies herba ignis nox orbis seges silva sol terra tempus ventus	do fero incipio pono possum refero sequor veneo video
Horace, 65 B.C. Sermons, I: 4, 6, 10; II: 1, 6 (thr. 1. 48); Epistle, II, 1 (thr. 1. 200); Ars. P., lls. 1-200; Odes, III: 1, 2, 3, (thr. 1. 20). (Loeb, ed. Fairclough), 1,200A-1,800N-1,200V (approx.)	bonus dignus magnus (30) malus medius parvus	amicus animus annus carmen deus honor nihil opus pater (30) pes poeta puer (20) res (20) sermo tempus verbum versus (20) vir vitium	dico do facio (30) fero possum (20) scribere video vivo volo
Ovid, 43 B.C. Metamorphoses, 500 lls., Her., 100 lls., Art of Love, 200 lls., Fasti, 200 lls., 1,210A-2,170N-1,230V.	altus longus	aer amor (20) annus (20) aqua ars caelum (20) causa deus (30) dies domus flumen locus manus mare nomen numen opus orbis os pars (20) pater populus puella res tellus (20) tempus terra (30) unda (20) verbum vir	dico (20) do (30) eo facio fero (20) maneo possum video

Juvenal, 60 A.D. Satires I, III, X, XI (thr. l. 141). (Loeb, ed. Ramsay), 1,160A-2,160N-1,140V.	bonus longus magnus (40) parvus qualis quantus summus	amicus caput deus domus (20) homo nihil (20) nox populus puer res urbs	credo dico do (20) eo facio fero opto possum timeo venio video volo
Beowulf, 8th c. (ed. Klaeber). 530A-1,950N-890V.	god heah heard leof	aetheling aglaeca bearn Beowulf (20) cynn (20) daed Dene dryten earl fela feond fyren folc frea God (20) guma geates Grendel haeleth Heorot Hygelac hond Hrothgar (20) hwilyth leode maeg mod monn (20) niht reced rinc scyldinges secg sith sweord theoden word	beran bidan cuman cunnan gan gefrem-man geseon gewitan healdan hyran magan methelian motan sculan secan standan thencan wenan weorthan witan
Roland, 11th c. (Ed. Bedier). 540A-1,380N-1,390V.	altre bels bon (20) cher destre dous fiers gent grant (40) saint saives	altre an argent barbe bastun battaille ber (20) chevalier Chrestiens citet cors cunseill cunte dux emperere (30) espee fils gent guant host hostage hour jur lei mains mes-sage mort muls nies or palies per pons puign quens rereguarde seigneur sire tere uncle vassal	aimer aler apeler chevalcher cumencer deveir dire duner enveier finer guarder juger laisser mander mettre muer murir ocire oir parler passer perdre poier porter prendre receivre remaneir respundre saveir tenir trover vedeir venir vuleir
Dante, 1265 520A-1,240N-1,240V.	alto (20) bello buono eterno grande (20) lungo molto novo solo tristo	aqua aere amore anima (20) bene cerebrio cielo core cosa dio duca gente (20) luogo maestro (20) mano mente mondo occhio ombra parola parte paura persona piede pieta poeta spirito tempo terra uomo via vita voce	andare cadere cominciare conoscere convenire dare discendere entrare giungere guardare intendere lasciare menare muovere parere parlare passare potere porre respondere sapere temere tenere togliare udire vedere (50) venire (50) volere volgare
Fior de Romances, c. 1285 (Wolf and Hyman, eds.) II. 390A-1,050N-820V.	bono grande lindo moro (30) todo (20)	amor (20) caballeros caballo captiva castillo cielo dios doncellos fior gente hermano mano mujer ojos padre palabras pie reina (30) rey (30) senor senora tierras vida	dar (20) hacer (30) ir (40) llever llorer (20) mandar matar mirar poner querer (20) saber tomar traer venir (20) ver (20)
Duque de Rivas, 1791 Romances, 1,080 lls. 660A-1,300N-650V.	alto blanco grande negro	alma amor caballero caballo calle cielo dia lado mar nube ojo ola oro pecho puerta reina rey tierra torre	correr dar decir dejar formar hacer ir llegar mirar parecer seguir tener tornar ver
R. M. Rilke, 1875 Das Buch der Bilder, 860 lls. 480A-910N-840V.	dunkel gross (20) gut klein (20) schwartz schwer (20)	Abend Ding Garten Grund Hand (20) Haus Kind Leben (20) Nacht Traum Wald Welt Wind	fallen gehen (20) halten kommen (20) legen machen nehmen sehen stehen wissen (20)
B. Brecht, 1898 Poems. 450A-1,260N-1,080V.	gross gut klein leicht	Abend Essen Fluss Herr Himmel (20) Liebe Mahagonny Mann (30) Mensch Nacht (20) Soldat (20) Stadt Tag Tier Vogel Wald Was-ser Weib Welt Whisky Wind Wipfel Zorn	bitten brauchen (20) fragen geben (20) halten kommen (40) lernen loben machen schrein schweigen schwimmen sehen singen sitzen spühren verfallen wachsen warten wissen (20) ziegen (20)
T. Gautier, 1811 Emaux et Camées. (Paris, 1888). 660A-1,500N-520V.	blanc (40) bleu noir rose vieil	air ciel doigt eau fleur flots grace jour larmes main marbre mer oeil or nuit peau pied voix	fair (30) prendre voir venir voulois

APPENDIX TO TABLE 2 (continued)

Poet, work and proportions of ANV	Adjectives	Nouns	Verbs
C. Baudelaire, 1821 Les Fleurs du Mal. 990A-1,910N-815V.	belle (30) doux grand (20) noir plein profond	air âme amour ange beauté (20) coeur (40) corps esprit fleur fond monde nuit parfum sang sein soir soleil (20)	aimer connaître donner passer trouver venir voir
Mallarmé, 1842 (Ed. Fry). 900A-1,700N-800V.	ancien azur beau blanc calme pale pur seul solitaire triste	cheveux ciel clarté coeur doigt eau enfant ennui femme feu fleur froid jour mort nuit oeil ombre or regard rêve rose soir vierge vol	aller baiser dire faire garder levre pentir savoir voir vouloir
Verlaine, 1844 Fêtes Galantes, ff. 790A-1,470N-780V.	beau blanche bon cher doux grand longue noir petite triste	âme amour bruit ciel coeur dieu enfant femme fleur homme jour lune mains rêve rose silence	aimer aller dormir faire mourir rêver tourner
J. Laforgue, 1860 Les Complaintes, Derniers Vers (Paris, 1894). 580A-1,600N-810V.	beau blanc bon doux grand mort petit pauvre unique	âme ciel coeur genoux lune monde nature oeil soir (20) soleil ton vent	aimer aller (20) danser dire faire (30) laisser mourir passer quitter savoir venir voir vouloir
Valéry, 1871 (Ed., MacIntyre). 900A-1,700N-900V.	beau calme doux éternel grand large noir nu profond pur seul sombre tendre	absence air âme (20) amour (20) arbre azur bois bras chair ciel coeur dieu doigt eau fleur forme fruit jour oeil main mer mort nuit ombre onde or pas regard rose secret sein silence soleil songe terre tresor vent	aller attendre boire briser chanter connaître dormir faire former fuir mourir passer porter savoir venir vivre
Federico Garcia Lorca, 1899 Romancero Gitano (2nd ed., Madrid). 520A-1,430N-500V.	alto blanco civil cuatro gitano grande lleno negro todo tres verde (40) viejo	agua aire caballo cielo ciudad cosa cristal estrella flor guardia luna luz mar monte niño noche ojo paz pecha plata puerta rama rumor sengre sombra viento voz	abrir buscar cantar correr dar decir dejar ir llorar mirar sonar subir tocar venir ver
Rafael Alberti, 1902 Poesia (1940, Buenos Aires). 410A-1,400N-400V.	alto azul blanco bueno frio muerto negro rojo	aqua aire (30) ala amigo arena barco barquero cielo corazon frente mar (80) marinero muerte (20) niño noche ojo pie puerto rio sangre (20) sireno sombra tierro toro (20) vela viento (20)	correr dar decir dejar dormir ir (40) mirar morir pasar querer (20) saber venir ver (20) volver
Ten seventeenth-century prose texts (first 8,000 words)			
Richard Hooker, 1554 Ecclesiastical Polity, thr. VI, 5. 660A-1,490N-890V.	able according being concerning eternal good great high natural (30) own perfect present	agent angel art cause course creature degree earth end God good heaven kind knowledge law (80) man (40) manner matter means name nature (30) nothing order other part perfection reason same sort spirit thing (70) time way will work working world	attain come consider give keep know let make observe see seem serve set speak take work
Francis Bacon, 1561 Advancement of Learning. 660A-1,660N-780V.	good (20) great (20) learned (20) like own true	age body business cause conceit duty end error example eye fault fortune God (20) government (20) hand knowledge (30) learning (40) life man (110) manner matter mind (20) nature person philosopher philosophy place pleasure point reason sense state thing time (30) work	give (20) let make (20) receive see take

John Donne, 1576 Sermons, 1617, nos. 5 and 6. 600A-1,560N-1,010V.	good great old own	affection bed beginning book Christ (50) Church creature (20) day (20) father God (80) grace Jesus (20) life Lord love (80) man (40) nothing one part person (20) place scripture sin soul (20) text thing (20) will wisdom (20) word (30) work world	begin bring cause express find (40) give know lose (70) love make (20) seek take think
Thomas Hobbes, 1588 Leviathan. 960A-1,830N-920V.	being diverse false great infinite like made own past present true waking	accident account action affirmation angle another body (30) brain cause conception consequence creature discourse dream (20) ear eye fancy (20) God image imagination invention kind man (80) manner matter memory mind motion name (60) nature nothing object one organ part (30) place (20) reckoning sense (40) sign sound speech (20) thing (70) thought (40) time (30) train triangle understanding use (20) word (40)	call (20) cause come conceive consider find know make (30) observe proceed produce see seem signify take think understand
Sir Thomas Browne, 1605 Hydriotaphia. 1,060A-2,070N-710V.	according (to) ancient found good great high large long noble old Roman sepulchral	account antiquity ashes body Britain burial coin conjecture country custom day dead death earth fire friend grave ground habitation interment king life love (40) man monument name nation part person piece place pope practice Romans Rome sepulchre substance time urne (50) way wood year	burn bury decline find (30) found (a city) hold leave lie make (30) seem
John Milton, 1608 Areopagitica. 900A-1,700N-1,040V.	good (20) great (20) new whole	age author book (70) city commonwealth evil God (20) good kind law learning licensing life (20) magistrate man (60) order reading reason sin state thing (20) time (20) truth virtue wisdom world writing	bring find give hear know (20) leave make read see take think write
Edward, Earl of Clarendon, 1609 History of the Rebellion and Civil Wars, I. 760A-1,680N-790V.	being good great (30) high new own whole	affair affection court (20) crown day duke (30) end highness house journey king (50) kingdom law lord majesty man (30) marriage matter mind nature occasion parliament (30) part people person (20) place power prince (50) reason sin Spain (20) thing time (20) treaty year	believe conclude find give know make (40) pass see take tell think
John Bunyan, 1628 Pilgrim's Progress. 52A-1,430N-1,350V.	good (30) little next own	back book burden (30) children city counsel death door dream fire gate gentlemen glory hand head heart heaven house life man (80) name neighbor one other place reason thing (30) time truth way (60) wife word work world [Christian (50) Despond Evangelist (20) Interpreter Obstinate Pliable Loyalty Passion Patience Slough Wiseman Worldly]	answer ask begin (20) bid call come (60) direct fall find get (20) give go (60) know lead look make meet read run see (60) seek set show speak stand (20) tell (20) take think turn

APPENDIX TO TABLE 2 (continued)

Poet, work and proportions of ANV	Adjectives	Nouns	Verbs
John Dryden, 1631 Preface to the Fables, thr. Chaucer. 720A-1,470N-900V.	being former good (20) great (20) little old own present same (20)	age author beauty book character countryman language man manner nature number opinion part poem poet (20) poetry reader reason sense tale thought time (20) verse word [Boccace Chaucer Homer Illiad Ovid Virgil]	call come find follow give know let live make (20) take think (20) translate understand write
John Locke, 1632 On Human Understanding, thr. 111, 5. 710A-1,260N-840V.	being certain equal evident general great impossible innate (60) necessary own same universal	assent (30) certainty child degree demonstration discovery extent faculty hearing idea (30) impression knowledge (30) man (50) mankind maxim mind (40) nature nothing notion object one opinion principle (30) proof proposition (30) reason (40) term thing (30) thought time truth (40) understanding (30) use (30) way word	assent (30) come (30) discover find give know (30) make observe perceive prove receive suppose take think understand
Ten twentieth-century prose texts (first 8,000 words)			
G. B. Shaw, 1856 Preface to St. Joan, thr. "he stuck at nothing." 910A-1,830N-940V.	mad masculine military sane social	fact fear imagination life (20) man mind nothing saint soldier vision voice woman [Joan (60)]	believe call come know live make (20) see throw understand
George Santayana, 1863 Three Philosophical Poets (Anchor), thr. "Lucretius," "would have vanished also." 800A-1,770N-1,040V.	great (20) happy human moral natural new possible universal	atom (20) consciousness death (20) experience fear force form ground life (50) love man materialism matter mind movement nature (40) nothing (20) part philosophy (20) poem poet poetry power soul substance (20) science space system thing (40) time truth way world (30)	arise call conceive fear live make pass produce prove seem think
Bertrand Russell, 1872 Unpopular Essays, "Phil. and Pol." thr. "Phil. for Everyman," "the best discipline is philosophy." 1,020A-2,120N-1,140V.	different general good great human liberal modern necessary obvious political practical present scientific theoretical	answer authority belief consequence democracy doctrine dogma government history idea (20) knowledge matter philosopher philosophy (70) problem question reality religion science (20) system thing thought war	accept become believe call consider develop give hold know (20) lead make (20) produce show think (20)
D. H. Lawrence, 1885 Studies in Classic American Literature. "Spirit of Place," thr. "invalidating his premises." 950A-1,850N-1,160V.	American (40) barbed dark deep different free (20) great (20) little (20) masterless moral new (20) old (40) pure real vast whole	artist Benjamin (30) Europe (20) forest freedom (20) God ideal liberty man (50) master (20) nature (20) people self slave soul (20) thing (20) truth wire (20) world (20)	come (20) get (30) go (20) hate know (20) like make (20) put read think try want work
Julian Huxley, 1887 Man in the Modern World. "Uniqueness of Man," thr. "Stone Age Men." 1,300A-2,060N-880V.	animal biological (30) conceptual (20) dominant early evolutionary great (20) high human (40) large social unique (30)	action (20) activity analysis animal (50) brain by-product characteristic consequence control development difference dominance evolution (20) experience group laughter life (20) man (70) object period primate process progress species (20) speech thought (20) tool tradition type (30)	acquire appear become (20) develop evolve provide reach

T. S. Eliot, 1888 Idea of a Christian Society, thr. "belief and understanding." 950A-1,590N-980V.	Christian (80) conscious different great modern negative pagan particular political (20) positive present religious small social (20)	behavior belief change Christian (20) Christianity (20) Church Community culture democracy faith form idea individual liberalism life (30) mind organization philosophy point problem relation religion society (60) state (20) subject system view	accept become believe concern live make mean see take think
Herbert Read, 1893 Anatomy of Art. 1,000A-2,020N-910V.	abstract aesthetic classical common formal geometrical good great greek human intellectual plastic psychological simple	arrangement art (160) artist (30) beauty (30) colour degree element (20) expression feeling form (40) harmony ideal mass mind object part pattern (20) perception period picture (20) portrait pottery process purpose rhythm section sense (20) sensibility shape space structure theory value word work (50)	become define express find give look make (20) take
Rebecca West, 1893 Black Lamb and Grey Falcon, p. 27 thr. p. 46, "to disclose next day." 860A-1,620N-1,210V.	afraid beautiful German good great (20) little old second-class young	business (20) businessman (20) carriage food German hand head husband (30) man (40) manufacturer night nothing people state ticket-collector time train wife (20) Yugoslavia year	begin come fall get go (30) know leave like look make (30) meet run see seem (20) take (30) think understand
George Orwell, 1903 "Pol. and Eng.," and "Reflections on Ghandi"; in Essays. 1,060A-1,680N-1,200V.	bad British clear good English human modern political possible true	effect English kind language life man meaning metaphor phase people sentence thing thought time unity war word writer	become call choose feel get give make (40) see take think use (20) write
John Wain, 1925 Contemporary Reviews of Romantic Poetry, Intro., thr. "of our own day." 900A-2,070N-920V.	English (20) good great literary (20) long modern political young	article author century (20) critic criticism (20) editor magazine review (20) reviewer standard time work	become begin find give make read take write

TABLE 3

CHRONOLOGY OF GENERAL USE: FIRST APPEARANCES

(First appearance is taken to be first major use followed by at least three with less than a century between each. Note that by this definition the first in the list will show many; and the last, few. Note how Wyatt, Sidney, Sylvester, among others, begin characteristic emphases. See also the table in Chap. 13.)

Minot, 1310, fair good great day god heart king knight lord man time word come find give go hear see take tell think
Gower, 1325, book eye hand law life love(n) thing way wit world know speak
Langland, 1330, heaven mercy people
Chaucer, 1340, high old gold lady make
Gawain P., 1350, dear look
Pearl P., 1350, grace ground
Hoccleve, 1368, lie
Lydgate, 1370, fresh fortune
James I, 1394, full sweet mind nature pain sing
Henryson, 1430, true face father flower night

Ballads, 146ff, son die
Skelton, 1465, noble
Dunbar, 1470, death light rise
Hawes, 1473, common fame head name begin call show
Douglas, 1474, gentle work(n)
Barclay, 1475, shepherd town live poor
Sternhold, 1480, foe glory power soul keep stand
Coverdale, 1488, faith sin spirit bear bring fall love(v)
Lindsay, 1490
Heywood, 1497, rich wise friend year

Wyatt, 1503, cruel desire fire place tear woe please seek
Surrey, 1517, beauty breast flame son thought teach
Churchyard, 1520, fear(n) seem sit
Crowley, 1521, blood hell
Baldwin, 1529, prince
Sackville, 1536
Googe, 1540, grief
Turberville, 1540, hope
Gascoigne, 1542, youth
Breton, 1545, kind little art

Spenser, 1552, new proud sad
Sidney, 1554, happy long muse sight virtue
Chapman, 1559, bright sacred grow
Daniel, 1562

Drayton, 1563
Sylvester, 1563, divine air earth sea
Marlowe, 1564
Shakespeare, 1564
Campion, 1567, joy part fly move
Fairfax, 1570, bold

Jonson, 1573, meet
Donne, 1576
Sandys, 1578, appear
Fletcher, 1582
Wither, 1588, pride voice
Herrick, 1591
Quarles, 1592
Herbert, 1593, praise(v) write
Carew, 1595
Shirley, 1596

Waller, 1606, care fate
Milton, 1608, wind
Suckling, 1609, wake
Cleveland, 1613
Crashaw, 1613, soft
More, 1614, sense shine
Denham, 1615, poet
Lovelace, 1616
Cowley, 1618
Marvell, 1621

Vaughan, 1622, cloud hour
Dryden, 1631
Roscommon, 1633, age wild
Oldham, 1653, vain
Blackmore, 1655, human various land sky
Creech, 1659
Garth, 1661
Walsh, 1663, charm
Prior, 1664
Pomfret, 1667, mighty delight

Addison, 1672
Somerville, 1675, nymph
Philips, 1676
Parnell, 1679
Young, 1683, fool scene
Gay, 1685, pass
Pope, 1688, maid
Blair, 1690
Dyer, 1700, deep wide behold
Thomson, 1700, mountain

Armstrong, 1709, green song breathe
Johnson, 1709, leave
Lyttelton, 1709

Shenstone, 1714
Gray, 1716, golden
Akenside, 1721
Collins, 1721, silent truth
J. Warton, 1722, dark field shade
Mason, 1725
T. Warton, 1728

Goldsmith, 1730
Cowper, 1731, foot
Churchill, 1738, home hold
Chatterton, 1752
Crabbe, 1754, own child pleasure feel
Blake, 1757, black pale morning sleep turn weep
Burns, 1759, mother
Bowles, 1762, cold white ear sorrow wave wood
Rogers, 1763, grey memory
Wordsworth, 1770, young tree pray

Coleridge, 1772, strange bird body moon water
Southey, 1774
Landor, 1775
Campbell, 1777
Moore, 1779, dream star woman
Hunt, 1784
Byron, 1788, blue
Shelley, 1792, dim
Hemans, 1793, the dead
Keats, 1795, wing

Hood, 1799
Horne, 1803, shadow
E. Browning, 1806, last
Tennyson, 1809
Tupper, 1810
R. Browning, 1812, house
Clough, 1819
Arnold, 1822
Meredith, 1828
Rossetti, 1828

Swinburne, 1837, dead bed watch
Hardy, 1840
Bridges, 1844
Hopkins, 1844
Henley, 1849
Wilde, 1856, red
Housman, 1859
Thompson, 1859
Phillips, 1864, rain
Yeats, 1865, stone

TABLE 3 (continued)

De la Mare, 1873
Masefield, 1878, hill
E. Thomas, 1878, grass
Lawrence, 1885

Muir, 1887
E. Sitwell, 1887
Aldington, 1892
Owen, 1893

Graves, 1895
Blunden, 1896

Auden, 1907, nothing

American

Trumbull, 1750, grave shore stream war
Dwight, 1752, pure peace
Freneau, 1752
Barlow, 1754, strong side
Halleck, 1790, warm hair music
Sigourney, 1791, holy
Bryant, 1794

Drake, 1795, river
Percival, 1795, clear
Pinkney, 1800
Emerson, 1803, rose
Longfellow, 1807, beautiful
Whittier, 1807, sound wall
Chivers, 1809, snow
Holmes, 1809, leaf
Poe, 1809

Very, 1813, walk
Lowell, 1819
Whitman, 1819
Timrod, 1820
Dickinson, 1830, small
Miller, 1839
Sill, 1841, let
Lanier, 1842, silence

TABLE 4

CHRONOLOGY OF MAJOR USE: NUMBER OF USERS
(In order of "first appearance"; see Table 3)

	Pre-1470	1470	1500	1530	1570	1600	1630	1670	1700	1730	1770	1800	1830	1870	1900	Am. 1770	1800	1830	1870	1900	Total
fair	6	4	1	9	4	8	3	7	7	2	4	2	3	1		6	4	6			77
good	9	8	8	10	9	8	5	1		4	3	5	2	3	1	1	4	6	4	2	93
great	9	7	7	10	7	8	8	6	2	5	1	6	4	5	5	2	2	3	4	5	106
day	9	7	6	9	9	6	7	7	9	7	10	7	9	9	7	7	8	9	7	8	157
god	9	8	7	7	6	7	9	5	6	5	4	8	8	5	2	4	6	7	7	4	124
heart	7	4	9	7	10	6	2	8	7	8	8	8	9	8	8	9	7	8	6	9	148
king	5	4	4	2	3	1	1	3	3	1	1	4	2			1		1			36
knight	4	6	1	1						1	1	1									15
lord	5	6	3	3	2		1	1			1	1	2	1			1	1		1	29
man	8	9	10	9	10	9	9	9	7	8	7	9	10	9	9	8	7	10	9	6	172
time	6	6	8	6	5	4	4	3	2	7	6	7	7	7	10	5	3	7	7	7	117
word	6	4	1	3	1	1	2				3	4	3	1	8		3	4	2	4	50
come	7	7	7	8	8	6	4	3	6	6	7	10	10	10	7	8	10	9	8	10	151
find	6	1	7	6	7	8	7	3	4	4	3	4	6	4	6	1	2	6	4	1	90
give	6	4	9	9	9	9	9	5	9	7	8	7	3	5	3	6	5	5	4	3	125
go	6	7	7	6	5	7	3	2	1	6	6	8	9	9	6	4	9	9	9	10	129
hear	5	1	3	4	6	3		5	5	6	6	6	8	6	3	5	8	5	4	6	95
see	8	8	10	9	10	10	6	9	9	9	8	9	9	10	8	9	10	9	9	10	179
take	7	8	7	8	7	5	6	2		4	2	6	5	5	6	5	4	2	4	4	97
tell	5	2	7	2	7	4	2	1	1	1	6		2	3		3	5	3	2		56
think	6	4	9	5	5	5	5	3		4	4	4	2	3	3	1	2	4	5	6	80
book	4	1																			5
eye	3	1	4	10	9	10	6	9	9	8	10	10	8	10	9	10	8	9	9	9	161
hand	5	4	4	5	4	1	1	7	8	3	7	7	6	8	6	8	6	8	5	9	112
law	3	1	1							1		1				2		1			10
life	7	5	5	6	4	1	6	6	5	8	5	8	8	6	6	8	7	7	7	6	121
love (n)	5	5	8	7	9	9	4	4	8	6	9	10	8	5	8	8	8	8	4	7	140
thing	6	6	9	3	5	6	4	2		2	2	6	8	4	3	2	4	6	7	2	87
way	3	1	3	1	1	1	2	1	2	4			2	3	2	3	2	6	1		38
wit	4	1	1	1		1	3														11
world	5	4	3	6	5	7	1	3	4	5	3	5	8	5	10	5	4	8	6	7	104
know	6	6	6	7	10	9	10	6	8	4	6	8	8	10	8	5	10	9	9	6	151
speak	3	3	2	2	2	3		1			1	4	1		3	1	2	1	3	2	34
heaven	4	2		8	4	6	6	6	7	4	6	5	3	2	2	8	5	3	2		83
mercy	2	2																			4
people	2	2	1				1							1					1		8
high	4	1	1	5	2	4	3	1	2	2	2	3	2			3	2		1		38
old	2	3	3	3	1	6	4	1	1	4	4	3	6	10	2	5	6	7	6	8	85
gold	3	2	1	1					1				1					1			10
lady	4	5	1	1							1	2					1				15
make	4	10	9	9	10	10	9	5	2	6	7	8	9	9	10	5	6	7	8	10	153
dear	2	2	1	2		1	1		1	3	1		3	1		1	2	4			25
look	2	2	1	3	3	2				1	6	8	7	4	4	5	6	5	5	4	68
grace	3	2	1	1	2	1					1		2				1				14
ground	2	1	1					1		1				1	1	2				1	11
lie	2	2	2	7	4	5		3		1	5	6	6	6	6	3	7	4	5	4	78
fresh	2	2											1								5
fortune	2	1	4	2						1											10
full	1	1		2	1	1	1				2		1			1		1		1	13
sweet	1	4	2	9	5	6		3	6	8	7	7	7	4		7	5	6	1	2	90
mind	1	3	5	3	1	1	1	3	4	3	2	3	3	2	4	5			5	2	51
nature	1	2	1	3	3	3	5	5	8	4	1	3	3		1	4	2	1			50
pain	2	2	5	1			3	1	1	3	1		1		3	1		2		1	27
sing	1	2	1	3	4	2	1	1	2	2	2	3	3	5		2	3	5	2	1	45

	Pre-1470	1470	1500	1530	1570	1600	1630	1670	1700	1730	1770	1800	1830	1870	1900	Am. 1770	1800	1830	1870	1900	Total
true	1	1	4	4	5	2	4				2	3	2		2		1	2	1		34
face	1		1		4	1					1	1	4	4	3	2		6	3	7	38
father	1	2	2				1			2	3	1	1	1	1	1	2	1	1	1	21
flower	1	2	1	1	1	1		1	4	1	2	3	1	4	1	3	3	2	3	1	36
night	2	1	2	7	2	4	3	6	2	2	5	6	8	9	7	4	6	8	7	9	100
son	1	2	1	1	1	2	1	1	1	4	1		1			3	1				21
die		2	3	2	4	3	2	3	2	3	3		3	4	2	3	3	3	1	4	50
noble		4		1		2	1			2							1				11
death		2	4	3	4	2	4	3		1		4	3	4	9	4	6	4	4	5	66
light		1		3	2	3	1	2			6	5	3	4	6	6	5	6	4	9	66
rise	1	2			3		3	5	9	4	4	2	1	2		8	4	1	1	3	53
common		1	1		1		1									1					5
fame		1	3				2	1	1							2	1				11
head	2	1	1	1		1	1	3	4	4	5	2	2	6	5	2		1	4	7	52
name		2	2		4	2	1	2	3			2		1		4	2			3	28
begin	3	2	2	1		1	1							1					1		12
call	1	2	1		2	2	2	1	2	1			3	1		2	1	1		1	23
show	1	4	3	2	5	4					1		1		1	1					23
gentle	1	1		2	2				2	1			1			1					11
work (n)	1	1		1			1	1						1							6
shepherd			1	2	2			1	2												8
town	2	1	1	1			2							2							9
live		2	3	3	3	4	3		1	4	2	2	3	1	1	2	2	1	3	1	41
poor	2	3	1	4	4	2	2	1		4	2		1								26
foe		1	1	1	2			1	1							1	1				9
glory		1		1	1			1	1		1		1		2	2	1	1			13
power		2		4	3	1	7	3	8	3	3	3			2	3	2	1	1		46
soul	1	1		4	7	6	5	6	7	1	8	7	6	4	1	6	6	7	1	2	86
keep	3	2	3		3	4	1			1	1		2	1	2		1	1	1	1	27
stand	1	2	1		3	4		3	2	5	2	4	7	5	2	3	4	5	1	6	60
faith		1	1	1	1											1	1	2	1		9
sin	1	1			3	1	1							1			1				9
spirit	1	1		2			1	1		3	6	5	4	1	3	1	4	4	1	2	40
bear	1	1	3	1	1			1	2	1	2		1		3			1			18
bring	2	2	3	2	3	7	4			2	2	2	1	1	1	2	1	1	2	1	39
fall	3	1	3	1	3		1	6		4	5	5	4	5	6	3	9	6	2	6	73
arm	1	1		2			4	2			1			1		3	1		1		17
love (v)	2	2	1	6	6	3	3		3	5	6	2	3	3	3	2	5	4	2	1	62
rich	2	1		3	1	2		1	1		1			1		2		1			16
wise	3	1		1		3	1	2			1	1					1				14
friend	1	1	2	1	1		5	3	7	6	4	3		2		2	1	2		1	42
year	1	1	1		2	1	1	1		4	2	1	4	4		2	5	6	2	3	41
cruel			4	1																	5
desire			2	3								1									6
fire			2	3	1	7	2	1		1			2		2	2		4		4	31
place			3		1	1				1			1	2	4		2	3	1	4	23
tear			2	1		3	2			2	3		2	1	1	2	1	1			21
woe	2		3		2				1	4	1										13
please			1	1			3		3												8
seek			6	2	1					1			1			2	1			1	15
beauty	1		2	6	2	1	1	1	3	1	1	1	2	5		3	4	3			37
breast			1	2	2	1	1	3	4	2	3			1		4	2	1		1	28
flame	1		2		2			1						1		3		2		1	13
sun			1	5	3	3	2	3	1	5	4	6	6	8	5	7	6	8	4	6	83
thought	1		1	8		1	3	2	3	4	4	3	3	1	4	4	2	2	1	1	48
teach	1		2		1	1	1		3			2				1					12
fear (n)			2		3	1	2	1		2	1		1		1					1	15
seem	1		3	2	1	3		2		2	3	3	4	6	5	1	5	4	4	1	50
sit	1		1	2	1	1	1		1	1	1		1	2			1	2		1	17
blood			2		4		2	1	1	1	1	1		1	2		2	1		4	23
hell			2	2														1			5
prince	1		3	1			1														6

TABLE 4 (continued)

NUMBER OF POETS PER ERA USING EACH WORD, IN ORDER OF APPEARANCE WITH FURTHER USE

	Pre-1470	1470	1500	1530	1570	1600	1630	1670	1700	1730	1770	1800	1830	1870	1900	Am. 1770	1800	1830	1870	1900	Total
grief			1	2	2					1							1			1	8
hope			1	3	1	1	1	1	1	4	1	2	3				2	2		1	24
youth	1		2	2			3	1	7	4	1	2		1	1	1		2			28
kind (a)	1		1	1		1	2														6
little	1		1	1	1	1		2	2	3	2	2	3	5	2	3	2	5	5	2	43
art			1	2	2	1	4	3	4	3	1		1			1		3			26
new	2			1	4	4	5	1	2	1		2		2	4	3	2	2	2	2	39
proud				2	1	2		2	2	1	2					3					15
sad				1	1	2	1	2	1	2	4	1	1			1	1	2			20
happy	1	1	1	4	1	3	3	1	2	3	1	1	2	1		3	2				30
long				1			1	3		1	2	2	3	5		2	2	2	2	4	30
muse				3	1		4		4	2						2					16
sight				3			1									1		1			6
virtue	1			2			1	2	4	2		1				1					14
bright	1	1		3		4	3	3	2	3	8	1	3	3		9	5	4	1		54
sacred				2			1	1	2	1											7
grow				1	2	3	3	2	1		1		5	4	4		2	3	4	1	36
divine				1			1		3	1	1						1	1			9
air				1		1		7	7	4	4	1	4	6	2	6	5	2	4	7	61
earth				2	5	4	2	2	1	1	4	6	6	4	4	7	7	2	5	2	64
sea				2		1	1			1	2		3	4	5	4	7	7	3	4	44
joy	3			1	1	1	3	3	4	5	4	3	2	1	1	6	1	2	1		42
part				1	2	3															6
fly				1	3	3	3	5	4	4	2					2			1		28
move				2		2			2						3						9
bold				1		1		1	1					1					1	4	10
meet					1	1	1		1	1						2		2			9
appear		1			2	2		1			1										7
pride	1				1		1		2	4						3					12
voice					1			1	1	2	2		1	2	2	2	2	2	2	2	22
praise (v)					1		1	2	1							2					7
write	1				1		3													1	6
care	2					1	2	1	1	2						1		1			11
fate						1	4	2	3	3					1	1		1			16
wind	1					1		2		2	4	1	5	6	5	3	1	5	3	6	45
wake						1		1		1	1					1					5
soft						1	2	5	6	3	4		1			1	1			1	25
sense						1	3			1		2									7
shine		1				3	1		2		1			1				3			12
poet		2				1	3		1		1		1				2			1	12
cloud							1	1		2	2			2	3	3	1	5		3	23
hour		1		1			2	1	2	4	5	2	1	3		4	3	4	1	1	35
age							2		1	2				1		1					7
wild							3	1	3	3	2	1	4	2	1	3	3	3			29
vain							4	2	2	1						1					10
human							1	1	2	1		2	1			1		3	1		13
various							2	2	1												5
land	1	1	2				1	1	1	3	1		2	2	1	4	4	2	2	3	31
sky		1					2	4	2	2	2		3	4	6	9	5	3	6	6	55
charm							2		1	3						1	1				8
mighty				1			1	2		1		1				1	1				8
delight			2	1			1			1			1	1			1				8
nymph								2	2	1		1									6
fool								1	1	1		1									4
scene								2	5	4	2					1	1				15
pass	2	1						1		2	1		1	5	1	1	2	3			20
maid		1		1				1	4	1	1	1					2	1			13
deep								2		1	5	3	1		3	2	6	3		1	27
wide								2	1		1					3					7
behold		1	1	1				1	2	2	1	1					1				11
mountain								1		3					2	2	2	1	2		13

	Pre-1470	1470	1500	1530	1570	1600	1630	1670	1700	1730	1770	1800	1830	1870	1900	Am. 1700	1800	1830	1870	1900	Total
green	2	1							2	1			2	5	3	2		1	3	2	24
song	1				1				4	2	2	2	4	2	1	3	1	5			28
breathe									1	1	1			1		1			1		6
leave		1	1						3		1		1	3	3		1	2	2	2	20
golden	1	1		3					4		2	4	2	3	2		3				25
silent									1	3	2	1	1								8
truth				1					3	1	2	2	1		1	1	1	1		1	15
dark						3			1	2		3	1	5	2	6	4	4	2	3	36
field		2		1					1	1			2	3		3	1				14
shade									2	2	1					2		2			9
foot						1				2	1		3	2	1		1	2	2	2	17
home		1								1	1		1	1	2	3	3	1	1	1	16
hold	2			1		1				1		1	1		3	1	1	4		1	17
own				2						1	3	2		1	1		1	1	2		14
child		1								2	1		4	2	8	1	4	4	1	4	32
pleasure		1	1	1						2	2										7
feel					1					3	3	6	1	2	3		5	3	1		78
black				1		2				1	1	1	2	2	2			1	2	5	20
pale										2	1		2	3		1			1		10
morning										2	1	1	1	1		1	3	1		1	12
sleep				1						1	1	1	2				1			1	8
turn	1									2	1		1	5	4	3	2	3	1	4	27
weep						2				4	2		1				1				10
mother		1								1	2	2	2		1	1	4	2			16
cold										2	2			5		3	1	2	1	2	18
white	1	1			1					1	2	3	2	5	3	2	4	3	7	4	39
ear	1			1	1					1	1	2					2		1	1	11
sorrow					1					1	3		1		1	1	1				9
wave										1			2		3	4	1	1	1	1	14
wood										2	1	2		2			1	1	1		10
grey										1			4	3	1		1		1		11
memory										1	1	1		2						1	6
young	1	3								1	1	1	4	4	1	3	3	3	1	1	27
tree		1						1		1	1	1	2	5	5	1	1	4	2	7	32
pray		1	1							1	2	1							1		7
strange			2								2	1	2	1	1			2			11
bird	1	1									2		2	5	4		1	2	2	4	24
body											1		1	2	3				1	3	11
moon											3	1	3	3	2		2	1	1	4	20
water	1	1		1	1						1		1	5	7	1	1		4	7	31
dream											2	4	4	3	3	1	3	5	4	2	31
star						1	1	1			3	2	3	2	2	2	3	6	1	1	28
woman				1		1					1	2	4	1		1	2	1	1	1	16
blue											2		1	2		2		2	3	3	15
dim											2		2				3				7
the dead											1		1	1	2						5
wing							1				1		2	3	1	1			2		11
shadow												2	2	2	2		1	1	1	1	12
last												1	1	2	1			1			6
house			1									1		3	2		1		1	2	11
dead			1		1					1			2	7	3		1	3	1	5	25
bed		1			1								2		2						6
watch													1	2	2			1			6
red	1	2								1			1	2	2		1	2		1	13
rain													1	3	2				1	1	8
stone	1									1			1	1	5		1		1	5	16
hill								2		1				3	2	4	1	3	1	1	18
grass						1								4	1		1			1	8
nothing				1			1								4		1		3	4	14

TABLE 4 (continued)

NUMBER OF POETS PER ERA USING EACH WORD, IN ORDER OF APPEARANCE WITH FURTHER USE

	Pre-1470	1470	1500	1530	1570	1600	1630	1670	1700	1730	1770	1800	1830	1870	1900	Am. 1770	1800	1830	1870	1900	Total
grave								1							2	2	2			1	8
shore										1						5	1				7
stream				1									2			4	2				9
war		1	1	1				1		1			2			2		1	1	1	12
pure				1			1	1								4	1	2		1	12
peace								1					1	1	1	2	2	1			9
strong		1		1	1			1			1	2				2		2			11
side				1												3		1		1	6
warm										1						2	1	2			6
hair								1								1	1	1	1	1	6
music				1				1				1		1		1	1	3	2		11
holy	1	3				3			1		1	1				1	2	1			15
river																1	1	2		3	7
clear		2										2		1		1	1	1		1	9
rose		1			1	1							1	2			3	1		1	11
beautiful										1			1	1			3		1		7
sound										1							2	1		2	6
wall													1	1	1		2	3	1	1	10
snow								1						2			1		2	2	8
leaf		1												1	1		2		2	4	11
walk										1				1			1	1	1	2	7
small			1		1									2				2	1	2	9
let	2		1	1	1										1			1		3	10
silence														1				3	1		5